Marlowe, Shakespeare, and the Economy of Theatrical Experience

Marlowe, Shakespeare, and the Economy of Theatrical Experience

Thomas Cartelli

upp

University of Pennsylvania Press

Philadelphia

Library of Congress Cataloging-in-Publication Data

Cartelli, Thomas.
  Marlowe, Shakespeare, and the economy of theatrical experience /
Thomas Cartelli.
     p.   cm.
  Includes bibliographical references and index.
  ISBN 0-8122-3102-3
   1. English drama—Early modern and Elizabethan, 1500-1600—History
and criticism. 2. Theater audiences—England—History—16th century.
3. Marlowe, Christopher, 1564-1593—Criticism and interpretation.
4. Shakespeare, William, 1564-1616—Criticism and interpretation.
I. Title.
PR658.A88C37   1991
792'.0942'09031—dc20   91-21173
                                                             CIP

For Jackie
    and the boys

Contents

Acknowledgments

This book owes much to the late C.L. Barber, under whose influence I did my first serious thinking about the plays of Marlowe and Shakespeare. In the decade since his death I have drawn heavily on the support and friendship of Michael Warren. Michael introduced me to the Shakespeare Association of America during the closing stages of my graduate work at the University of California at Santa Cruz, and that organization has since functioned for me as an invaluable resource for collegial interaction and scholarly feedback. Early versions of Chapters Four and Six were expressly written for SAA seminars, and my conception of the book as a whole developed out of the SAA seminar on Marlowe and Shakespeare that I was permitted to direct at the 1985 meeting in Nashville.

My membership in the Marlowe Society of America has also contributed much to this book's development. Sections of Chapters Three, Five, and Seven were presented at MLA sessions sponsored by the MSA, and at the First and Second International Marlowe Conferences which met at Sheffield and Oxford, respectively. I owe a special debt to the former president of the Society, Matthew Proser, for repeatedly demonstrating confidence in me and my work.

Other colleagues whose help and encouragement I would like to acknowledge are Jean Howard who has long been a source of intellectual inspiration and professional support; Harry Berger, Jr., sometime mentor and inveterate gadfly; David Kastan who wrote me my first and only fan letter; Maurice Charney, whose wit and charm invariably enrich our professional encounters; Jim Bloom who has been keeping me intellectually honest since we were undergraduates at Bennington; David Much who has rescued large portions of this book from computer oblivion; my two anonymous readers at Penn whose reports provided the most informed and constructive criticism I could hope to receive; and, last but by no means least, my fellow comparatist and agent, Jim Shapiro.

Muhlenberg College has awarded me several travel and summer research grants to support my work on this project, along with a sabbatical leave which allowed me to spend an indispensable semester of research at the

British Library. I would especially like to acknowledge the role played by the late Dean of the College, Robert Williams, in providing me with what was at the time an unprecedented reduction of teaching responsibilities during a make-or-break stage of this book's development. The present Dean and former Chair of the English department, Nelvin Vos, has been similarly gracious and consistent in demonstrating faith in me and my productions.

Earlier versions of Chapters Four and Six were published in *Theatre Journal* 35:3 (1983) and *ELH* 53:1 (1986) respectively. They are reprinted by permission of The Johns Hopkins University Press. Chapter Seven is a revised version of an essay that originally appeared in *"A Poet and a Filthy Playmaker": New Essays on Christopher Marlowe* (New York: AMS Press, 1988), edited by Kenneth Friedenreich, Roma Gill, and Constance Kuriyama. Material from the earlier essay is used with permission of AMS Press. Much of Chapter Eight was first published in *The Bucknell Review* 29:2 (1985), and is reprinted with permission of the Associated University Presses.

I reserve a last word of acknowledgment for my sons, Philip and Gregory, who have taught me much about the meaning of pleasure, and for my wife, Jackie Miller, whose indulgence in the area of childcare gave me the freedom to write a book to stand up beside her own.

A Note on Texts

Quotations from Marlowe are generally taken from Irving Ribner, ed. *The Complete Plays of Christopher Marlowe* (New York: Odyssey Press, 1963). In Chapter Three, I have employed the New Mermaids edition of *Tamburlaine the Great, Parts 1 and 2*, J.W. Harper, ed. (New York: Hill & Wang, 1973).

Quotations from Shakespeare are generally taken from David Bevington, ed. *The Complete Works of Shakespeare* (Glenview, Ill.: Scott, Foresman & Co., 1980). In Chapter Four, I have employed the Arden edition of *Macbeth*, Kenneth Muir, ed. (London: Methuen, 1980); in Chapter Eight, the Arden edition of *Timon of Athens*, H.J. Oliver, ed. (London: Methuen, 1959).

Prefatory Note

This book addresses several collateral subjects and concerns. It is, most prominently, a book about the structure of exchanges—psychological, social, and political—that were negotiated between audiences and plays in Elizabethan public theaters in a period ostensibly dominated by Shakespeare but strongly rooted in Marlowe. It is also a book that attempts, somewhat presumptuously, to re-assemble critically—through the medium of an applied model of audience response—theatrical experiences that are neither specifically my own, nor (for the most part) directly attributable to historically specific individuals or audiences. While the interactions between audiences and plays that I construct are largely hypothetical, they have (I will argue) a very plausible basis in the design of the playtexts in question, in the conditions of their production, and in the range of responses that were available to Elizabethan playgoers.

Another concern of the book is to apply its interest in theatrical experience to plays by Marlowe and Shakespeare that do not usually "speak" to each other in comparative estimates of their work, which generally focus on style, theme, or influence. I have chosen to link Marlowe and Shakespeare to the theoretical concerns of this project not only because their names are associated with a particularly provocative set of plays, but because they have traditionally functioned as embodiments of opposed and often irreconcilable ideas about theatrical experience. It is not my purpose here to reconcile them in a single, all-embracing interpretive economy. Rather, I intend to explore distinct moments of their participation in a shared theatrical enterprise—to which they both gave shape and which shaped their productions—in an effort to translate the comparatist debate into theatrical terms. In the process, I intend to demonstrate that their plays were jointly situated in the "web" of a theatrical apparatus that characteristically complicated the translation of apparent authorial intentions into predictable effects.

The book is divided into four parts of two chapters each, and includes a brief introduction in which I take issue with traditionally polarized estimates of Marlowe and Shakespeare in an effort to establish a more complementary perspective toward their respective productions. In the opening chapter of Part 1, I develop a model of theatrical experience, the contours of which are Freudian in orientation but which is grounded in a detailed reappraisal of the attacks leveled against the Elizabethan theater by such contemporary polemicists as Stephen Gosson and Anthony Munday. I begin by taking the position that pleasure, not moral enrichment, is the prevailing aim of Elizabethan playgoing and that engagement, not resistance, is the primary medium through which playgoers experience pleasure. I then advance the argument that an audience-oriented methodology is more apt than a text-centered methodology to "recover" the pleasures of Elizabethan playgoing: pleasures that may be traced (as the antitheatricalists contend) to the presence of transgressive or heterodox material in the plays themselves and in the conditions of their performance.

In my second chapter, I attempt to bring an audience-oriented theory of reading to bear on a revised estimate of the psychic disposition of Elizabethan playgoers and on the social psychology of Elizabethan playgoing. I undertake this revision in the interests of broadening our conception of the range of plausible responses an Elizabethan playgoer could conceivably entertain in the face of pointed theatrical challenges to moral and political orthodoxies. While I continue to employ ideas drawn from the modern critical repertory—especially from recent theories of cinematic spectatorship—I rely throughout on contemporaneous accounts of Elizabethan habits of mind and behavior, as well as on some of the most exacting recent work in Elizabethan social history.

Parts 2–4 offer a series of applications of the model of audience/play relations delineated in Part 1, and are organized in a manner designed to address both parts of my critical agenda. Each section consequently includes a chapter devoted to a play or group of plays by Marlowe and Shakespeare that "stages" one of three positions I advance regarding Elizabethan theatrical transactions: namely, their encouragement of audience engagement with transgressive fantasy material; their capacity to demystify established structures of belief and behavior; and their operation as correctives to readerly defined habits of taste and judgment.

In Chapter Three, I focus on the contemporary perception of Marlowe's Tamburlaine, and explore the range of responses the Tamburlaine phenomenon seems to have elicited from Marlowe's audiences, as well as its status as a powerful, but socially divisive, cultural fantasy. In the ensuing chapter on *Macbeth*, I offer a more broadly psychological appraisal of that play's construction of audience response, which explores the transgressive effects of the playgoing subject's sustained engagement with Macbeth. Chapters Five and Six share a concern with the responsiveness of Marlowe and Shakespeare to the kind of social and political analysis their contemporaries generally associated with Machiavelli. I suggest that for Marlowe Machiavellism operates, in *Edward II* and elsewhere, as a particularly enabling source of theatrical energy that informs both his demystification of prevailing structures of power and standards of behavior and his corresponding valorization of power and the powerful. In the chapter that follows, I discuss Shakespeare's comparatively more dialogic, but comparably incisive, participation in the enterprise of demystification. I contend that Shakespeare's work in this vein often involves the interrogation of ideologies in which he was presumably invested, and the cultivation of audience resistance to the same political and social fantasies he seems committed to defending and elaborating in such plays as *Henry V* and *The Merchant of Venice*.

In Chapters Seven and Eight, I directly address some of the book's primary methodological claims in the process of demonstrating how such allegedly corrupt, and theatrically unorthodox, playtexts as *The Jew of Malta* and *Timon of Athens* construct positions for their audiences to inhabit that make their normatively repellent protagonists the privileged subjects of audience regard. The book concludes with a brief meditation on the limits of my own methodology in which I acknowledge the largely imaginary status of the audiences for and of whom I presume to speak, but insist on their need to be heard.

Introduction: Marlowe and/or Shakespeare

In his introduction to *Marlowe and the Politics of Elizabethan Theatre*, Simon Shepherd writes that he has "pushed Shakespeare to the edges" of his book "because our thinking about Renaissance drama is so Shakespeare dominated that he becomes a principle, an obstacle, not a set of rhetorical structures, and positive discrimination is needed to move out of the intellectual trap." As a first step in moving out of this trap, Shepherd advocates the "study of the critical construction of Marlowe-who-isn't-Shakespeare" (1986, xiv). I would like in the following pages to pursue such a study, but want to do so without assembling another trap in which the Marlowe-who-isn't-Shakespeare plays the subversive antagonist in a dramatic competition devoted to the decanonization of the Shakespeare-who-isn't-Marlowe. I would like, in other words, to avoid the tendency, apparent in almost all comparative studies of Shakespeare and Marlowe, to use the one playwright simply to demonstrate the radicalism or conservatism, hollowness or wholeness, of the other.

I oppose especially an interpretive strategy made explicit by Wilbur Sanders in *The Dramatist and the Received Idea* where he confesses that he has "cast Marlowe to play [the] unenviable role" of the lesser man in the comparative transaction (1968, 18). Sanders makes his casting choice on the basis of Marlowe's "already distended reputation"; the artistically "unavailing" nature of Marlowe's "alertness to the currents of contemporary life"; and Marlowe's alleged lack of "inner stability." Sanders's choice of words betrays a disapprobation of Marlowe and his work that is at once moral and ideological in orientation, and that is premised on a valorization of Shakespeare's "broad and profound humanity" (19) in which the critic himself is deeply invested. Marlowe's critical subordination to Shakespeare is, in fact, so often explained in terms of the latter's "richer tonalities, and subtler nuances of human relationship" (Harry Levin 1976, 263) that the comparison serves to deny Shakespeare, as well as Marlowe, any opportunity to deviate from the rule or paradigm the critic sets for him.

Shakespeare's status as a stable and dependable source of humanistic wisdom and understanding has, of course, become much unsettled of late, thanks to the efforts of revisionists of every shape and variety. Critical treatments of Marlowe, however, continue to run along the well-worn lines of accommodation and demonization, which collectively constitute a form of institutional denial.[1] The Marlowe who is "other" than Shakespeare is denied not only when he is demonized and his work is evaluated in relation to standards of dramatic decorum and psychic wholeness established by Shakespeareans. He is denied also when he is accommodated as a genius of the second order who contributed the "mighty line" to English blank verse drama and whose "experimental" approach to the stage opened up a series of new dramatic prospects for his successors to realize.[2] This tendency to domesticate Marlowe, to cast him as a leading figure of the first phase of the Shakespearean master narrative, operates in alternation with his demonization to discourage any sustained encounter with his difference or otherness. Although Stephen Greenblatt's inspired essays on Marlowe have considerably altered these traditional lines of inquiry, only a few recent commentators have, for example, been willing or able to entertain the homoerotic nature of Marlowe's dramatic orientation in *Edward II*, one that simply cannot be accounted for or explained by traditionalist assumptions that seek either to mystify or marginalize what deviates from a Shakespearean norm.[3] And even Greenblatt himself, albeit in a more sophisticated manner, reproduces the either/or habit of mind when he writes that whereas "Shakespeare approaches his culture . . . as dutiful servant, content to improvise a part of his own within its orthodoxy," Marlowe approaches it as "rebel and blasphemer" (1980, 253).

In many respects, a demonized Marlowe operates as a pre-condition for a canonized Shakespeare. Isolating Marlowe's difference or otherness to the realm of the neurotic, rebellious, or blasphemous helps substantiate the identification of Shakespeare with psychic wholeness, political orthodoxy, and artistic balance and perfection. It enforces a comparative habit of mind that privileges Shakespeare as rule and represses Shakespeare's capacity to demonstrate the exceptional freedom from artistic or moral constraint conventionally attributed to Marlowe. With Marlowe operating as the privileged purveyor of marginal or contestatory impulses, Shakespeare is generally denied the opportunity to participate in his own "strangeness"

(Barber and Wheeler 1986, 39), or to lay a claim of his own to heterodox political and social opinions. The old Shakespearean chauvinism that speaks of his "richer tonalities," his comprehensiveness of vision, and "humanely original" perspectives, all at the expense of Marlowe, leads one to suspect that if there were no Tamburlaine with whom to compare Henry V, no Barabas with whom to compare Aaron the Moor or Shylock, we might well be entertaining a more radical Shakespeare than we entertain at present. I do not, on this account, advocate a collapsing of all differences into an identification that would give us a Shakespeare-who-is-Marlowe. To do so would deny the Shakespeare-who-isn't-Marlowe the capacity to do anything other than manage our fantasies, control our nightmares, or tell us what mercy really means. And it would confirm Marlowe's assigned status as merely the bogeyman of Shakespeare's imagination, the only conceiver of what he sets out to subdue. Jill Levenson has noted that "criticism which approaches Marlowe by the light of Shakespeare persistently distances audiences from Marlowe's plays."[4] I ask whether criticism that approaches Shakespeare by the light of a demonized or devalued Marlowe might not distance us with equal persistence from Shakespeare's plays.

2

In the context of such considerations a project committed to the critical construction of the Marlowe-who-isn't-Shakespeare must inevitably involve the concomitant reconstruction of the Shakespeare-who-isn't-Shakespeare. This may be equivalent to saying that one wishes to invent, as others have done, an alternative Shakespeare, one who stands opposed to most of what has been said or done in the name of "Shakespeare" in the 370 years since his death. At the risk of sounding disingenuous, I would prefer to say that I aim to recover, not to reinvent, Shakespeare. But I will also confess that the Shakespeare I intend to recover is, like Marlowe, largely irrecoverable. One of the prevailing problems in both traditional and revisionist Shakespeare scholarship is the treatment from a predominantly text-centered perspective of plays that were, at their moment of production, much more dynamically interactive enterprises than many scholars would lead us to believe. Even the most exacting work on staging techniques, playhouses, and audience composition stops short of encounters with plays in performance. It does so largely because such encounters can only constitute imagined and, hence, imaginary re-creations of what is constitutionally indeterminate and indeterminable. Such scholarship knows and acknowledges its limitations, and understandably consigns to the domain of invention work that strays beyond the parameters of what is practically knowable.

Nevertheless, I prefer the term "recovery" because although no authoritative re-creation of an Elizabethan audience's responses to Shakespearean plays in performance may be possible, just such an effort at re-creation is needed if we intend to make better use of the layers of commentary and information that have set the Shakespeare-who-isn't-Shakespeare at so great a remove from apprehension. What is required is a kind of critical archaeology that can re-establish the theatrical priorities of Shakespearean texts, re-orient the institutionalized discourse that obscures them, and, finally, reanimate them into performative life. This would not allow us to recover in any final sense what is irrecoverable, or give us anything we could claim as the "real" Shakespeare. But it would, I believe, bring us into contact with deeper structures of Shakespeare's art.

Getting at the "historical" Marlowe would appear to require less in the way of excavation since the institutions that have evolved around his work have been few and far between. However, because the chief medium through which Marlowe's work is presently read and disseminated is the Shakespeare industry (in the form of university course offerings, RSC productions, etc.), the interpretive equivalent of revisionist historiography may be needed to recover both the Marlowe-who-isn't-Shakespeare and the Shakespeare that "Shakespeare" has repressed. The case for Marlowe can best be made by abandoning the Marlowe *or* Shakespeare formulation that operates as the hidden agenda in comparative estimates of their work. If we view Marlowe less as an alternative to Shakespeare than as a formidable contemporary with whom Shakespeare was, for a few years, actively competitive and by whom Shakespeare was, for a longer time, preoccupied, we may move a step closer to reconstructing some of the formative conditions of Elizabethan theatrical experience which Marlowe played a powerful role in shaping.

3

In offering his own review of comparative studies of Marlowe and Shakespeare that "needlessly reiterate Shakespeare's superiority to Marlowe," Maurice Charney observes that "Dramaturgic criteria are likely to yield more positive results than those drawn from an ideational, thematic, or strictly verbal approach" (1979, 43). In taking Charney's injunction to heart, I would add that *theatrical* criteria, that is, observations drawn from an informed reconstruction of the interactions of plays and their audiences, are likely to yield even more positive results than dramaturgic approaches. I make this adjustment in Charney's position because I believe that the failure to attend to the distinctiveness of Marlowe's and Shakespeare's respective approaches to their audiences has played a pivotal role both in Marlowe's critical subordination to Shakespeare and in the institutionalization of a prescriptive Shakespearean aesthetic, and because I feel that it is on the level of theatrical experience that a sustained study of Marlowe and Shakespeare can be most profitably conducted. Plausible reconstructions of interactions between audiences and plays best indicate how the textually apparent aims and intentions of plays are negotiated and transformed into theatrical effects. And it is, I submit, mainly through the exploration of theatrical effect that we will become able to alter and re-direct the tendency to ground our appraisals of the plays of Shakespeare and Marlowe in preconceptions about their author-functions.

Were we able, through a fortuitous conjunction of documentary and interpretive procedures, to effect the reconstruction of audience responses to Marlowe and Shakespeare I envision, we would find that what conspicuously distinguishes the one playwright from the other are the specific strategies each develops to appeal to his audience and to organize the central fantasy content of his plays. I make this claim in the form of a provisional conclusion that epitomizes both the nature and direction of the methodologies I intend to employ in the course of this book. My purpose here is to resituate the comparatist debate about Marlowe and Shakespeare by directing critical attention to the often complementary structure of theatrical exchanges set into motion by their plays. I intend to reformulate traditional critical evaluations of Marlowe's allegedly "amoral" approach to the stage and Shakespeare's "socially responsible" art in terms of distinctions that are responsive to the broad range of effects generated by plays in performance. While I do not plan to abandon entirely a comparative terminology or apparatus, the alternating "readings" of selected plays of Marlowe and Shakespeare I will offer are not designed to assemble a counter-narrative that seeks to displace the master-narrative of Shakespearean predominance, or to advance a theory or thesis regarding poetic influence. They variously represent attempts to reconstitute the interactive dynamics of audiences and plays in performance and to bring into focus theatrical strategies and preoccupations that may be construed as characteristic of each playwright's approach to the problems and issues in question. Their cogency finally depends on how convincing a case I can make for the application of an eclectic critical methodology that draws on both historically specific material and subjective perceptions, but that is grounded in something I choose to call the "economy of theatrical experience."

Part I

The Economy of Theatrical Experience

1. The Terms of Engagement

The Pleasures of Engagement

In the first of two articles devoted to exposing the weaknesses of stage-centered readings of Renaissance dramatic texts and to demonstrating the strengths of text-centered readings, Harry Berger, Jr. concludes a characteristically deft piece of analysis by observing that "Performance asks us to submit to its spell, and the text asks us to examine the implications of that submission" (1982, 53).[1] Berger persuasively builds his case by contending that a play in performance "does not allow us the leisure to interrupt, challenge, or question" and, hence, prevents us "from carrying out central interpretive operations that presuppose our ability to decelerate the text, to ignore sequence while accumulating synchronic or paradigmatic clusters of imagery" (51–52). He rightly notes that we "find ourselves forced to listen selectively when at theater" and "tend to ignore the superflux which the spoken language shakes down about our ears, so that we may remain attentive to the 'happening' that moves ever forward and waits on no auditor's leisure" (52). And he concludes that if "It is hard for us to believe that playgoers understand all the figurative acrobatics executed by Shakespeare's language as it flies by, . . . it is equally hard to believe that Elizabethan spectators . . . were not in the same plight" (52).

I quote Berger at such length both because he makes so strong a case against the representational claims of stage-centered criticism and because his rhetoric betrays many of the limitations of the position he is attempting to advance. Berger correctly observes that there is far more in any Shakespearean text than can be taken in, much less precisely understood, by even the most attentive playgoer. Our experience of plays in performance *is* apt to focus our attention on the "happening" at the expense of verbal nuance and well-cultivated patterns of imagery. But Berger's tendency to privilege the latter at the expense of the former—which is not, in the first place, an exclusively verbal event—reveals not only his desire to protect what is, after all, the constitutive site of textualists like himself, but also a distrust of the shaping power of drama in performance which contests his claim to interpretive priority. This distrust is grounded in the critic's resistance to the "spell" performance "asks us to submit to," a spell that threatens the critic's ability to maintain control over or distance from an experience designed to engage the spectator. In refusing to submit to the spell of performance and in attributing to the text the request that "the implications" of submission be examined, Berger commits himself to the study of Shakespearean playtexts from the vantage point of resistance, a position from which engagement must always seem suspect and self-mystifying, indeed, must always seem like submission to a spell.[2]

Unlike the stage-centered "new histrionicists" Berger takes to task in his more recent *Imaginary Audition* (1989, 3–42), I plan to proceed without surrendering my own resistance to the spell of performance since resistance is as much a component of theatrical experience as it is the enabling medium of text-centered criticism. It is, however, my intention to explore the implications of submission primarily from the perspective of engagement, and to delegate a more active role to spectatorship than Berger would allow even in the reformulated arguments he advances there. While I accept Berger's assertion that "The Shakespearean intention constituted by the reader and the interpreted text will differ from the one constituted by the spectator and the performed script" (1982, 53), I believe that even readerly oriented critics can produce interpretations of playtexts that plausibly recreate the conditions of performance experienced by spectators, and hence can reconstitute Shakespearean intentions in the context of dramatic effects.[3] But it is only by subordinating resistance to engagement in the economy of our own interpretive procedures that we can hope to provide a more faithful reconstruction of theatrical experience than Berger seeks or supplies.

I advance this claim for a number of reasons. Theatrical experience is, to begin with, generally far more permissive than our socially regulated experience of everyday life. It is especially conducive to the representation and entertainment of fantasies that are usually relegated to the background of our consciousness outside the theater. As a result, it is particularly geared to satisfy a playgoer's longing for a release from normative constraints. As Freud observes:

> Being present as an interested spectator at a spectacle or play does for adults what play does for children, whose hesitant hopes of being able to do what grown-up people do are in that way gratified. The spectator is a person who experiences

too little, who feels that he is a "poor wretch to whom nothing of importance can happen," one who has long been obliged to damp down, or rather displace, his ambition to stand in his own person at the hub of world affairs; he longs to feel and to act and to arrange things according to his desires—in short, to be a hero. ("Psychopathic Characters" 1942 [1905 or 1906], 305)

This interested spectator described by Freud is predisposed to let his or her hold on one world slip in order to enjoy temporarily the pleasures of inhabiting another, more satisfying reality. Letting the world slip does not, in this respect, require a complete submission of the imagination to this alternative playworld so much as it involves a consciously willed surrender to the playworld's logic or mode of definition. In the process of this surrender, the spectator's hold on a normative persuasion is loosened; the characteristic defenses or resistances normally brought to bear against foreign or threatening experiences are voluntarily lowered or weakened; and the fantasies usually held in check by such devices are given freer rein to seek fulfillment. While the theatrical enterprise also requires a variety of strategies to structure, manage, and control the fantasy material that constitutes a given play's performance appeal, it is on that play's capacity to satisfy its audience's desire for psychic release or fantasy fulfillment that its dramatic—and commercial—success will largely depend.

It is, of course, the critic's prerogative to operate at some remove from the playgoer's immersion in plays in performance. But it does not necessarily follow, as Berger contends, that playtexts merely ask us to examine "the implications" of "submission" to the "spell" of performance. As a scripted supplement to the performances it maps and records, the playtext also asks us to reconstruct the dynamics of audience engagement from the point of view of the audience itself, an audience that, in the Elizabethan period, may well have been more restive and contentious than the audiences Berger has in mind. Berger's choice of words suggests that all acts of audience engagement are premised on submissiveness, that all performances are potentially spellbinding, and that it is the duty of the critic to operate as a kind of counter-fantasist committed to freeing the reader from the mystifications of aesthetic identification suffered by playgoers. Rather than distinguish between one playgoer's voluntary immersion in a compelling fantasy and another's "mechanical and unfree" submission to a spell (see Jauss 1982, 154), Berger views playgoing itself as a constitutionally uncritical activity that cannot sustain the watchful regard of an engaged spectator. In so doing, he reproduces in small "the conceptual history of

'catharsis' " that, according to Hans Robert Jauss, "appears as the ever renewed attempt to undermine the direct evidence of aesthetic identification
and to impose on the recipient the effort of negation so that his aesthetic
and moral reflection may be set free and not succumb to the fascination of
the imaginary" (1982, 94). In order to avoid this tendency to separate the
emotional content of audience reception from its intellectual components,
we would do better to assume, with Jauss, that "emotion and imagination
participate in the same psychic process" (118) and that both may participate
as well in the critical reconstruction of theatrical experiences.

Readings of Elizabethan playtexts that aim to cultivate this middle
ground need to focus on the ways in which playwrights like Marlowe and
Shakespeare approached such constituent elements of theatrical production as the combined commercial and artistic status of plays; the intimate
yet expansive physical layout of the public playhouse; and the position of
the playhouse as a "new place apart" (Barber and Wheeler 1986, 20; see
Mullaney 1988, esp. 1–59) that answered the London playgoers' need for a
focus for their opposing interests and collective aspirations. These readings
also need to focus on the variety of interactions between audiences and
plays that could be provoked by the operation of enormously suggestive
material upon a public that was sophisticated with respect to the conventions of playgoing but that could also respond uncritically to the most audacious appeals. To approach Elizabethan playtexts from such
perspectives, it is necessary to adapt even stage-centered methodologies to
the vicissitudes of a medium designed to appeal to a paying auditory of
clients or customers on a regular, profitmaking basis. I suggest nothing
new in noting, after Carol Rutter, that "The Elizabethan playhouse was
organized to make money" (1984, 28). But the instructiveness of Rutter's
observation and of Andrew Gurr's to the effect that "The playhouses were
not places for art or culture, and their poetry was the very impure poetry
of money" (1970, 3) has generally gone unheeded by scholars and critics
whose resistance to such seemingly unhumanistic propositions often implies a corresponding resistance to drama in performance. One is certainly
right to resist the reductiveness of Gurr's identification of the business of
playhouses with the business of playwrights, as well as his implicitly elitist
separation of "art or culture" from the domain of a commercial and popularly oriented enterprise. Playwrights like Marlowe and Shakespeare assuredly made art of the highest order in meeting the demands of both their
employers and audiences for commercially viable entertainment. But one
would be wrong to subordinate the primary aim of playwright and play-

house—that is, the aim to satisfy or please (which may be understood on a number of different levels, as I hope to demonstrate)—to one's own quest for meanings or morals that may well have been marginal to the interests that prevailed in what Gurr terms "the environment" of a play's performance.

If we linger for a few moments over some of the more interesting attacks on and defenses of theater in the last decades of the sixteenth century, we may better appreciate the role played by pleasure in Elizabethan theatrical transactions, and why pleasure is the overt and hidden enemy, respectively, of Elizabethan antitheatricalist and modern textualist alike. Puritan objections to plays on such bases as their confusion of male and female roles and their abridgement of Biblical commands governing representation are too well known to require rehearsal here, although the possibility that their indiscriminate literalism harbors a more specific anxiety regarding the pleasures of theatrical transvestism surely needs to be acknowledged. We need also do no more than register how radically the characteristically shrill and formulaic attacks on playmaking distort the actual matter and manner of plays in performance. It is, however, well worth observing that while scholars have been eager to accept the blandishments of a Nashe regarding the moral import of theater at face value, they have been generally unwilling to grant any validity to the positions taken or advanced by such gifted polemicists as Stephen Gosson. An important exception is Michael Bristol who contends that "The late sixteenth-century polemic against the stage actually takes account of [the] radical potentiality of the theater," while "The much weaker humanistic defenses of the theater overlook [it], concentrating instead on making a case for literature and the literary artist as the reason for the playhouse's existence" (1985, 113).[4] For this reason among others, I would submit that we have more to learn about the prevailing economy of Elizabethan theatrical experience from some of the theater's detractors, especially from Gosson and Anthony Munday who once played an active role in the theater itself, than we do from its defenders.[5]

Gosson's attacks on the theater proceed from a series of assumptions that are, admittedly, prejudicial to any objective estimate of theatrical experience. He assumes, for example, that "every pleasure" we may encounter should be construed as a possible temptation of the devil (*Playes Confuted*, 172–73) and that "a plaie can bee no looking glasse of behaviour" (187) insofar as it blends evil with good and, hence, makes it impossible for an audience to extract a clear-cut guide to moral behavior. But Gosson's resistance to pleasure and moral ambiguity also makes him highly attuned to the ways in which even well-meaning plays manage to penetrate the defenses of their auditors and lodge their matter in the recesses of a playgoer's mind or imagination. As Gosson writes in *The School of Abuse*:

> [The players] seeke not to hurt, but desire to please: they have purged their Comedyes of wanton speaches, yet the Corn whiche they sell is full of Cockle: and they drinke that they drawe, overcharged with dregges. There is more in them thenwe perceive, the Devil standes at our elbow when wee see not, and woundeth sore when he raseth no skinne, nor rents the fleshe, . . . the abuses of plays cannot be showen, because they passe the degrees of the instrument, reach of the Plummet, sight of the mind, and for trial are never brought to the touch-stone. (1579, 37–38)

Gosson employs moral and religious discourse here to describe what we today would translate into psychological terms. Plays are dangerous, according to Gosson, not because they are consciously or explicitly subversive, or because players or playwrights are devils. Rather, the danger of plays resides in an imaginative superflux that cannot be confidently identified or traced. Plays put a devil of suggestiveness inside the heads of their audiences which, once safely ensconced, can neither be brought to justice nor exorcised. In a vision of psychic economy that he shares with Freud, Gosson suggests that the thoughts, images, and fantasies that leak out of plays into what amounts to the unconscious of the playgoer are psychically conserved and, ultimately, translated into abuses whose source or origin remains mystified.

In describing plays as carriers of an invisible disease that spreads its germs in the same imperceptible manner as the Black Death, Gosson is himself doing more than mystifying otherwise undocumentable abuses of the theater. He is calling attention to the affective power of theatrical suggestiveness in a manner that undercuts the eloquent defense of the drama's instructiveness offered by Nashe when he contends that "no Play . . . encourageth any man to tumults or rebellion, but layes before such the halter and the gallowes; or praiseth or approoueth pride, lust, whoredome, prodigalitie, or drunkennes, but beates them downe vtterly" (*Pierce Penniless*, 214). While Nashe speaks on behalf of dramatic intention, Gosson focuses his attack on dramatic effect. Although Nashe is on firm ground with respect to the majority of Elizabethan plays which ultimately, if not successfully, aim to "shew the ill successe of treason, the fall of hastie climbers, the wretched end of vsurpers, [and] the miserie of ciuill dissention" (*Pierce Penniless*, 213), he does not speak directly to Gosson's critique of the imagi-

native residue plays leave in their wake. Nor does Nashe speak to the fact
that the variableness of plays has its analogue in the variableness of playgoers, some of whom may prove unresponsive to the lessons preached by
expressly didactic plays or may become immunized against the moral messages that more subtle plays often reserve for their closing moments, having found the theatrical appeal of vice sufficiently attractive to assure its
staying power.

It is to such possibilities that Anthony Munday addresses himself in the
following passage from the *Third Blast of Retrait from Plaies*:

> When [our youth] are out of sight of their maisters, such government have they
> of themselves, that what by il companie they meete withal, & il examples they
> lerne at plaies, I feare me, I feare me their harts are more alienated in two houres
> from virtue, then again maie wel be amended in a whole yeare. (134–35)

Munday's anxiety about the transformative effects of plays on the minds of
untutored youth may sound to some a little too like the calls for censorship
of popular music we have been hearing with increasing frequency in our
own time. We may, accordingly, choose to classify it as unduly alarmist
and may also choose to apprehend it as advancing, along with Gosson's
writings, a propagandistic cause that has little finally to say about the actual
experiences of playgoers. But Munday also shares with Gosson a preoccupation with the psychological consequences of dramatic effect that the drama's defenders choose either to ignore entirely or to present only in the
most favorable manner. Both polemicists significantly advance a reading of
theatrical experience in which audience engagement with the pleasures of
plays maintains a decided edge over engagement with their moral import.
They find the formal structures of plays insufficient to provoke the resistance to their tempting pleasures that must be sustained to prevent the
playgoer's alienation from virtue and embrace of vice. Nashe does not, of
course, ignore the possibility that playgoers will actively engage themselves
with the fantasy content of a given production. In fact, he provides the
best known instance in Elizabethan dramatic criticism of the potential intensity of such engagement when he writes of Talbot triumphing anew in
1 Henry VI, with "his bones newe embalmed with the teares of ten thousand spectators at least (at seuerall times), who, in the Tragedian that represents his person, imagine they behold him fresh bleeding" (*Pierce
Penniless*, 212). But his choice of so indisputable an example of the enriching effects of plays impels one to wonder how Nashe would have moralized

the applause that attended the triumphs of Marlowe's Tamburlaine which encourage all that Munday feared and Gosson suspected.

More modern moralizers of Elizabethan drama typically relegate such displays of engagement to the domain of the much-abused groundlings, thereby reserving for the more privileged playgoer a conscious habit of thoughtful detachment that resembles their own.[6] Detachment in the face of a triumphing Talbot or of so powerful a theatrical phenomenon as Tamburlaine is, however, hardly the kind of response Shakespeare and Marlowe aimed to produce if they did, in fact, aim to satisfy their audiences. And, as I intend to demonstrate, even when Marlowe and Shakespeare attempted to encourage their audiences to resist the theatrical appeal of such morally unsavory characters as Faustus and Richard of Gloucester, they can hardly have hoped to erase entirely the psychological residue of the audience's probable engagement with them. It is this self-constituted incapacity of plays to dissipate the very energies they evoke that Gosson and Munday remark and that Nashe denies. Whether Nashe issues his denial in complete sincerity or out of the same politic regard for his safety that sent him into two years of self-exile after the Isle of Dogs controversy is impossible to determine. But statements such as "no Play encourageth any man to tumult or rebellion, but layes before such the halter and the gallowes," although consistent with the texts of such popular works of the time as Richard III and Doctor Faustus, are inconsistent with a theatrical economy that privileges engagement at the expense of resistance.

Marlowe's and Shakespeare's skillful management of their own expressiveness has contributed greatly to our sense of the textual balance of such works while simultaneously inhibiting our ability to establish meaningful contact with the fantasy material their artistry both evokes and contains. Since the formally defensive strategies employed by Marlowe and Shakespeare in their most potentially volatile plays—e.g., the morality trappings of Doctor Faustus, the invocations of Providence in Richard III—are also consistent with the received ideas a conservative scholarly tradition has maintained about Elizabethan orthodoxies, and the theatrically appealing fantasies of necromantic and Machiavellian self-aggrandizement are identifiable with ideas that the same tradition has considered subversive, it has been easy to assume that what we discern on the level of textual economy reflects the broader economy of Elizabethan theatrical experience. As Michael Bristol observes:

The subsequent success of the great Elizabethan playwrights and the prestige accorded to their work have made it difficult to appreciate the priority of a het-eroglot theater, its capacity to arouse genuine political anxiety, and its impact on social discipline and the structure of authority. (1985, 123)

Indeed, before the last ten years of scholarly revisionism, it was difficult to place what I term the fantasy content of plays in any context other than fantasy. The present breakdown of a critical consensus regarding Elizabethan orthodoxies, particularly as it has been fostered by a new school of cultural materialists and a new generation of social historians, now allows us to entertain ideas about the actual experiences of audiences at plays which make more explicable the anxieties of the city fathers and burghers of London regarding truant apprentices, masterless men, and the status of playhouses as breeders of tumult and disorder.[7]

As we begin to read against the grain of textuality and to explore the extra-textual effects of plays in performance, we begin to notice how readerly strategies that attempt to slow a text down or to rewind it work against the development of psychic impressions an engaged playgoer was likely to experience. The viewing and listening habits of Elizabethan playgoers are largely lost to us, but we can at least assume that the impressions of plays we draw most vividly to consciousness today—Faustus trying to make himself immortal with a kiss, Richard of Gloucester peremptorily calling for Hastings's head before sitting down to eat—made equally vivid impressions on them even as they were compelled to register the religious and moral consequences of such actions. We may also assume that our comparative immunity from the compulsion to register such consequences may characteristically insulate us from the full cathectic force of such provocations. Stephen Greenblatt's well-known formulation—"There is subversion, no end of subversion, only not for us" (1981, 57)—may be re-situated in this context to remind us that what is "not for us" may have operated to far more volatile effect for Elizabethan playgoers.

By sensitizing ourselves to what cannot be lost in even the most moralized translation, we may re-establish contact not only with such established masterworks as *Richard III* and *Doctor Faustus*, but with the arguably humbler fare Elizabethan audiences consumed on the five out of six playing days when works by Marlowe or Shakespeare were not performed. It is such work, drawn from an earlier and presumably less sophisticated repertory, that so aroused the hostility of Gosson and Munday, and that the anonymous *Life and Death of Jack Straw* (1594) may be held to exemplify. In examining such an overtly didactic work, we notice that even as it repeatedly subjects the riots and rebellions of Jack Straw and company to criticism and ridicule, and endows the young Richard II with the patience and charity of a saint, it cannot unsay words or retrospectively erase actions that a contemporary audience was apt to find suggestive or memorable. Marlowe's eloquence and Shakespeare's artistry were not required to plant ideas in the minds of playgoers that efforts at containment were incapable of completely rooting out. When a character clearly headed for the gallows says, at the start of *Jack Straw*, "The Rich have all, the poore live in miserie," it is easy to say in retrospect that his sentiments are discredited with his character. But could an itinerant playgoer who felt deeply the truth of such a statement be made to forget this feeling even after John Ball's head rolls?[8] Were *Jack Straw* to appear on Gosson's short-list of approved moral and cautionary models, he would no doubt say of it as he says of the others, "These Playes are good playes and sweete playes, and of al playes the best playes . . . yet they are not fit for every mans diet: neither ought they commonly to be shewen" (*Abuse*, 41).

Gosson's objection even to the "best playes" is based on a distinction between the wise and, therefore, "protected" playgoer, on the one hand, and what he elsewhere calls "the meaner sort"; and between plays in print and plays in performance. His assertion that "Whatsoever such Playes as confere good matter, are set out in print, may be read with profite, but cannot be playd, without a manifest breech of Gods commandement" (*Playes Confuted*, 198) is integrally tied to his demonstration of why what moralizes in the study operates to opposing effect in theaters. There, "[the meaner sort] take up a wonderfull laughter, and shout altogether with one voyce, when they see some notable cosenage practiced, or some slie conveighaunce of bawdry brought out of Italy, whereby they show themselves rather to like it then to rebuke it" (*Playes Confuted*, 183–84). Although one may disqualify Gosson's observation on the basis of his polemical intentions and his class condescension, it is difficult to disavow it as a valid depiction of the disparity between dramatic intention and dramatic effect which is as commonly perceived in theaters today as it was in Gosson's time. The source of this disparity is that theater—as a commercial medium licensed to operate at a privileged remove from the constraints of everyday life—is better equipped to educate through engagement than through the cultivation of resistance, and, therefore, has the capacity to qualify or subvert the aims of even the most didactic playtexts when those aims fail to appeal to their audiences with the same intensity as do the actions they seek to inhibit. In liking rather than rebuking the practice of "some notable cosenage," Gosson's "meaner sort" may well be demonstrating their ignorance and susceptibility to vice. But they may also be demonstrating the capacity of what I would like to call the "theater-function" to make the responses of all sorts of playgoers arbiters in the negotiation and realization of dramatic intentions.

This is a lesson learned and articulated in our own time by Bertolt Brecht who often found his politically didactic intentions undermined by a theatrical apparatus that "theatres down" everything (Willett 1964, 43). In his effort to produce audiences capable of collaborating with him in "appoint[ing] a new function for the theatre," Brecht noted that "the theatre itself resists any alteration of its function" and consequently advised the spectator to "read plays whose aim is not merely to be performed in the theatre but to change it: out of mistrust of the theatre" (43). The consistency of Brecht's position with Gosson's antitheatricalism and advocacy of reading as an alternative to performance is rooted in a shared mistrust of the theater's capacity to translate authorial intentions into predictable effects. It was largely to counteract the transformative potential of theatrical representation that Brecht developed his well-known aesthetic of alienation and the guidelines for dramatic speech and action required to advance it. That Brecht required so wide an array of devices to encourage his audience's resistance to the "theatre apparatus" attests to his grudging appreciation of the centrality of engagement in the theatrical enterprise.

Engagement and Resistance

My reference to Brecht is timed to coincide with a slight shift in perspective of my own. I have in the above attempted to lay the foundation for a model of theatrical experience and have employed a terminology of engagement and resistance to set the parameters of our discussion. In demonstrating the intense preoccupation of Elizabethan antitheatricalists with the problem of audience engagement, I have attempted to redirect critical attention from the readerly oriented margins of theatrical experience to its center. This "center" I take to be that point of contact or field of engagement between audience and play that cannot, as Gosson claims, be graphically mapped and confidently patrolled, but can be located only in the give-and-take of theatrical performance. Since no critic can be sure how what is given by a play will be taken by its audience, any theoretical model of such transactions must be both speculative and general in orientation. Allowance must be made not only for the extent to which an individual playgoer's gender, class, occupation, and religious beliefs contribute to his or her responses to plays, but also for the variety of ways in which plays may be presented. Our difficulties are compounded when the model we seek to establish is constructed on the irrecoverable responses of audiences as removed from us in time and space as are their structures of feeling and belief. One is easily tempted, as Alan Sinfield (1981) has noted, to superimpose what one feels and believes in the present on contexts of the past that would, if put to the test, probably resist any and all attempts at appropriation.

To minimize the unavoidable effects of appropriation, I have thus far depended—and will continue to depend—on observations drawn from even the most questionable sources of Elizabethan dramatic criticism. But since such sources are too limited and provide too limiting an account of Elizabethan theatrical experience, I intend to venture farther afield than a studied dependence on documentary resources would permit. Reconstructing plausible accounts of audience encounters with the plays of Marlowe and Shakespeare requires the deployment of a critical methodology grounded in an appreciation of the material conditions of Elizabethan theatrical production and of the performative orientation of Elizabethan playtexts, but that is also attuned to the psychological frameworks of theatrical experience and to the network of political and social constructions in which they are embedded. Given the representational constraints of a more positivist model, it is only by assuming the operation of a substructure of psychological exchanges that we are able to account for and describe the powerful effects that plays in performance have on their audiences, to understand why, in the words of Francis Bacon, "the minds of men in company are more open to affections and impressions than when alone."

While Bacon was convinced of the powerful effects of collectively received impressions, he also acknowledged that the source of their influence on "the minds of men in company" was "a great secret in nature" (cf. Gurr 1987, 135–36). Since Nietzsche's efforts to recover the Dionysian spirit of Greek tragic drama and Freud's seminal essays on the psychology of aesthetic experience, we are in the position to tease out with greater assurance than Bacon the secret of audience responsiveness to plays. As Freud writes:

If, as has been assumed since the time of Aristotle, the purpose of drama is to arouse "terror and pity" and so "to purge the emotions," we can describe that purpose in rather more detail by saying that it is a question of opening up sources of pleasure or enjoyment in our emotional life, just as, in the case of intellectual activity, joking or fun open up similar sources, many of which that activity had made inaccessible. ("Psychopathic Characters," 305)

What to Bacon appears "a great secret in nature" is for Freud rendered unmysterious by the assumption that drama offers playgoers an outlet or channel for the entertainment of feelings or fantasies that would otherwise remain inaccessible to them. Drama "gives people the sense, which they so much desire, of a raising of the potential of their psychical state" (305). It does not so much take people out of themselves as persuade them that there is more in themselves than they had previously imagined.

In translating Aristotle's philosophic prescription regarding pity and terror into a psychological description of pleasure or enjoyment, Freud is not simply substituting one kind of terminology for another. He is focusing on the capacity of drama to offer audiences a variety of sensations that terms like pity and terror cannot adequately describe. According to Freud, plays offer the playgoer the opportunity "to give way without a qualm to such suppressed impulses as a craving for freedom in religious, political, social and sexual matters, and to 'blow off steam' in every direction in the various grand scenes that form part of the life represented on the stage" (306). In other words, they offer their audiences an open invitation to fantasy fulfillment, an opportunity to satisfy vicariously cravings and longings whose range of expression they must ordinarily inhibit.

In advancing this avowedly therapeutic model of playgoing, Freud is careful to note the equally integral role played by resistance in the economy of theatrical experience. Following Nietzsche who had contended that "tragic insight, . . . merely to be endured, needs art as a protection and remedy" (*The Birth of Tragedy*, 98), Freud observes that "the dramatist will provoke not merely an *enjoyment* of the liberation [of fantasy fulfillment] but a *resistance* to it as well" (309). In the most sustained recent attempt to develop a Freudian theory of literary response, Norman Holland substitutes the word "defense" for resistance and describes its function in the following manner:

Defense, in a literary work, takes one of two general modes: meaning or form. Typically, the unconscious fantasy at the core of a work will combine elements that could, if given full expression, give us pleasure, but also create anxiety. It is the task of the literary "work" to control the anxiety and permit at least partial gratification of the pleasurable possibilities in the fantasy. The literary work, through . . . "form," acts out defensive maneuvers for us: splitting, isolating, undoing, displacing from, omitting (repressing or denying) elements of the fantasy. Meaning, whether we find it or supply it, acts more like a sublimation, giving the fantasy material a disguised expression which is acceptable to the ego, which "makes sense." (1975, 189)

Holland's elaboration of Freud's comparatively less schematic model of theatrical experience dilutes somewhat Freud's grander claims about the playgoer's unqualified surrender to "suppressed impulses." In so doing, it makes a more persuasive case for their application to the "system of built-in balances" which Maynard Mack attributes to the Elizabethan theatrical enterprise (1962, 277) than it does to the system of *im*balances described by Gosson and Munday.

For antitheatricalists like Gosson and Munday, the Elizabethan stage more closely inspired the kind of audience engagement envisioned by Freud. From their vantage point, plays satisfied all too well their audiences' "craving for freedom in religious, political, social and sexual matters." The only way that "meaning" could fulfill the function delegated to it by Holland would be for the reader of a playtext to discover it in complete isolation from the seductive apparatus of the playhouse. The casting off of audience inhibitions which Freud, Gosson, and Munday so vividly envision cannot, however, be construed to be the only or primary characteristic of Elizabethan playgoing. As Freud himself suggests, we require, instead, a model that at least acknowledges the competing claims of resistance, one that places a play's invitation to fantasy fulfillment in competition with a system of defenses that is not only built into plays themselves, but also contributed by playgoers who seek both stimulation and *protection* from anxiety provoking material.

No model of theatrical experience can, of course, be constructed in either an historical or formal vacuum. When Nietzsche speaks of art as providing protection against tragic insight, he is speaking specifically of the potent ritual drama of fifth century Athens, as, for that matter, is Freud in the first half of his essay. And when Holland discusses the subtle "defensive maneuvers" of *literary* works, he is not specifically taking account of the broader effects generated by plays in performance. A potentially more serious objection may be raised against my own application of "the universalist claims of psychoanalysis" to the study of Elizabethan drama: claims that, in the words of Stephen Greenblatt, generally remain "unruffled by the indifference of the past to its categories" (1986, 215). According to Greenblatt, "psychoanalytic interpretation" is "causally belated" since it "seems to follow upon rather than to explain Renaissance texts." But insofar as it is also "causally linked" to "the legal and literary proceedings of the sixteenth and seventeenth centuries, . . . its interpretive practice is not irrelevant to those proceedings, nor is it exactly an anachronism." He concludes that "psychoanalysis can redeem its belatedness only when it historicizes its own procedures" (221). While such a project is beyond the scope of the present discussion, attempting to locate and identify discursive links between the language of psychoanalysis and the language of Elizabethan theatricality can at least help us to distinguish those procedures that speak to Elizabethan cultural practices from those that do not. It is in the interest of establishing such links that I have already given considerable interpretive weight to the pre-emptive psychologizing discourse of antitheatricality.

Turning from the antitheatricalist critique of playmaking to a more overtly Freudian appraisal of playgoing, however, does require contending with the arguably unbridgeable gulf between different historical constructions of the subject. As Herbert Blau writes:

> To update Nietzsche's question about the Greeks, do we look similarly from generation to generation? Or within a generation, regardless of class or sexual difference or—with our new zeal about difference in the discourse of desire—concepts of desire and subjectivity, hence spectatorship as well? (1990, 63–64)

In order to address such questions, one is tempted to make some of the same universalizing claims about spectatorship that are made in the name of psychoanalysis. We must, consequently, proceed with caution as we begin to assemble a model of what I have, with equal caution, termed *theatrical*, as opposed to *dramatic*, experience. I ground my differentiation of the theatrical from the dramatic on that of the ubiquitous Harry Berger who observes that "Where drama is a certain kind of action capable of representation in a variety of media, theatre is a particular medium—primarily visual (not primarily verbal) which embraces the network of actual circumstances and participants who cooperate in representing and observing a particular action" (1968, 4). Theatrical spectatorship is, then, a condition produced by the interaction of a specific set of enabling circumstances. It is, as it were, framed by the formal properties of plays and playhouses, the proprieties of acting and scenic representation, and the repertoire of responses encouraged by the same. These properties and proprieties do not, of course, remain constant over differences in time and space. Yet just as the generally uniform conditions of moviegoing have contributed to the development of an identifiable reception psychology, so too may a fairly consistent model of spectatorship be distilled from the conditions of playgoing.

In the following appraisal of the relationship between "the cinematic apparatus" and the cinematic spectator, John Ellis provides a cogent example of how a specific format may construct a framework for the viewing subject that effectively "subjects" the viewer to a predictable pattern of engagement:

> Commercial cinema . . . provides an image that is large, usually substantially larger than the individuals watching it. It also provides a particular set of circumstances for watching this image: the audience is seated in rows, separated from each other to some degree, and the image is projected in near-darkness. This induces a particular kind of mental state in the commercial cinema viewer: a concentration of psychic activity into a state of hyper-receptivity. . . . Sitting still in the dark has overtones of sleep and dreaming: indeed, it is easier to fall asleep in a film than is often admitted. But it is dreaming from the outside: the images are coming from a source other than that of dream images, which are produced from the unconscious. . . . Images and sounds are received in a state where the normal judging functions of the ego are suspended to some degree (near to sleep), so that what is seen is not subject to the usual expectations of plausibility that we apply to everyday life. (1982, 40)

Ellis goes on to equate the position of the cinema's viewing subject with that of the voyeur in noting that "The spectator is involved in looking at something that does not (except in very exceptional circumstances) look back at the spectator" (45). And he adds an astute psychological insight to Bacon's observation regarding the susceptibility to "affections and impressions" of the "minds of men in company" when he writes that "The individual spectator is secure in the knowledge that his or her position as voyeur is unthreatened" since "everyone else present is committing the same offence, if, indeed, it can be called an offence in these circumstances" (45).

As in this instance, much that Ellis has to say about the conditions of cinema viewing may be directly applied to an appraisal of theatrical experience. Much else, however, radically departs from what we know of the conditions that obtained in the Elizabethan public playhouse where the viewing subject was more apt to stand in the light than sit in the dark and where a state of "hyper-receptivity" could easily be transformed into hyper-activity. The notable differences between the viewing conditions of the public theater and those that prevail in the contemporary cinema may, nevertheless, help us to determine which psychological paradigms best represent the construction of the Elizabethan playgoing subject. It is, for example, often casually assumed that the same kind of voyeurism that characterizes cinematic spectatorship may be held to characterize the Elizabethan playgoer's response to plays. But if we examine voyeurism in the context of another psychoanalytically charged concept—namely, fetishism—we may conclude that the latter more accurately represents the mode of spectatorship encouraged by the conditions of performance in Elizabethan public theaters. As Ellis writes in arriving at his own distinction between voyeurism and fetishism:

> Where voyeurism maintains (depends upon) a separation between the seer and the object seen, fetishism tries to abolish that gulf. . . . This process implies a different position and attitude of the spectator to the image: It represents the opposite tendency to that of voyeurism. . . . Fetishistic looking implies the direct acknowledgement and participation of the object viewed. . . . With the fetishistic attitude, the look of the character towards the viewer . . . is a central feature. . . . The voyeuristic look is curious, inquiring, demanding to know. The fetishistic gaze is captivated by what it sees, does not wish to inquire further, to see more, to find out. . . . The fetishistic look has much to do with display and the spectacular. (1982, 47)

We need not accept either the particular concept—fetishism—or Ellis's distinction to acknowledge a direct connection between specific enabling conditions and specific psychological effects. By simply projecting ourselves into the domain of the public playhouse—a site whose openness, light, and divisible boundaries between playgoer and performer are diametrically opposed to the conditions of cinematic viewing—and into the domain of the plays associated with that playhouse—whose interest in display and the spectacular is well known—we may better appreciate how much spectatorship is the symptom, product, or construction of the prevailing conditions of production and, consequently, how much it owes to intramural as well as to extramural considerations.[9]

Ellis's distinction between voyeurism and fetishism may be extended to the different varieties of spectatorship that different versions of the theatrical apparatus "sponsor" or produce. Just as most films separate the gaze of the viewer from the gaze of the viewed, so too do plays that operate within the parameters of an illusory "fourth wall" and are thereby transacted beyond the participatory range of their audiences. Although even these plays will occasionally extend themselves into that liminal area where play and audience meet and imaginatively coalesce, the plays we associate with the Elizabethan public playhouse inhabit and exploit this interactive terrain with a good deal more frequency. This is as much to say that plays like *Macbeth*, *Richard III*, and *Tamburlaine the Great* more actively solicit the participation of their audiences in fulfilling the fantasies they set to work than do plays that generally limit their interactive range to the confines of the stage, thereby maintaining that "separation between seer and object seen" which Ellis associates with voyeurism. While the substructure of psychological exchanges, schematized here in terms of engagement and resistance, will make itself felt in each instance, the more conspicuously theatrical play will attempt to "abolish that gulf" between "seer and object seen" and, hence, will generally prefer the more immediate effects of audience engagement to those generated by resistance.

Since Elizabethan drama is too various and insufficiently theorized to be classified in the manner of Brecht's epic theater or of such self-conscious movements as the French theater of the absurd, we are generally restricted to a language of genres and conventions in our efforts to distinguish or draw connections between plays and between the performative transactions they encourage. We may, for example, note that the Elizabethan public theater favored a "non-illusory" style of dramatic representation that did not aspire to realistic dramatic portraiture and did not insist on strict demarcations between the space occupied by actors and the space occupied by playgoers (Styan 1975, 180–81). This style or convention would seem especially conducive to the theatrical exploitation of the space between audience and play. A less obvious, but equally significant, convention is the collateral movement of play and playgoer into and out of a formally directed indulgence in fantasy which may well be held to have informed many Elizabethan and Jacobean productions, but which seems to have functioned in a particularly enabling manner for Marlowe and Shakespeare. This convention is most prominently displayed in Shakespeare's festive comedies and pastoral romances which implicitly identify their own patterns of withdrawal and return with the overall structure of their audience's experience.[10] But it is also discernible in each genre Shakespeare cultivates, most notably in such histories as *Richard III*, and in the tragedy

Macbeth. What distinguishes the effect of this convention on audiences is the distinct manner in which individual plays stage their competition between the gratifications of fantasy fulfillment and the satisfactions offered by the opposing pull of resistance. The operation of a theatrical economy of engagement and resistance is, in other words, coordinated (though not finally controlled) by the choices the artist makes in the disposition of his fantasy material. Since it is out of a play's fantasy content that a play's performance appeal is largely constituted—as Gosson, Munday, and Freud appear to suggest—we may say that audience engagement would most likely be generated when a playwright cultivates fantasy material of a particularly compelling variety and presents it in a powerfully appealing manner. Engagement would, on the other hand, be discouraged by the repeated and clearly perceptible efforts of the playwright to mediate, qualify, or oppose, either on the level of form or meaning, the performance appeal of fantasy fulfillment. In Shakespeare, such efforts are usually textually framed or structured in a manner consistent with what may be termed "the normative persuasion" of his audience, that is, with morally and politically orthodox habits of feeling and belief. While a similar opposition between performance appeal and normative persuasion can also be considered characteristic of Marlowe's art, Marlowe does not generally offer his audiences as balanced a disposition of his fantasy material as does Shakespeare. The two parts of *Tamburlaine* and *The Jew of Malta* do not, for example, offer the playgoer many incentives to remain attached to normative states of mind and feeling.

In Shakespeare, the claim of the normative makes itself conspicuously felt in the formal pacing and structure of plays like *Richard III* and *Macbeth* as they move towards closure and attempt to foreclose the continued operation of the fantasies that animate them, and in the affective privileging of politically and morally orthodox states of mind and feeling. In Marlowe, we notice the same privileging of the orthodox in a play like *Doctor Faustus*, but we also notice there, and in the Tamburlaine plays in particular, that a great deal more theatrical energy is devoted to maintaining the bond of engagement between audience and play than to arousing audience resistance. Marlowe's plays usually encourage their audiences to engage to the utmost in fantasy fulfillment: to engage, moreover, in fantasies opposed to the orthodoxies of a moral order to which most members of the audience would at least be expected to subscribe. Shakespeare's work in this mode is much less straightforward. It is often complicated by formal or moral restraints that alert the audience to the socially destructive and personally corrupting consequences of aggressively commanding behavior. It is also complicated by an approach to the cultivation of fantasies that is generally more critical than Marlowe's. Shakespeare tends to encourage an audience to fulfill its wanderlust only up to a point before attempting to pull it back to a sense of proportion in which political or social considerations—not always of a morally "normative" or orthodox variety—take precedence over the pleasures of fantasy fulfillment.

In most instances, the competition between engagement and resistance that Marlowe and Shakespeare set into motion in their most theatrically oriented plays should not be expected to resolve itself in any clearcut manner. Although Shakespeare may attempt more strenuously than Marlowe to dissolve or qualify the bonds of engagement he so assiduously cultivates, he cannot finally command the outcome of the competition he has evoked. This is the case because the very process a playwright activates is, as Gosson and Munday contend, a matter of resonances and suggestions that continue to ramify in a playgoer's mind long after play's end. This may, perhaps, only be another way of saying that plays in performance are better at generating incidental effects than they are at realizing determinate or intended meanings. But it is also a way of emphasizing that not even the most obvious conjunctions of cautionary aims and carefully structured effect—such as we find at the beginning and end of *Doctor Faustus* and in the closing movement of *Macbeth*—can summarily erase the enlivening experiences of vicarious abandonment and aggression in which an audience's pleasure is often rooted. We do not, on this account, need to entertain images of a subversive Shakespeare or a heterodox Marlowe in order to contend that their plays had the capacity to foster subversive and heterodox impressions in the minds of their beholders. We need merely to resist the idea that textual intention or dramatic closure can inhibit minds stimulated by powerful fantasies or by striking interventions in established belief from continuing to stage such plays in their own imaginations. The effects of such transactions may not be as decisive as Munday claims in asserting that "The webs of [of plays] are so subtilie spun, that there is no man that is once within them, that can avoide them without danger" and that "None [who] come within those snares . . . maie escape untaken, . . . such force have their inchantments of pleasure to drawe the affections of the mind" (*Third Blast*, 142). But neither can Nashe's assertion that "no Play . . . praiseth or approoueth pride, lust, whoredome, prodigalitie, or drunkennes, but beates them downe utterly" be taken with half the confidence with which it is made.

Pleasure and Transgression

Nashe can be of more help to us in negotiating the next phase of our discussion if we pursue for a moment one of his more bitter attacks against Puritan antitheatricalists. As he writes in *Pierce Penniless*: "All Artes to them are vanitie: and, if you tell them what a glorious thing it is to have *Henrie* the fifth represented on the Stage, leading the French king prisoner, and forcing both him and the Dolphin to sweare fealty, I, but (will they say) what do we get by it?" (213). The immediate object of Nashe's attack is the alleged materialism of Puritans, their "filthie vnquenchable avarice" and hunger for "execrable luker" which he opposes to the "true Nobilitie" advanced and embodied by the "aduenturous mindes" one may encounter in plays. But in the process of indicting the boorishness of Puritans, Nashe also objectifies the capacity to take pleasure in fantasy possessed by sophisticated theatergoers like himself. The vividness with which Nashe expresses his enjoyment of what is at once, from his point of view, both a theatrical and a historical triumph suggests that he was not unqualifiedly committed to the highly moralized conception of theatrical experience he elsewhere advances. While he depicts Henry V's triumphs in decidedly patriotic terms, and presents them as conducive to the moral enrichment of the playgoer, he also seems to experience a sense of vicarious empowerment in the prospect of Henry "leading the French king prisoner and forcing him and the Dolphin to sweare fealty." What Nashe "gets by" his theatrical experience is certainly nothing as material as he alleges his puritan antagonists crave. But his pleasure has its source in the material conditions of Elizabethan theatrical production which both allow for and encourage the kind of fantasy fulfillment Nashe describes.

In presenting itself as a "new place apart," the Elizabethan theater constituted a space that was distinctively other than the world outside its walls. As Steven Mullaney observes:

> When Burbage dislocated theater from the city, he established a social and cultural distance that would prove invaluable to the stagecraft of Marlowe and Shakespeare: a critical distance . . . that provided the stage with a culturally and ideologically removed vantage point from which it could reflect upon its own age with more freedom and license than had hitherto been possible. (1988, 30)

According to Mullaney, "The place of the stage was a marginal one" in several senses of the word, not least among them being its topological setting in the margins or Liberties of the city of London (9). Playgoers making their way out of the city proper, through the Liberties and into the public playhouse, would conceivably experience a growing sense of freedom from the constraints of prescribed orders of behavior that were, in many respects, officially opposed to the very liberty they had set out to enjoy. As is the case with respect to many varieties of spectatorship, the act of separation that is performed by playgoers as they pay their admission fee constitutes an imaginatively enabling event, an initiation into a world of what Victor Turner has called "liminoid phenomena" (1977, 44). These phenomena are not, according to Turner, "centrally integrated into the total social process." Instead, they "develop most characteristically *outside* the central economic and political processes, along their *margins*, on their *interfaces*, in their 'tacit dimension' " (44). In crossing into this second world or place apart, the playgoer passes from one framework of experience into another which has its own logic and defining conditions, in some ways similar, in others directly opposed, to those of "ordinary experience."[11] Some consciousness of the implications of this rite of passage may even serve to motivate the playgoer to attend a play in the first place.

One might assume that the marginality of the Elizabethan playhouse served to blunt any material impact that plays might have on the world outside the theater. But the very otherness of theatrical experience may have enabled the transaction of fantasies even the theater's aristocratic patrons might have attempted to suppress had such transactions taken place in a less mediated manner (cf. Mullaney, ix–x). These fantasies, moreover, may well have contributed to the formation of ideas and opinions that had a decidedly material impact on prevailing social practices. Indeed, what so disturbed critics like Gosson was the invisibility of the subversions and seductions they detected, their elusive status as impressions or suggestions that the overt actions of plays only *seem* to "beat down" and which they cannot, in any event, erase.

These seductions were specifically attuned to exploit and satisfy the audience's desire for release from normative constraints and its wish to explore vicariously abnormative or heterodox states of mind and feeling. In plays like *As You Like It* and *A Midsummer Night's Dream*, this desire for release is satisfied by the engagement of the audience in fantasies which, though enlivening, are neither particularly transgressive nor threatening (though it may well be argued that both plays occupy oppositional positions with respect to patriarchal dominance). On the other hand, plays like *Richard III*, *Macbeth*, *Tamburlaine*, and *The Jew of Malta* are posed to appeal to their audiences in a distinctly transgressive manner. The fact that the most performatively appealing characters in such plays are usually the most morally outrageous suggests a direct correlation between the audience's experience of pleasure and the enactment of transgressive and often violent fantasies. It is in the context of such considerations that Freud rather opaquely but suggestively observes that "the neurotic instability of the public and the dramatist's skill in avoiding resistances and offering fore-pleasures can alone determine the limits set upon the employment of abnormal characters on the stage" ("Psychopathic Characters," 310). In the plays of both Marlowe and Shakespeare, however, we may notice that a great part of the psychical charge experienced by audiences seems designed to derive less from the simple predominance of "fore-pleasures" and avoidance of "resistances" than from the clash of strong, theatrically privileged inducements to fantasy fulfillment with equally strong, but normatively defined, inducements to resistance. Thus, the pleasures of fantasy fulfillment are often directly tied to the transgressive status of the fantasy in question. Rather than attempt to avoid resistances rooted in a playgoer's normative persuasion, Marlowe and Shakespeare make their transgression the basis of the performance appeal of such characters as Tamburlaine, Barabas, and Macbeth. The pleasure a playgoer experiences through vicarious participation in the fantasies of aggression and moral abandon such characters enact draws directly on the forbidden or illicit status of their behavior.

What permits the playgoer to overcome a predictable resistance to such provocations is, to adapt Freud's observation, the dramatist's skill in making such agents of provocation as Barabas and Tamburlaine more theatrically appealing than characters who may be said to represent a normative field of reference. The appeal of such characters is rooted in any number of factors, but is perhaps best explained in terms of the character's embodiment of the play's central fantasy content, and in terms of the success he enjoys in commanding the resources of the stage and in demonstrating his mastery of the theatrical apparatus. In the course of *The Jew of Malta* and the Tamburlaine plays, Marlowe persuades his audience to "read" his production in terms of how his privileged characters represent it. Playgoers interpret the play in the way it is interpreted for them by its preferred or favored agents. To say that playgoers "identify" with such characters would be equivalent to saying that they recognize in these characters or in the positions they advance something that serves to enlarge or validate a prevailing conception that playgoers have or hold about themselves, much as

Nashe projects into the triumphs of Henry V a sense of his own empowered and empowering Englishness. But this need not always be the case.

I make this qualification because it is conceivable that even the most temperate and socially orthodox playgoers may find themselves engaged by the transgressive actions of a Marlovian overreacher or a Shakespearean villain like Richard of Gloucester. Such engagement may be transacted in one of two ways. Playgoers may, as a condition of their playgoing, consciously permit Tamburlaine to construct for them a vision of the world radically other than the world they ordinarily inhabit, one whose logic makes Tamburlaine the choicest spirit in it. Or they may unconsciously permit Tamburlaine's words and deeds to play upon what Freud would term "deeper psychical sources" of enjoyment of which they may remain unaware even as they find themselves pleasurably aroused by Tamburlaine's transgressions. In neither instance do we need to say that playgoers "identify" with Tamburlaine. It may, in fact, be more correct to say that in the one instance they *select* Tamburlaine as the most compelling embodiment of positions the playworld advances, and that in the other *they are selected* by Tamburlaine as the unsuspecting objects of a psychological seduction. They choose or are chosen.

As John Ellis writes with respect to the analogous dynamic of identification in the cinema:

> The spectator does not . . . "identify" with the hero or heroine: an identification that would, if put in its conventional sense, involve socially constructed males identifying with male heroes, and socially constructed females identifying with women heroines. The situation is more complex than this, as identification involves both the recognition of self in the image on the screen, a narcissistic identification, and the identification of self with the various positions that are involved in the fictional narration: those of hero and heroine, villain, bit-part player, active and passive character. It involves the identification of the public, external phantasies of the *fiction* with personal phantasies. Identification is therefore multiple and fractured, a sense of seeing the constituent parts of the spectator's own psyche paraded before her or him. (1982, 43)

The priority Ellis gives to "the various positions that are involved in the fictional narration" in situating the responses of both male and female spectators is consistent with my earlier claim regarding the role played by the theatrical apparatus in structuring spectatorship. But it may also appear to underestimate the contribution of sexual difference to the development of audience responses. A few of Laura Mulvey's "afterthoughts" on "visual pleasure and narrative cinema" may help to clarify both Ellis's position and my own habit of allowing gender-neutral language to repress the differential claims of female spectatorship. Mulvey grounds her analysis of "cultural convention and trans-sex identification" on a "narrative grammar" that contemporary cinema and Elizabethan drama may be said to share:

> Andromeda stays tied to the rock, a victim, in danger, until Perseus slays the monster and saves her. It is not my aim, here, to debate on the rights and wrongs of this narrative division of labour or to demand positive heroines, but rather to point out that the "grammar" of the story places the reader, listener or spectator *with* the hero and that the woman spectator in the cinema not only has her own memories but an age-old cultural tradition adapting her to this convention, which eases a transition out of her own sex into another. (1981, 13)

After enriching this insight with a series of carefully considered emendations of Freud's concept of " 'masculinity' in women" and of "the ego's desire to phantasise itself in a certain, active manner," Mulvey concludes that "as desire is given cultural materiality in a text, for women (from childhood onwards) trans-sex identification is a *habit* that very easily becomes *second Nature*" (13). I intend to reserve for a later discussion Mulvey's qualifier to the effect that "this Nature does not sit easily and shifts restlessly in its borrowed transvestite clothes" (13). For now it should be sufficient to note the extent to which her observations contribute to a broader conception of trans-class, trans-cultural, trans-race identification in the Elizabethan playhouse: one that renders a normative appropriation of the term suspect or misleading.

For these reasons among others I have, in the course of this chapter, preferred to use the term "engagement," instead of "identification," when speaking of the playgoer's immersion in the affective field of fantasies, emotions, and attitudes associated with a strong central protagonist or generated by a strong theatrical experience. There are, of course, playgoers who are actively disposed to identify directly with theatrical figures and events that satisfy their "craving for freedom in religious, political, social and sexual matters," and it is the psychic disposition of the same that I intend to explore, especially in the next, but also in subsequent chapters. I would, in the meantime, like to bring this chapter to conclusion by briefly examining an expressly brutal scene from *King Lear*—III.vii, in which the blinding of Gloucester is enacted—in order to provide a preliminary example of theory in practice.

Although it is no doubt true that a normatively sensitive playgoer will be repulsed and outraged by Gloucester's blinding, I would contend that this scene can also generate some manner of theatrical pleasure. It is too easy to assume—as would most readerly oriented critics—that Gloucester's blinding can be vicariously felt only from the point of view of the sufferer himself or from that of a sympathetic witness. In the context of a play in which physical and emotional violence is inter-generational, in which at least one son and daughter suffer greatly at the hands of their fathers and the rage of the remaining siblings is arguably grounded in feelings of paternal neglect, it is possible that violence delivered from any quarter may prove "enlivening" at best, perversely satisfying at worst. The playgoer's hold on his or her normative sympathies can probably never be sundered in the face of such an action. But if the same playgoer has consciously come to terms with the otherness of the theatrical event and has licensed the play in question to enjoy the same freedom of expression he or she has exercised in coming to the theater, then the playgoer may well be able to entertain responses that would seem decidedly abnormative outside the theater. I would, accordingly, like to make a case for the audience's participation in this scene of suffering from the point of view of the aggressor.

Shakespeare clearly takes pains to preclude such a possibility, first, by having the otherwise unappealing Cornwall, instead of the more theatrically attractive Edmund, perform the deed in question; and, second, by having Cornwall's servant heroically die in the effort to prevent it. But the servant can no more prevent Gloucester's blinding than Shakespeare can prevent its transgressive resonances from filtering through his audience's already weakened capacity to resist anxiety-provoking material. Nor can Shakespeare prevent the theatrical apparatus itself, attuned as it is to cater to the audience's desire for enjoyment, from transforming an act of supreme perversity into an occasion for perverse satisfaction. (In a recent National Theatre production of *Lear*, a very audible pop accompanied the bursting of Gloucester's first eye, encouraging the kind of ghoulish thrill or *frisson* one generally associates with the effects of horror films.) One may also detect in Cornwall and Regan's joint acts of aggression the displaced activity of parricidal fantasies that operate to similar effect in *Macbeth*, compelling one's feelings of resistance, moral outrage and indignation to compete with the theatrically privileged pleasures of vicarious transgression.

As noted above, defenses against the unsettling fantasies a given play cultivates are usually inscribed in the formal structure or moralizing cues of the playtext itself. Even without the intervention of Cornwall's servant, the spectator of Gloucester's blinding is given ample notice that the action witnessed is evil; that identifying with the agent of such villainy is wrong; and that such actions have consequences that will eventually "plague the inventor."[12] However, the fact that the spectator can generally depend on a drama's formal structure to keep the play of fantasy within containable limits also eliminates the need to hold tight to normative defenses. Hence, the drama's very structure enables the playgoer to entertain the fulfillment of fantasies whose realization would prove positively disabling in the framework of ordinary experience. Thus freed of normative constraints by the dependence on theatrical convention, the playgoer is able to turn the occasion of someone else's suffering into an occasion of pleasure.

This feeling of pleasure need not derive, as is usually the case in Marlowe, from any conscious or unconscious engagement with the aggressor in a violent action. As Ellis observes:

> It is equally possible for pleasure to be gained from scenes of humiliation and defeat as it is from scenes of success and victory. In both cases, the pleasure comes from the fulfillment of a wish (for we wish what we fear as well as what we desire), and from seeing the fulfillment of that wish in the other. (1982, 86)

Pleasure may also be "due to masochistic satisfaction" and have its source in the playgoer's identification with the victim of aggression ("Psychopathic Characters," 306). What ultimately determines a playgoer's position in relation to scenes of suffering or transgression is the interplay of his or her normative psychic disposition, the (probably more permissive) psychic disposition brought to bear on the viewing of plays, and the specific nature of a given play's approach to the same. Plays that traffic in transgression and suffering—and most plays that are tragic in orientation will belong to this category—traffic as well in a broad array of compensations designed to satisfy the playgoer's desire for pleasure. As Freud writes:

> Suffering of every kind is . . . the subject-matter of drama, and from this suffering it promises to give the audience pleasure. Thus we arrive at a first condition of this form of art: that it should not cause suffering to the audience, that it should know how to compensate, by means of the possible satisfactions involved, for the sympathetic suffering which is aroused. ("Psychopathic Characters," 307)

Although Freud draws this conclusion in relation to Greek tragedies in which "Heroes are first and foremost rebels against God or against something divine; and pleasure is derived . . . from the affliction of a weaker being in the face of divine might" (306), it can also be profitably applied to the study of Shakespearean drama where the lines of conflict are less strictly demarcated and distinctions between victims and aggressors are often confused. Indeed, it is precisely this blurring of roles that makes it so difficult to determine the affective aims and ends of plays like *King Lear* and *Macbeth*.[13]

It is, for example, sufficiently clear that when Tamburlaine threatens the virgins of Damascus with sudden death in the first part of Marlowe's play, imaginative engagement with a seemingly omnipotent human aggressor, capable of making his will his act, guarantees far more pleasure to the audience than sympathetic suffering. Whatever resistance the audience may require to defend itself from countenancing so abnormative an action has long been broken down by a play expressly designed to allow the audience to fulfill vicariously its own fantasies of omnipotence. However, in *King Lear*, sympathetic suffering is so systematically evoked that the only compensatory satisfaction Shakespeare can offer his audience is the prospect of looking on as the aggressors are destroyed with their victims. Faced with this prospect of largely masochistic satisfaction, the audience may well find itself more powerfully enlivened by the sadistic ministrations of the play's aggressors. What mediates the movement of audience engagement in such instances will have much to do with the psychic disposition of the playgoer, whose capacity to resist such an alternative is tested and challenged by the failure or refusal of the drama to provide a more acceptable source of pleasure. The capacity of the playgoer to find satisfaction in scenes of suffering cannot, finally, be measured in any but speculative terms. But if the plays that a playgoer attends on a regular basis repeatedly depend on a high degree of responsiveness to violent or transgressive subject matter, then it can be inferred that some integration of pleasure with fantasies of aggression is likely.

The Elizabethan repertory is, of course, characterized by a large body of plays that traffic broadly in violent effects and appear to encourage audience engagement with their featured agents of transgression. In this context, the critical privileging of audience resistance to characters like Tamburlaine, Selimus, and Richard of Gloucester constitutes a willful disregard of the prevailing conditions of Elizabethan dramatic production and consumption. What we need instead of a critical perspective premised on disapproval and denial is a way of understanding why such plays exerted so strong an appeal on their playgoing public and, more specifically, why the playgoing public could be expected to respond favorably to representations of transgressive behavior and ideas. It is this that I hope to supply in the following chapter.

2. The Audience in Theory and Practice

While I have attempted to ground my model of theatrical experience on observations drawn from the attacks on and defenses of playmaking of the 1580s and 1590s, I have also relied on formulations that are indebted to more modern habits of thought and feeling, and have often appropriated insights drawn from psychoanalysis and contemporary film theory in an effort to develop a collateral model of theatrical spectatorship. I have specifically deferred coming to terms with the problem posed by different historical constructions of the subject, preferring to privilege the Elizabethan theater's construction of a *playgoing* subject rather than contend with the "bafflement" likely to be generated by a more probing exploration of Renaissance culture (see Greenblatt 1986, 210). In referring in the above to the defenses an interested spectator at a performance of *King Lear* could be expected to bring to bear against anxiety-provoking material, I have, for example, failed to consider the extent to which those defenses may differ from those the Elizabethan playgoer may have summoned up in the face of similar provocations. I have, moreover, assumed (in the "unruffled" manner of the psychoanalytic claimant) that a mechanism commensurate with defensiveness played a role in the psychic procedures of the Elizabethan subject.

Although I harbor no illusions regarding the ability of even the most astute analyst to classify and measure so hypothetical a construct, I do think that valid observations can be made regarding the psychic dispositions of Elizabethan playgoers, and that such observations can be legitimately addressed in the "historically belated" languages of contemporary critical practices. Such observations will necessarily depend on what Simon Shepherd terms "guesswork" in his own effort to clear out space for what I would prefer to call informed speculation. As Shepherd writes:

> Many documents survive and have often been analysed, but it is harder to know what the [Elizabethan] audiences thought of the theatres —why they went, what they thought they were watching, how they perceived the theatre's relationship

with the rest of their lives; most work here is guesswork, and it is worth the reader remembering that when I (or anyone else) assert that a particular text is radical or whatever, there are very few grounds for knowing if any or all of the audience saw it that way (which doesn't mean that they didn't either). (1986, xiv–xv)

It is for such reasons that much of what I will have to say about particular plays in subsequent chapters will seem highly subjective, and will depend on an answering responsiveness on the part of the reader who will have to substitute for the missing link in this transaction, namely, the Elizabethan playgoer. Some measures can, however, be taken to give that playgoer a more collaborative role in this project.

One means of compensating for the silence of the absent playgoer is to indicate how the kinds of responses we delegate to guesswork may have been prompted by both explicit and implicit directives in the playtexts that survive them. A second is to correct some of the misconceptions about Elizabethan playgoers that have been fostered by a critical reliance on a prescriptive historicism which has presumed to speak for them. While this may well involve the cultivation of an entirely new set of misconceptions that later scholars will have to dislodge, contending with the vexed question of the historical subject cannot be infinitely deferred. Finally, we will need to integrate what we can learn from the playtexts themselves and from newer approaches to the historical moment of Elizabethan drama with the model of theatrical experience I have outlined above.

The Audience in Theory

The performative orientation of much recent dramatic criticism has already done much to illumine the previously dark corners of audience response by focusing on the playwright's attempt to control, shape, and "orchestrate" the effects of his art. As Jean Howard writes:

Shakespeare's plays . . . give every evidence that he thought a great deal about audiences: their potential recalcitrance and suggestibility, the techniques by which the dramatist wins or forfeits control over them, the potential abuses and benefits of such control; . . . he also created scripts that reveal his constant concern with guiding the perceptions and responses of those who watched his dramas. (1984, 8)

It is, of course, easier to determine how a given playtext attempts to guide "the perceptions and responses" of an audience than it is to determine how the audience in question—which is not a unitary group but an assembly of often clashing temperaments and moods—actually received and responded to the play in performance. For example, when Leontes, in the first act of *The Winter's Tale*, seems to move out of his state of jealous self-absorption to address the audience directly, it would appear that Shakespeare intends to challenge the audience's predictable resistance to Leontes's misbegotten fantasy and to bring it into the orbit of his obsessiveness:

> There have been
> Or I am much deceiv'd, cuckolds ere now;
> And many a man there is, even at this present,
> Now while I speak this, holds his wife by th' arm,
> That little thinks she has been sluic'd in 's absence
> And his pond fish'd by his next neighbor, by
> Sir Smile, his neighbor.
>
> (I.ii.190–96)

Shakespeare's success at spreading the contagion of Leontes's jealousy to the male playgoers in the audience-at-large depends on his character's ability to arouse at least the tacit ackowledgment of a corresponding suspicion in his auditors. It depends as well on the predisposition of these playgoers to be aroused in a manner that is likely both to provoke the kind of anxiety that is presumably inimical to the pleasure they normally seek in plays and to transform that feeling of anxiety into a sensation of pleasure. How such playgoers did, in fact, respond to this presumptive assault against their complacency is lost to us. But if we are willing, on the one hand, to forgo the easy answers a moralizing tradition of criticism provides and, on the other, to entertain some of the possibilities opened up by a more performative orientation, we may be able to recover at least a rough idea of audience response to this and other highly charged theatrical moments.

The moralizing tradition to which I refer has an abstract solution to such material dilemmas. Proceeding from a sense of history gleaned, as Michael Hattaway writes, from "literary and printed sources," from "philosophic and theological tracts" (1982, 2), it would view Leontes's attempted abridgment of the confines of dramatic space as consistent with his inversion of his own psychic hierarchy, and would extend that view to all members of the audience (apart, perhaps, from the long-suffering groundlings).

Leontes's attempt to engage the audience's participation in the anarchy of his own perceptions would be interpreted as an exaggerated symptom of psychic disturbance which the audience has been taught neither to share nor to countenance. The audience would, in short, become even more distanced from a character it already finds extremely alienating.

A performative orientation which privileges psychological effects over paraphrastic meanings supplies a decidedly different reading of the same action. From a performative perspective, Leontes's address to the audience would first need to be placed in relation to the dramatic economy of the play's first movement, within which it offers an area of relief or release from an unveering focus on his psychic and emotional isolation. All that precedes and succeeds Leontes's brief aside appears expressly designed to alienate both male and female playgoers from the scene of Leontes's fantasy. However, in so doing, it also serves to inhibit their capacity for engagement with the one character onstage who commands the kind of theatrical energy to which audiences are likely to prove responsive. Prior to Leontes's outburst, the play exists at a psychic and physical remove from the protected space occupied by the audience. If not precluded altogether, audience engagement with the play's fantasy content is at best deferred or deflected into sympathetic concern for the innocent characters who are soon to become Leontes's victims, most notably, Hermione. Upon Leontes's outburst, what has been deferred may suddenly be spurred into life. Leontes's direct address to the audience may even stimulate a bout of "fetishistic looking" in which the audience's "gaze is captivated by what it sees, does not wish to inquire further, to see more, to find out" (Ellis 1982, 47). The audience need not meet Leontes's challenge with an answering affirmation of shared suspicion for engagement to occur. It need merely register the tempering of its own resistance to a fantasy that has now outgrown the boundaries of the stage and Leontes's self-absorption alike. As the spectator turns (as well *he* might) to catch the knowing look of "Sir Smile, his neighbor," the play itself turns a corner, having made a small inroad into the imagination of its beholders, one that will possibly energize their succeeding encounters with the play's protagonist and his formerly incomprehensible rage.

I add the parenthetical qualifier—"as well *he* might"—because this scene also brings into focus Laura Mulvey's qualification of her argument regarding the female spectator's habit of trans-sex identification "that very easily becomes second Nature" but "does not sit easily and shifts restlessly in its borrowed transvestite clothes" (1982, 80). Indeed, it is difficult to imagine any female spectator being "carried along . . . by the scruff of [this] text," which seems designed to make her feel "so out of key with the pleasure on offer, with its 'masculinisation,' that the spell of fascination is broken" (12). The restless shifting that Mulvey envisions during otherwise successful acts of trans-sex identification in the process of cinematic viewing might, in the context of a mixed-sex viewing of *The Winter's Tale*, result in a restive disinclination on the part of female playgoers to yield to the logic or grammar of Leontes' sexually degrading fantasy. Such shifting might lead to a predominantly gender-specific response to the scene in question, casting Leontes's generation of male anxieties about female sexuality in direct opposition to newly generated female anxieties about male violence. At this point, the audience might be as divided in its perceptions of the stage action as Leontes is estranged from Hermione.

In the course of this meditation, I have, admittedly, left the inscrutable Jacobean audience behind and have replaced its unknowable responses with perceptions of my own.[1] My reading of this scene has focused less on what Leontes's lines "mean" than on what they do or, more correctly, seem intended to do when performatively realized before an attentive and, perhaps, unusually responsive audience. I have, however, proceeded without reference either to a specific performance of *The Winter's Tale*, or to an actual audience whose consensual responses to this sequence could be accurately determined. Instead, I have, constructed a hypothetical performance of *The Winter's Tale* consistent with the dramatic directives embedded in its playtext, and have reconstructed the kinds of audience response such a version of the play would conceivably elicit.

Both strategies are problematic. My performative model of this sequence may distort or misinterpret the playtext's directives (there is, after all, no explicit cue for an *aside* in the playtext itself). And my reconstruction of audience response to a sequence I have myself set into motion may be too subjectively charged to lay any claim to consensual validity. The problem of consensual validity is, of course, a central one, and has been the focus of many recent debates about the various forms of reader-response criticism, an enterprise that has much in common with the project I have undertaken here. Unfortunately, most proponents of reader-response criticism have confined themselves, in theory and practice, to the consideration of texts whose performative function is completely "transacted" by the reader alone, in isolation from the powerful stimulus provided by actors on a stage and from the more subtle influence exerted by a playgoer's membership in a company of consenting others.[2] In attempting to adapt the readerly persuasions of critics like Norman Holland, Stanley Fish, and Wolfgang Iser to the specific demands of a dramatic text, it thus becomes necessary to begin by acknowledging the peculiar position that the playtext holds in relation to the interpretive process.

As noted earlier, the dramatic text operates as a scripted supplement to the performances it maps and records, as a secondary source to primary experiences it closely resembles but with which it can never become synonymous.[3] Transacting a reading with this text alone is a perfectly legitimate exercise insofar as the performances to which the text points or refers can never be reconstituted to satisfy everyone's sense of their validity or authority. However, no response to a dramatic text that proceeds in the absence of performative considerations can also claim to respond to the *play* that is the elusive signified of the textual signifier. A play performed in a uniquely public space, constructed with a conscious regard for bringing audiences into proximity to speaking pictures and animated emotions, necessarily claims a more active role in shaping and manipulating audience response than has been claimed for nondramatic texts, which are considered passive accomplices to the interpretive act itself.[4] The active role that plays take in shaping audience response requires the audience-oriented critic of dramatic texts to construct a provisional mean between the two extremes embodied by fixed texts which we alone can animate and by irrecoverable performances which animated their original audiences. Lacking a representative performance model of a play like *The Winter's Tale* to which we can refer with the same graphic consistency as we refer to its text, we are compelled to operate in a middle ground that is largely of our own making, but that is also shaped by a disciplined regard for the historically specific conventions of theatrical performance and a sustained responsiveness to the peculiar economy of theatrical experience. The validity of this operation finally depends on whether audience-oriented critics and *their* audiences agree about what these conventions are and what this theatrical economy actually entails; it depends, that is, on whether they are—to borrow Fish's phrase—"member[s] of the same interpretive community" (1976, 485).

The problem of validity is compounded when we dare to speak on behalf of yet another interpretive community, namely, the Elizabethan audience, whose responses to plays are either irrecoverable or too enmeshed in polemical considerations to be trusted. Nevertheless, I do mean to make a claim for the capacity of at least some members of the playgoing public to experience and sustain the sensation of pleasurable provocation

Shakespeare seems to want to elicit through Leontes's address, and more generally, for that public's capacity to appreciate psychic disturbance as psychic arousal. In order to substantiate these claims and to contravene some of the objections often leveled at the avowedly subjective practitioners of reader response criticism, I intend to extend the range of audience oriented criticism into the domain of historically specific audiences, beginning with the following effort to revise conventional views of the Elizabethan interpretive community.[5]

The Elizabethan Interpretive Community

In *The Birth of Tragedy*, Nietzsche draws a direct correlation between the popularity of the deeply unsettling matter of Greek tragedy and the psychic health of Greek culture. He does so in part to criticize and belittle what he considers to be the degraded culture of his contemporaries who prefer the quietizing pleasures of sentiment and romantic posturing to the provocations of tragic experience.[6] Were we to apply Nietzsche's remarks to a comparative study of Elizabethan drama and the decidedly less provocative drama of the Restoration and the eighteenth century, we would be able to isolate some important characteristics of early modern theatrical culture. The Nahum Tate sentimentalization of *King Lear*, which has analogues in Dryden's earlier rewritings of *Antony and Cleopatra* and *Troilus and Cressida*, could provide an exemplary case in point, as could the general critical designation of Shakespeare as a native genius in-spite-of-himself who required the corrections that a more decorous age stood ready to deliver.

Every age reshapes the productions of the past in a manner designed to ensure continued access to and enjoyment of them. In some instances, the teeth of such productions are sharpened to assure that the bite they once commanded will still be felt by an auditory dulled either by overfamiliarity or unfamiliarity with them. A systematic effort to dull or to soften the effects of specific Elizabethan plays seems, however, to have motivated Dryden and the adapters of the eighteenth and bowdlerizers of the nineteenth centuries. I take these efforts to have been made not only out of a concern for what could continue to give pleasure to a contemporary audience, but also out of an anxiety about what that audience could be expected to endure. That these audiences could be expected to endure less than the playgoing Elizabethan, and that what they construed as endurance could on no account be considered conducive to pleasure, suggests a change in

temperament and psychic disposition, a shift in preference from engagement to resistance, openness to denial, in the context of theatrical transactions.

Although the apparent psychic restraint of eighteenth-century playmak-
ers and playgoers tells us nothing definite about the psychic disposition of
Elizabethan audiences, it does indicate that the latter at least maintained a
broader range of responsiveness to plays. The repertory of surviving plays
tells us a great deal more about the specific kinds of dramatic material to
which the playgoing public was responsive. And the pre-eminence of
works by Marlowe, Shakespeare, Jonson, and Webster in that repertory
tells us that what we today consider the masterworks of the age were (with
a few significant exceptions) similarly construed by the playgoing public.
But even if, as Andrew Gurr writes, "the successes among the better plays
were made by the consistent judgments of a long series of audiences" who
"could hardly be called bad judges" (1970, 153), our reasons for valuing such
works may be different from those of Shakespeare's contemporaries. It
may, for example, please us to think that the popularity of *Doctor Faustus*,
The Spanish Tragedy, and *Hamlet* testifies to the Elizabethan audience's enjoyment of the same kind of psychic health in the face of suffering that
Nietzsche attributes to the understanding auditory of fifth-century Athens.
The popularity of such works may, however, just as well document the
responsiveness of audiences to plays that traffic in devils, ghosts, and the
violent effects of revenge. In short, we still need to meet some of the challenges Simon Shepherd delegates to guesswork. And the most formidable
of them is to see whether something substantive can be added to informed
opinion regarding the psychic disposition of Elizabethan playgoers.

Despite Andrew Gurr's recent effort to collect all extant references to
"Playgoing in Shakespeare's London" in his book of the same name (1987),
we are still as far as ever from any authoritative conclusion regarding the
mental and social composition of Elizabethan playgoers. The enterprise
itself is fraught with ideological assumptions that color and distort both
the recovery and transmission of the information that we do possess.[7] Such
is the case even with regard to the documents that scholars like Alfred Harbage and Ann Jennalie Cook have employed to support their respective
theses. As Gurr observes in his earlier book, *The Shakespearean Stage*
(1970):

> Shakespearean London more than most conurbations had a many-headed public
> divided against itself, and the images its members painted of playhouses and

playgoing were highly variable and of very doubtful reliability, particularly from the non- playgoing 80 per cent. The spokesmen for Puritan London described the audiences as riotous and immoral; the playwrights described them as ignorant and wilful; the City Fathers regarded them as riotous and seditious. (141)

Yet, as Gurr concludes, "If any of these images had been in any large degree true the playhouses would have been closed much earlier than 1642" (141).

In his most recent book, Gurr contends with the limitations and *lacunae* of his own information oriented approach by offering an estimate of audience composition that is, finally, based less on documentary evidence than on guesswork:

> I am inclined to believe that despite the infrequent reference to their presence citizens were the staple, at least of amphitheatre audiences, throughout the period. . . . Given the number of citizens in London, their relative affluence, and their proximity to all the playhouse venues, it may not be wildly wrong to think of them and their lesser neighbors the prosperous artisan class as a kind of silent majority of the playhouses. (1987, 64)[8]

That Gurr bases his belief on an inclination he hopes is not "wildly wrong" does not encourage confidence. It does, however, constitute an honest appraisal of the difficulties involved in making such a determination, and also offers a corrective to Ann Jennalie Cook's more confident claim that the majority of playgoers in Shakespeare's London were drawn from the privileged classes (1981). Cook's thesis has been roundly criticized by other scholars, though by none more convincingly than Martin Butler who observes that "the size of the ratio between population and theatre capacity seems to point very strongly in the opposite direction from Cook's conclusion, towards inclusiveness rather than exclusiveness" (1984, 298). Butler concludes that "It is patently obvious . . . that the unprivileged did go to plays in quantities, and that at least some of the time or in some theatres they constituted the principal audience" (300).[9]

In another appraisal of Cook's "hypothesis of primarily elite spectators" as "one fraught with logical and empirical problems," Walter Cohen takes Butler's conclusion one step farther, contending that "an insistence on a heterogeneous audience with a plurality of artisans and shopkeepers, and a majority consisting of these groups and the ones beneath them—servants, prostitutes, transients, soldiers, and criminals—is compatible with the existing evidence and hence considerably more plausible" (1985, 168). Cohen may appear to recuperate here Alfred Harbage's well-known conception of

Shakespeare's audience as "literally popular, ascending through each gradation from potboy to prince" (1941, 159). But his own notion of the "literally popular" is pointedly committed to a *descending* model of a largely artisanal theater that reaches down to embrace representatives of the Elizabethan underclass.

Rather than contribute an interested hypothesis of my own, I choose to accept Butler's general argument on behalf of inclusiveness but prefer not to choose between Gurr's estimate of audience composition and Cohen's since both are, to varying degrees, designed to advance a class-oriented argument. Attempting to make distinctions regarding the class-composition of Elizabethan audiences is, assuredly, a worthy activity. Knowing to whom a play like *Tamburlaine* was primarily addressed would immeasurably enrich our understanding of Marlowe's intentions. Whether Tamburlaine's aggressive rise from humble origins to shake the inherited thrones of the mighty would primarily excite the emulation of the propertyless worker, inspire the admiration of the upwardly bound merchant, or exasperate the propertied aristocrat is a subject of profound interest that I will address in my next chapter. But the search for a predominant audience also involves the quest for the kind of single, predominating response which may have been incompatible with the economy of Elizabethan theatrical experience and with the dynamic (and divided) nature of Elizabethan society. If the Elizabethan playhouse did, in fact, cater to a broad range of social types, the conflicts that characterized their encounters outside the theater may have played a similarly divisive role in the context of theatrical experience. Thus, a play like *Tamburlaine* could be said to have simultaneously addressed itself in different ways to different constituencies.

While the division of the Elizabethan playgoing public into discrete classes with specific social or political points of view may appear to offer a promising method of reconstructing audience response, it also has the effect of channelling playgoer responses into predetermined, socially constructed categories. Even were we able to identify the interests of citizens with the thematic conventions of domestic comedy or the interests of apprentices with the more violent fare of revenge tragedies, we would still have to account for the proven capacity of playgoers to find satisfaction in dramatic material that is clearly foreign to their practical interests and preoccupations. For such reasons it is finally less important to identify who comprised the Elizabethan audience, from what social classes and walks of life they were drawn, than it is to determine what motivated people of all classes to attend plays, what effects plays might have had on them, and what such people brought to their successive acts of playgoing. To make such determinations, we must continue to rely to a large extent on informed speculation. But we may also use historical resources that supersede the kind of evidence assembled by Gurr who, in his chapter on the "Mental Composition" of Elizabethan audiences, seldom ranges beyond the confines of theatrical literature and fails entirely to address either the psychological disposition of playgoers, or the social and political conditions of Elizabethan England (1987, 80–114).

It is not, for example, simply guesswork to call attention to the rapid economic and demographic changes in late sixteenth-century English society, to observe that "the ideal of a static, paternalistic society . . . was threatened by growing commercialism and individualism, which the state was unable to control," or to note that "Contemporaries were acutely aware of these challenges to the social order" (Beier 1974, 27). Nor is it guesswork to allege that the corresponding shifts in traditional social relationships these changes engendered—especially in London, that "centre of conspicuous consumption"—would be felt as keenly by the Elizabethan playgoer as by any other contemporary Englishman.[10] As Lawrence Stone writes:

> The rapid economic changes of the period were upsetting old social relationships, creating new classes of persons who no longer fitted into the old, ordered hierarchical system. There were now very much larger numbers of ruthless entrepreneurs who were disturbing public order by their materialist drive for economic gain. (1972, 86–87)

Stone makes this statement in the context of his well-known argument that "the rise of the gentry . . . is politically the single most important social development of the age" and that "the rise of the professional classes is . . . not far behind it" (75), an argument we need not accept in full to make use of the evidence from which it is drawn.[11] Such evidence depicts an England where formerly strict social distinctions were becoming blurred, where the "thrusting materialist drive for economic gain" was at once a source of social division and a shared interest for a broad range of social types.

We possess, of course, many other pictures of Elizabethan society, drawn from a number of competing and complementary perspectives, and should not, perhaps, privilege one over the other. But Stone's provides a particularly apt point of departure for a reconstruction of the psychic landscape of the Elizabethan playgoer insofar as his emphases fall on some of the same social and economic concerns with which the Elizabethan theatrical industry was preoccupied. In his portrait of Francis Langley, builder and owner of the Swan playhouse, William Ingram provides an interesting case study of one of the more disruptive social types Stone sees emerging at this time, namely, the "ruthless entrepreneur." According to Ingram:

> Langley early developed a kind of haughtiness or disdain of those around him, perhaps in emulation of the social positions adopted by the Londoners of rank and position he knew as a youth.
>
> He also developed a kind of arrogant ruthlessness, . . . the behavior manifested itself in a deliberate refusal of compassion for the plight of inferiors, coupled with a readiness to take advantage of them whenever the opportunity might present itself. In this he pursued a mode of conduct that he might easily have observed around him. London was never devoid of exemplars for this sort of behavior, and they could be found at all levels of society. (1978, 3–4)

While Ingram clearly wishes to make the unsympathetic Langley appear more representative an Elizabethan than he may have been in fact, Ingram is also careful to add that if Langley was "in many ways the embodiment of his times," he did not, "like Sir Philip Sidney," embody the age's "aspirations" so much as its "actualities," one of which was the predisposition to violence (7). This disparity between the age's aspirations and its actualities has also been remarked by Joel Hurstfield, who writes of the "tension between things as they seemed and things as they were" with particular application to "such violence as existed in Tudor England" (1973, 66), and by Anthony Esler for whom it provides a key to understanding why "the Elizabethan younger generation" tended to "lavish their highest idealism on objects which to more orthodox minds seemed sordidly materialistic" (1966, 160).

Langley's case not only provides a point of reference for Stone's observations regarding economic ruthlessness and the attractions of social mobility, and for Hurstfield's and Esler's regarding the age's apparent contradictions; it also closely corresponds to some of the less flattering perceptions of contemporary visitors to England about Englishmen in general. One account portrays Englishmen as "extremely proud and overbearing" and indiscriminately violent (1 Wirtemberg in Rye 1865, 7–8); another as "not vindictive, but very inconstant, rash, vainglorious, light and deceiving, and very suspicious" (Van Meteren in Rye, 70). Although such perceptions may appear symptomatic of the defenses any foreigner will erect against new and seemingly threatening experiences (a charge that may not, however, be applicable to Van Meteren who lived in England throughout Elizabeth's reign), they grow to something of great constancy as one reads through them, especially in their repeated emphasis on the *in*constancy of the English temperament and on the susceptibility of Englishmen to imaginative suggestion and sudden acts of violence. For example, a Venetian envoy to London writes in 1559 that

> The English are universally partial to novelty, hostile to foreigners, and not very friendly amongst themselves: they attempt to do everything that comes into their heads, just as if all that imagination suggests could be easily executed; hence a greater number of insurrections have broken out in this country than in all the rest of the world, . . . (in Hurstfield and Smith 1972, 32)

The same envoy adds that "during the last twenty years three Princes of the blood, four Dukes, forty earls, and more than three thousand other persons have died by violent death." He concludes that it may "be easily imagined that no foreigner could rule this kind of people, when even their own countrymen are not safe" (33). That a fondness for precipitous involvement in ill-conceived political ventures continued to beset the English at the end of Elizabeth's reign is illustrated by the seditious activity of the Earl of Essex—who, like Elizabeth herself, may be said to have fully appreciated the influence of plays on receptive minds—and the frustrated complots traditionally associated with Guy Fawkes and his confederates.

Other accounts testify to a populace "desirous of novelties" who changed "their fashions every year, both men and women" (Van Meteren in Rye, 71) and quickly redressed offenses, both real and imagined. As Jacob Rathgeb, private secretary to Frederick, Duke of Wirtemberg, writes in 1592:

> . . . because the greater part [of the inhabitants of London], especially the trades people, seldom go into other countries, but always remain in their houses attending to their business, they care little for foreigners, but scoff and laugh at them; and moreover one dare not oppose them, else the street boys and apprentices collect together in immense crowds and strike to the right and left unmercifully without regard to person; and because they are the strongest, one is obliged to put up with the insult as well as the injury. (Rye, 7–8)

The possibly oversensitive Rathgeb also reminds us that violence was not simply the work of tradespeople directed against foreigners when he notes the "thirty-four heads of persons of distinction stuck atop London Bridge"

(Rye, 9) and explains why most English cities lack fortifications. Describing a visit to Reading, he observes that "what was fortified and strong has long ago been razed and destroyed, in order that the subjects, who are naturally inclined to sedition, should in no case find an opportunity to rebel and rise up against the government" (Rye, 13).

The sight of the same thirty odd heads of persons of distinction inspired Thomas Platter in 1599 to note that what was apparently intended to constitute a warning to all other presumptuous conspirers against the state actually functioned as a source of self-esteem for those spectators who could "identify" with the executed noblemen:

> At the top of one tower almost in the centre of the [London] bridge, were stuck on tall stakes more than thirty skulls of noble men who had been executed and beheaded for treason and other reasons. And their descendents are accustomed to boast of this, themselves even pointing out to one their ancestors' heads on this same bridge, believing that they will be esteemed the more because their ancestors were of such high descent that they could even covet the crown, but being too weak to attain it were executed for rebels; this they make an honor for themselves of what was set up to be a disgrace and an example. (Clare Williams, ed., 1937, 155)

The ability of these "interested" spectators to transform such conspicuous reminders of the mortal consequences of political transgression into "an honor for themselves," provides a revealing insight into what could constitute a legitimate aspiration for privileged Elizabethans and a habit of mind for privileged playgoers.[12] At the very least, it supports the antitheatricalist claim that Elizabethan playgoers could be expected to transform "into example of imitation" the very actions proscribed by the most morally and politically didactic plays.

What Rathgeb attributes to the natural inclination of Englishmen to sedition, and Platter attributes to pride, is elsewhere identified with an excess of animal spirits, as is the case in the following excerpt from "Paul Hentzner's Travels in England" (1598):

> [The English] are powerful in the field, successful against their enemies, impatient of anything like slavery; vastly fond of great noises that fill the ear, such as the firing of cannon, drums, and the ringing of bells, so that in London it is common for a number of them that have got a glass in their heads to go up into some belfry, and ring the bells for hours together, for the sake of exercise. (Rye, 111)

Hentzner's observation that the exuberance of English bell-ringers was fueled by drink may be placed in the broader field of reference provided by Keith Thomas, who notes that the average consumption of alcohol at the time in question works out to a pint-a-day for every man, woman, and child in England (1971, 18). Whether it was a natural seditiousness, overweening pride, a simple taste for liberty, or the mood altering effects of alcohol that made the English "impatient of anything like slavery," a composite picture of Elizabethans drawn from such evidence would feature a volatile populace at virtually every social stratum, sudden and extravagant in its expressions of anger and pleasure; highly susceptible to suggestion; haughty and anti-authoritarian; and strongly responsive to novelty and changes of fashion.[13]

According to Thomas, such a picture would only be the outward manifestation of deeper currents of thought and feeling which were themselves the products of lives that "were, by our standards, exceedingly liable to pain, sickness and premature death" (5). After observing that " 'Drink' was built into the fabric of social life" and "played a part in nearly every public and private ceremony, every commercial bargain, every craft ritual, every private occasion of mourning and rejoicing" (17), Thomas notes, for example, that "Alcohol was . . . an essential narcotic which anaesthetized men against the strains of contemporary life" (19). Notable among these strains were the repeated visitations of the plague; the "capricious" and unmanageable danger of fires (17); and the "lifetime of intermittent physical pain" survivors of the same "could anticipate" (6).[14] But what is most noteworthy in Thomas's review of English living conditions is the failure of any of these strains to prompt the great mass of English people to hold the material world in contempt and to place their faith in the solace of the afterlife promised by Christian belief and devotion.

The reports of foreigners regarding the pride, volatility, inconstancy, and propensity for violence of Elizabethans are complemented, on this account, by domestic reports of the irreverent approach of the populace to religious rituals and beliefs. As Thomas observes:

> Presentments made before the ecclesiastical courts show that virtually every kind of irreverent (and irrelevant) activity took place during divine worship. Members of the congregation jostled for pews, nudged their neighbors, howled and spat, knitted, made coarse remarks, told jokes, fell asleep, and even let off guns. Preaching was popular with the educated classes but aroused the irritation of others. (161)

Thomas's last comment suggests that behavior of the kind described in such presentments may have largely been confined to the uneducated, some of whom "remained throughout their lives utterly ignorant of the elementary tenets of Christian dogma" (159). But the series of examples Thomas advances also suggests that irreverence was not symptomatic of religious ignorance alone or confined to the domain of "heath and forest" where many "knew more about Robin Hood than they did about the stories in the Bible" (164). The antitheatricalists, of course, alleged that irreverence had established a particularly strong footing on the Elizabethan stage where plays might compete with sermons for the allegiance of even the most privileged members of society. As Richard Schilders writes in his preface to John Rainolds's *The Overthrow of Stage Playes* (1600):

> . . . the gentlewoman that sware by her trouth, *That she was as much edefied at a play as ever she was at any sermon, etc.* will, ere she die, be of another minde, though it may be shee saied true then, in regard of her owne negligence and backwardnes in not giving eare to the word of God with reverence. The like may fall out also to those men too, that have not bene afraid of late dayes to bring upon the Stage the very sober countenances, grave attire, modest and matronlike gestures & speaches of men & women to be laughed at as a scorne and reproch to the world (A3v–4r).

According to Thomas, irreverence was also symptomatic of the "wide degree of heterodoxy" (166) that embraced rich and poor alike in the period in question. It could be expressed in such curiously inspired statements as that attributed to Thomas Aston of Ribstod-with-Bewdley to the effect that "stage plays were made by the Holy Ghost and the word of God was but man's invention" (170), or in the learned provocations attributed to Marlowe in the Baines deposition. The fact that Marlowe's alleged contentions regarding the strategically mystifying basis of religious belief and enforcement could be anticipated in 1578 by a ploughwright's remarks regarding the invented basis of the New Testament—which he termed "but mere foolishness, a story of men, or rather a fable" (171)—testifies to the possible pervasiveness of such thinking in the late sixteenth century and also indicates the possibility of a responsive auditory for thoughts of a similarly heterodox variety that were expressed on the contemporary stage. The fate of the ploughwright—one of eight persons burned at the stake between 1548–1612 for holding anti-Trinitarian beliefs—leads Thomas to conclude that such "evidence of widespread religious skepticism is not to be underrated, for it may be reasonably surmised that many thought what they dared not say aloud" (171).[15] If, with Thomas, we add to "this self-conscious rejection of religious dogma . . . the incalculable forces of worldliness and apathy," which ordinarily oppose themselves to religious practices, we may also be prepared to acknowledge that "a substantial proportion of the population regarded organized religion with an attitude which varied from cold indifference to frank hostility" (172).

Evidence also suggests that some Elizabethans of the lower classes harbored deep resentment against prevailing social, political, and economic arrangements. As Keith Wrightson observes:

> Anonymous libels and seditious utterances testify to the existence among at least some of the common people of a bitter hatred of the rich whom they regarded as exploiters: "Yt wold never be merye till some of the gentlemen were knocked down" was the opinion of one prospective leader of an abortive Oxfordshire uprising in 1596. (1982, 150)

This opinion so closely echoes that of one of Jack Cade's comrades in Shakespeare's 2 Henry VI—"Well, I say it was / never merry world in England since gentlemen came / up" (IV.ii.7–9)—that one wonders whether the Oxfordshire man was presenting it as a contemporary solution to the problem posed there. As Buchanan Sharp writes with respect to the Oxfordshire disorders: "The dislike of gentlemen was so strong that when an attempt was made to recruit followers from among the servants of the gentry, the ringleaders felt sure of success because they believed the servants were kept like dogs and would welcome the opportunity to rise and cut their masters' throats" (1980, 39). In noting "that London experienced unprecedented social problems in the late Elizabethan period" and that "hundreds of young, male vagrants . . . were loitering around the streets," A.L. Beier observes that "the socioeconomic groups in London most prone to vagrancy were servants and apprentices" and contends that "the leading causes of vagrancy among servants and apprentices were conflicts with their masters" (1978, 214–17). Since approximately 12 percent of London's apprentices "were the sons of knights, esquires and gentlemen," with "the remainder . . . being drawn largely from the middling ranks of rural and urban society" (Wrightson 1982, 28), it is likely that dissatisfaction with the economic order and defiance against constituted authority were not restricted to the lower classes. When one considers that servants and apprentices were most frequently singled out from the general mass of "masterless men" as participants in, and instigators of, disorders in the immediate vicinity of Elizabethan playhouses, the possibility that such people were also regular playgoers must contribute to our developing profile of the Elizabethan interpretive community.

Two of "three large-scale riots that occurred during Whitsuntide 1584" began outside theaters and, along with additional evidence, suggest that theaters may well have served as sites for the expression of class resentment. As Roger Manning writes:

> The first riot began on Monday evening when a gentleman did a pirouette on the stomach of an apprentice who had been sleeping on the grass at the entrance to a theatre. . . . The next day a crowd of 500 apprentices attempted to rescue imprisoned companions. On Wednesday a riot, provoked when a serving-man wounded an apprentice with his sword at a theatre door, drew a crowd of 'near a thousand people'. . . . Continuing disorders . . . led to the closing of theatres (1988, 202–3).

Manning also notes that "Between 1581 and 1602" the previously orderly city of London "was disturbed by no fewer than 35 outbreaks of disorder," twelve of which "can be attributed to economic distress," though the "largest category . . . consists of the 14 insurrections and riots which protested the administration of justice" (187, 202). Manning adds that "Of the nine remaining instances of disorder during this period, four riots were directed against gentlemen and lawyers" (202).

Such a state of affairs, viewed in the context of the reports on the English temperament offered by foreigners and the presentments of heterodox opinions, has fairly obvious implications for a study of dramatic reception. The observations assembled above make a persuasive case for altering received opinions regarding the Elizabethan interpretive community, especially with respect to what may have constituted the Elizabethan playgoer's psychic disposition. It has long been alleged by friend and foe of the theater alike that the behavior of audiences in Elizabethan playhouses was permissive in the extreme (see Gurr 1987, 44–49 for the latest list of examples). Even advocates of a largely privileged auditory are quick to remark the repeated instances of unruliness countenanced by the same, though, with important exceptions, generally attributed to the undisciplined activity of groundlings or the high-spirits of truant apprentices. But the Elizabethan playhouse traditionally entertained by Shakespeareans in and through their readings of plays has also long been the domain of an arguably imaginary auditory whose alleged moral restraint and religious and political orthodoxy fail to correspond to the general tenor of reports about audience behavior and to the picture of unrestraint, impiety, and occasional sedition assembled here. Although selectively drawn, this picture has the virtue of being based on primary sources and on the exhaustive research of social historians, instead of on officious prescriptions regarding appropriate moral, religious, and political behavior and on the historical observations based on them. Its potential at least to adjust and, hopefully, to broaden received ideas about the Elizabethan playgoer's psychic disposition and the range of responses a playgoer might have been capable of entertaining, may be enhanced if we return for a moment to the Elizabethan debate about playgoing and playgoers, and begin to consider the audience in practice.

The Audience in Practice

Thomas Nashe advances his famous defense of plays in the context of his "complaint of sloth" in *Pierce Penniless* (208ff). Working from the general premise that "Sloath in Nobilitie, Courtiers, Schollers, or any men, is the chiefest cause that brings them in contempt" (210) and contending that "it is very expedient they haue some light toyes to busie their heads withall, cast before them as bones to gnaw vpon, which may keep them from hauing leisure to intermeddle with higher matters" (that is, "affayres of the State"), Nashe concludes that "the pollicie of Playes is very necessary, howsoeuer some shallow-braind censurers (not the deepest serchers into the secrets of gouernment) mightily oppugne them" (211–12). Rationalizing plays as providing an effective means of social control over those who might otherwise make their idleness the occasion for antisocial behavior, Nashe nominates "men that are their owne masters (as Gentlemen of the Court, the Innes of the Courte, and the number of Captaines and Souldiers about London)" as most likely to profit from the pastime of plays (212). Besides offering these men a preferred alternative to "gaming, following of harlots, [and] drinking," plays constitute "a rare exercise of vertue," according to Nashe, who also asserts that "there is no immortalitie can be giuen a man on earth like vnto Playes" before moving on to attack his Puritan antagonists who "care not if all the auncient houses were rooted out, so that . . . they might share the gouernment amongst them as States, and be quarter-maisters of our Monarchie" (212–13).

As noted earlier, it is difficult to distill what Nashe actually believes from what Nashe says in defense of plays. His justification of what he terms "the pollicie of Playes" on the ground that plays provide a necessary distraction for those inclined to politically seditious thoughts may, for example, deliberately exaggerate the threat to the state posed by slothful "Courtiers, Nobilitie, and Schollers," especially given Nashe's warning about the anti-aristocratic and anti-royalist position of Puritans, who would appear to pose more obvious threats against the kingdom's peace. On the other hand, Nashe may be candidly (and honestly) acknowledging the potential seditiousness of these privileged playgoers in order to endow the enterprise cf playmaking with the trappings of official policy, and may make the threat posed by Puritans appear greater because it is not mediated by a similarly "deep" insight "into the secrets of gouernment." It is at least clear that in presenting the joint enterprise of playmaking and playgoing as a "pollicie" of social control, and in generally restricting his remarks on audience composition to "men that are their owne masters," Nashe is at once acknowledging and deflecting "perceptions which are consistently borne out everywhere in habits of speech about the theatres" (Butler 1984, 302). These perceptions, howsoever motivated by the social, religious, or economic interests of their respective spokesmen, repeatedly testify that playhouses "drawe together the baser sorte of people" (Chambers 1923, vol. IV, 311); provide an opportunity for "the refuse sort of evill disposed & ungodly people . . . to assemble together"; and serve as "the ordinary places for all maisterless men & vagabond persons that haunt the high waies to meet together & to recreate themselves" (Chambers, 318). Nashe virtually concedes the antitheatricalist argument regarding playhouses as "resorts of idleness" in order to advance his claim that plays in practice regularly transform the occasion of idleness into "an exercise of virtue." But in making his case for the redeeming effects of plays on privileged playgoers, he conspicuously understates the number of "the meaner sort" who attended plays and consequently overstates the capacity of plays to "beat downe utterly" temptations to "tumults and rebellion" (214). In so doing, he attempts to deflect what were, after all, the most frequent and threatening charges lodged against theaters.

Like Nashe before him, Heywood in his *Apology for Actors* (1612) writes as if "the pollicie of Playes" guaranteed a single, unitary effect on their beholders; as if the response of an audience to a play were equivalent to that of a pious congregation to a didactic sermon:

> Playes are writ with this ayme, and carryed with this methode, to teach the subjects obedience to their King, to shew the people the vntimely ends of such as

haue moued tumults, commotions, and insurrections, to present them with the flourishing estate of such as liue in obedience, exhorting them to allegeance, dehorting them from all trayterous and fellonious strategems. (F4)

Heywood not only writes against the grain of complicated effects elicited by a play like *Macbeth*, which only superficially conforms to the orthodox pattern of meaning he describes; his attempt to address the antitheatricalist concern about the negatively exemplary effects of the dramatization of "tumults, commotions, and insurrections" operates at a privileged remove from all but abstract considerations. Even when Heywood offers more graphic observations on theatrical experience, he operates from a partial position that privileges only those aspects of "liuely and well spirited action" that have the "power to new mold the harts of the spectators and fashion them to the shape of any noble and notable attempt" (B4).

If we place Heywood's remarks alongside a letter written by the Lord Mayor of London to Lord Burghley in 1594, we may better appreciate the limitations of Heywood's position. While the Lord Mayor's letter conforms in many ways to the characteristic style and content of these annual pleas for the suppression of plays, it also specifically responds to Nashe's defense of plays and succinctly describes how the presentational style of a play and the nature of its auditory may affect its overt aims and intentions:[16]

> I am not ignorant (my very good L.) what is alleadged by soom for defence of these playes, that the people must haue soom kynd of recreation, & that policie requireth to divert idle heads & other ill disposed from other woorse practize by this kynd of exercize. Whereto may bee answeared . . . that as honest recreation is a thing very meet for all sorts of men, so no kynd of exercise, being of itself corrupt & prophane, can well stand with the good policie of a Christian Common Wealth. And that the sayed playes (as they are handled) ar of that sort, and woork that effect in such as ar present and frequent the same, may soon bee decerned by all that haue any godly vnderstanding & that obserue the fruites & effects of the same, conteining nothing ells but vnchast fables, lascivious divises, shifts of cozenage, & matters of lyke sort, which ar so framed & represented by them, that such as resort to see & hear the same, beeing of the base & refuse sort of people or such yoong gentlemen as haue small regard of credit or conscience, draue the same into example of imitation & not of avoyding the sayed lewed offences. (Chambers, vol. IV, 316–17)

Rather than refute Nashe on the ground of the express meaning of plays, the Lord Mayor chooses to focus on "the fruites & effects of the same," which are generated not so much by the plays themselves as by how "they are handled" and how their matter is "framed & represented." In so doing, the Lord Mayor strongly suggests that moralized representations of theatrical experience—like those offered by Heywood and Nashe—do not register the actual effects on audiences of plays in practice. While audiences in theory should privilege the cautionary "ayme" and "method" of plays that treat "shifts of cozenage, & matters of lyke sort," audiences in practice "draue the same into example of imitation." This is the case, according to the Lord Mayor, because the seductive matter of plays is "so framed and represented" as to arouse the audience's capacity for engagement and because audiences themselves are predisposed, as much by their "small regard of credit or conscience" as by their idleness, to enjoy rather than to avoid "the sayed lewd offences."

The Lord Mayor's remarks on audience composition, like the general format of his letter itself, are, perhaps, too predictable to be noteworthy. But his linkage of the responses of "the base & refuse sort of people" with those of "such yoong gentlemen as haue small regard of credit or conscience" indicates that playgoers of opposing classes could be drawn to plays for many of the same reasons, and that "men who are their owne masters" and masterless men were equally susceptible to the influence of a play's performance appeal. And his subsequent delineation of "such as frequent the sayed playes"—in which he singles out "vagrant persons & maisterless men that hang about the Citie, theeues, horsestealers, whoremongers, coozeners, connycatching persones, practizers of treason, & such other lyke" and identifies "this vngodly sort" as "the very sinck & contagion not only of this Citie but of this whole Realm" (317)—suggests that the problem posed by playgoers was but a local manifestation of a broader social phenomenon. While his rhetoric is partisan and polemical, the Lord Mayor's observations regarding Elizabethan playgoers are confirmed, in ways that Heywood's and Nashe's are not, by virtually all the evidence I have assembled on the subject of Elizabethans in general, most notably by Thomas Platter's remarks on the response of privileged Elizabethans to the cautionary aims of the prospect of impaled heads on London Bridge. Although the Lord Mayor generally restricts his identification of the "ungodly sort" to representatives of the lower classes, it can, on this account, hardly be assumed that only "such other lyke" and "such yoong gentlemen as haue small regard of credit or conscience" would prove responsive to plays that were clearly designed to interest gentlemen and servants alike, to exploit their susceptibility to suggestion, and to satisfy their desire for novelty and excitement.

In preferring the Lord Mayor's depiction of "the fruites & effects" of playgoing to those offered by Nashe and Heywood, I am effectively determining which contemporary testimony about the effects of plays on audiences can be reconciled with a revised estimate of the psychic disposition of the Elizabethan interpretive community; with the model of theatrical experience I have advanced above; and with Elizabethan playtexts that are arguably heterodox or transgressive in orientation. Surely, Heywood's stirring depiction of a playgoer's likely response to the bravado of an actor playing Edward III or Henry V *can* be reconciled with both the historical evidence and psychological model:

> what English blood seeing the person of any bold English man presented and doth not hugge his fame, and hunnye at his valor, pursuing him in his enterprise with his best wishes, and as being wrapt in contemplation, offers to him in his hart all prosperous performance, as if the Personater were the man Personated, so bewitching a thing is liuely and well spirited action, . . . (*Apology*, B4)

But were we to attempt to apply Heywood's statement that "Playes are writ with this ayme, and carryed with this method, to teach the subiects obedience to their King," or Nashe's to the effect that plays constitute "a rare exercise of virtue," to a contemporary audience's experience of *Richard III*, *The Jew of Malta* or the two parts of *Tamburlaine*, we would soon register the irreconcilability of such positions with both the psychic disposition of Elizabethan playgoers and the economy of Elizabethan theatrical experience.

In the very practice of playgoing, Elizabethans of every class registered their receptiveness to "bewitching" representations of both licit and illicit fantasies and inclinations, as well as their predisposition to respond to plays in a fashion more attuned to a play's performance appeal than to its didactic intentions. The Lord Mayor was not alone in discerning this silent conspiracy between the audience's capacity to transform cautionary aims into "lewd" effects and the nature of the theatrical apparatus itself. Playwrights themselves, including Nashe, regularly attacked the audience's incapacity to comprehend and emotionally sustain a play's express meaning or intentions, though they usually attributed the audience's lack of understanding to ignorance or inattentiveness.[17] I think we would do better to attribute the audience's taste for "the pomp of proud audacious deeds," for

"*Tales*, *Tempests*, and such like drolleries," for the "fond and frivolous gestures," which were "greatly gaped at, what times they were showed upon the stage in their graced deformities," by "some vain, conceited fondlings," and which the printer of the first edition of *Tamburlaine* (1590) chose to excise from his version of Marlowe's play, to a psychic disposition incompatible with the moral prescriptions of the theater's defenders and with the aesthetic demands of some of the theater's more sober-minded playwrights.[18] Characteristics that have been traditionally considered constitutive of the Elizabethan interpretive community—and which would be conducive to the edifying effects of plays promoted by Heywood and Nashe—either may have failed to maintain their hold on the Elizabethan playgoer in the context of theatrical experience, or may not have had the same hold on playgoers as they had on those who did not regularly attend the theater, or may have been contested by habits of mind and feeling that could lay equal claim to normative status.

Given the privileged status of the Elizabethan playhouse, playgoers probably approached the occasion of playgoing as a release from the constraints of ordinary experience, and came to the theater prepared to suspend their inhibitions against provocative or potentially threatening fantasy material. It is also likely that the regular playgoer maintained a normative persuasion that was at once more morally and psychically permissive than that of his or her fellow Elizabethan who consciously decided not to attend plays. But it is just as likely that the range of attitudes, opinions, and feelings that may be construed as normative was actually much broader—and more variable—than has traditionally been assumed, and that playgoer and non-playgoer alike may have been equally capable of entertaining irreverent attitudes, skeptical opinions, and the most worldly or material ambitions and aspirations. I include the non-playgoing public in this formulation because it would hardly be reasonable to assume that the playhouse functioned as the exclusive outpost for the expression and entertainment of ideas and fantasies that were inconsistent with officially countenanced beliefs and opinions. The playhouse functioned as a *medium* for the expression and entertainment of a *range* of ideas and fantasies, some orthodox, some heterodox, some potentially seditious, some expressly patriotic, some conducive to social change, some committed to social control. And only by broadening our notion of the normative to include attitudes and opinions that traditional scholarship would classify as abnormative will we become able to do justice to the full range of effects such a medium could generate.

What we know of the practices and presentments of Elizabethans in general suggests that many Elizabethan playgoers were capable of entertaining the kinds of responses to plays that have been considered either historically implausible or incompatible with their ostensible intentions. While we have few specific records regarding audience reception, broadening our conception of the psychic disposition of Elizabethan playgoers allows us to reconstruct the responses of audiences whose possible irreverence, skepticism, and desire for social and economic advancement made them particularly susceptible to the influence of plays that made such attitudes and desires seem particularly appealing. It also allows us to consider that those pious and orderly subjects who (the Lord Mayor's remarks to the contrary) conceivably attended the theater with a corresponding regularity, and who would otherwise be expected to respond to such appeals in a censorious fashion, may have found themselves pleasurably aroused by the prospect of participating vicariously in experiences that might oppose their own quotidian values and beliefs, but did not depart entirely from their range of reference. As Robert P. Adams observes:

> In the most notable tragedies of state, with Kyd and Marlowe as the pioneers from about 1586 onward, great tyrants are by no means . . . "always presented as usurpers," nor are they "invariably" defeated and replaced by morally virtuous "model kings." . . . Such establishment approved thinking on tyrants versus good kings in late Elizabethan times was, as Lever has said of the concept of the great chain of being, in "an advanced state of rust." When the best tragic writers went to history—often, daringly, to very recent history—for their mirrors of the modern state, what they and their politicized audiences could see depended not only upon what they had been officially instructed to see; their tragic vision also related to what they had grown *prepared* to see as an alternative. (1977, 77)

The position established by a scholarly tradition that predicates audience reception on the respective moral and political prescriptions of Christian homilies and official Tudor pronouncements cannot account for the variety of perspectives likely to be entertained by a sophisticated audience or to be fostered by the complex interplay of theatrical experience. And this is especially the case with respect to audience reception of plays that either fail to provide a strong moral framework to hold the appeal of performance in check, or that oppose Elizabethan orthodoxies while promoting positions that had no official status and, hence, have been construed to be abnormative or heterodox.

The plays of Marlowe in particular have been especially vulnerable to critical distortion and denigration because their apparent challenges to Elizabethan orthodoxies are held to be irreconcilable with received ideas about Elizabethan belief systems. Their ostensibly heterodox approach to official moral and political prescriptions regarding social advancement, self-aggrandizement, and homosocial activity seems so at odds with "the dominant ideologies of Elizabethan England" that the theories they advance have been repeatedly "devalued, misrepresented, and opposed" in most commentaries on his work (Shepherd, 87). One of the prevailing sponsors of Marlowe's critical reception has been the persistent attribution to Marlowe's audience of a set of impenetrable inhibitions which makes the audience seem incapable of responding to Marlowe's plays in the way Marlowe appears to want his audiences to respond. Even as astute a critic as Jonathan Crewe believes that "the very poetics of Elizabethan drama would inhibit [Marlowe's] capacity to idealize [his] 'appalling' figures." According to Crewe, "The conception of the dramatic protagonist, whether tragic or comic, as a negative exemplum is too powerfully entrenched in the sixteenth century for any simple reversal to be probable either at the level of poetic theory or even at that of audience response" (1984, 325). But Crewe's eventual concession that the seemingly abnormative Tamburlaine "at least becomes thinkable as the embodiment of the culture's true image(s)" and, even, culturally "normalized" to some extent (327) suggests that Crewe's original resistance to such possibilities was based more on his reliance on prescriptions drawn from official culture than on evidence drawn directly from the plays of Marlowe and his contemporaries.[19]

To restore to a playwright like Marlowe the responsive auditory that the success of his plays and the extent of his influence on other playwrights may justly claim, it is necessary not only to broaden our conception of the range of responses his plays may have elicited, but also to attend closely to the ways he attempts to shape or manipulate audience response. One of the reasons that the debate on audience composition can be of little help to us here is, as Moody Prior writes, "not merely that any given audience is made up of individuals representing many varieties of temperament and attitude," but that "the same group of people will respond differently and become a different audience under distinct influences" (1951, 104–5). Another is that the situation of an audience in a theater cannot be wholly identified with the social profile of its members outside the playhouse. As Shepherd contends:

[A play] addresses its audience and in addressing them it constructs for them positions from which to view or read the artwork. . . . Of primary importance here is how the playtext addresses its audience, what picture of themselves it encourages them to recognise, and where it tells them they are situated in the social order. (1986, 43–44)

An audience capable of inhabiting the variety of positions different plays construct for it is a necessary correlary to such observations. Such an audience would need at times to surrender on demand its investment in the values and assumptions that otherwise define it in exchange for the pleasure promised by theatrical engagement. It would need to be able to be shocked out of its religious indifference or complacency by a play like *Doctor Faustus*; to be drawn into the amoral abandon of Machiavellian posturing by plays like *Richard III* and *The Jew of Malta*; to be caught up in the fantasy of omnipotence cultivated by *Tamburlaine the Great* and in the collective dream of national assertion generated by *Henry V*.

In the face of so wide a variety of provocations, an audience will require a correspondingly wide repertory of responsiveness, one that is not limited to the attractions of orthodoxy or heterodoxy, daring or restraint. And if it is truly a receptive auditory, it will also need to become skilled in knowing just when and how it is being provoked, and what its submission entails.[20] A receptive auditory need not be a mystified auditory, incapable of breaking the spell an entire play or a single character attempts to cast over it when that spell is dramatically contested or, for that matter, when its own interests are at stake, as I hope to show in the second of my chapters on Shakespeare. For now, I would like to turn our attention to what is arguably the most expressly spellbinding play in the Elizabethan repertory, and begin to turn theory into practice.

Part II

The Webs of Plays

3. The Tamburlaine Phenomenon

The Moment of *Tamburlaine*

If, as J.L. Styan maintains, a given society's drama "tells us a great deal about the people who go [to the theater], why they go and what happens to them" (1975, 109), then a play that occupies as prominent a position as *Tamburlaine the Great* occupies in the Elizabethan repertory is bound to tell us much about its own enabling conditions. The extraordinary success and influence enjoyed by *Tamburlaine* tell us that Marlowe's approach to his material made it strike an unusually responsive chord in his audience. Why this was the case may be traced in part to Marlowe's decision to dramatize the rapid rise to a position of virtually uncontestable worldly power of an aspiring commoner, a theme that seems to have been of considerable interest to the playgoing members of a society whose "most fundamental characteristic . . . was its high degree of stratification, its distinctive and all pervasive system of social inequality" (Wrightson 1982, 17). Marlowe plots his course to audience engagement with such a figure very carefully, conditioning his audience to consider Tamburlaine's effortless command of the resources of the stage as the most significant indication of his dramatic status. Tamburlaine earns the audience's unqualified regard by repeatedly demonstrating his mastery of opponents who are, by comparison, unskilled in the arts of theatrical persuasion. That his opponents are largely drawn from the ranks of hereditary royalty and nobility makes Tamburlaine's presumption at once a socially volatile and psychologically provocative construction. The danger that Tamburlaine courts in "managing arms" against the reigning gods of this earth becomes a source of transgressive pleasure for an audience whose more mundane ambitions are recast in the form of heroic aspiration.

Marlowe's success in making the vicarious participation in Tamburlaine's triumphs imaginatively enlivening for an audience greatly depends on that audience's capacity to identify its own interests with a character who stands opposed to many of the prescribed values of "official"

Elizabethan culture and on his ability to turn potential resistance to the Tamburlaine phenomenon to theatrical advantage. Richard Levin's recent article on the contemporary perception of Tamburlaine offers convincing evidence that *Tamburlaine* "evoked a positive response in contemporary audiences," one probably characterized more by "amoral wonder" than "moral approbation," but positive nevertheless (1984, 53).[1] Levin's evidence not only makes a strong case for audience responsiveness to Tamburlaine's appeal, but also suggests that Marlowe exploited a revealing current of class-interested feeling in his audience. The episodes that Levin identifies as having had the most memorable effect on Marlowe's contemporaries—which include Tamburlaine's "defeat and humiliation of Bajazeth (Part I, IV.ii); and his harnessing the captured kings to his chariot (Part II, IV.iii)" (57)—are, however, also among those most frequently cited by Marlowe's more traditional critics in order to demonstrate the negatively exemplary aspects of Tamburlaine's appeal. These critics take their interpretive cues from the moral and political prescriptions of the "official" documents of the period—which, as Mark Burnett has argued, offer a "wholly inaccurate and inadequate picture of Elizabethan society" (1987, 309)—and attempt to subsume conspicuously heterodox plays like *Tamburlaine the Great* into what they take to be the overarching master-text of Elizabethan ortho-doxy.[2] Even critics who are disposed to entertain a more theatrically faith-ful impression of Tamburlaine have had difficulty in countenancing Tamburlaine's behavior in these episodes which the best of them represents in terms of antisocial aggression that appeals to "the evil and disruptive" forces "within our nature" (Steane 1964, 84).

I believe there is more to Marlowe's success in making such moments memorable to his audience than a simple catering to brutal and bullying fantasies and impulses (though I am not opposed to accepting the same as a motivating aim of the episodes in question). The humiliation of Bajazeth and the harnessing of the captive kings enacted by a self-made scourge of God would surely provide Marlowe's audience with wonderfully exagger-ated images of their own ambitions for mastery given the freest and most sovereign expression. And the extremity of Tamburlaine's inversion of the orders of political succession with which the audience would be most fa-miliar would give an heroic gloss to the audience's more modest exertions to rise in the world. What may appear to some as sadistic bullying may actually have been experienced by Marlowe's audience as a holiday licens-ing of social, political, and psychological unrestraint, and may have pro-vided a focus for their expression of frustration with prevailing institutional arrangements. Tamburlaine operates, in this respect, as much in the manner of a lord of misrule as in that of a scourge of God.

It is impossible to determine whether Marlowe created the taste for "high astounding terms" and "proud audacious deeds" that his imitators and appropriators attempted to satisfy, or simply found himself in the position of giving his audience what it wanted at the most opportune of moments. But as David Riggs has stated in his own attempt to come to terms with "the puzzling relationship that obtains between Marlowe's hero and the social attitudes of his audience":

> When a "literary" or rhetorical ideal elicits this kind of response, and exhibits this degree of resilience, one gathers that it has managed to involve itself with cultural ideals as well. (1971, 63)

The relationship between *Tamburlaine the Great* and the cultural ideals of Elizabethan England on the eve of the defeat of the Spanish Armada has often been addressed, with the coincidence of an outright fantasy of omnipotence and a fact of sudden military predominance providing perhaps too much fodder for the scholarly imagination. It is, nonetheless, clear that many of the fantasies Marlowe cultivates in the domain of the aspiring mind could find an objective correlative in the growing political and economic fortunes of an aggressive and increasingly self-assured nation-state that was making discernible inroads into Spanish presumptions of world sovereignty well before the defeat of the Armada.

That Marlowe composed the Tamburlaine plays with a sure hand on the pulse of his times seems beyond question, as the very existence of a sequel to *Tamburlaine the Great* (seemingly even more popular than its namesake) demonstrates. Such plays could hardly have achieved the popular acclaim they enjoyed had they been either eccentric projections of their author's power fantasies or cautionary tales on the excesses of pride and vainglory. With explorers crossing the oceans, vast sums of wealth being carved out of the new world to serve both new and old desires, a seductive figure like Machiavelli (as he was popularly understood) stimulating the imaginations of many, and established systems of social and economic relationships yielding to the forces of aggressive individualism and an emergent capitalism, it would seem only fitting for Marlowe to exploit the appeal of a character who was the obvious embodiment of energies and ambitions with which both prosperous and merely aspiring Elizabethans would be familiar. As Stephen Greenblatt has observed:

> If we want to understand the historical matrix of Marlowe's achievement, the analogue to Tamburlaine's restlessness, aesthetic sensitivity, appetite, and violence, we might look not at the playwright's sources, not even at the relentless power-hunger of Tudor absolutism, but at the acquisitive energies of English merchants, entrepreneurs, and adventurers, promoters alike of trading companies and theatrical companies. (1977, 42)

This is not to suggest that Marlowe's appeal to his audience establishes itself as a simple rehearsal of contemporary aspirations, or that the popular basis of that appeal is grounded in any populist assumptions Marlowe may have harbored about his audience. If the Tamburlaine plays can be said to dramatize a Renaissance version of the will to power, it is probable that something like a will to power had already become (or was in the process of becoming) a popular fantasy that could be exploited and enlarged upon in a theatrical context.[3]

According to Anthony Esler, the Tamburlaine phenomenon appears to have brought into focus "a new view of ambition," one that Esler associates with "the aspiring mind of the Elizabethan younger generation" (1966, 80), but which may well have animated individuals from all classes of Elizabethan society. In this sense, the larger than life figure of Tamburlaine, rising from obscure origins by the aggressive exercise of his native talents, may be said to represent the stage-projection of what David Riggs has called "the real, but highly suspect, aspirations of a large part of Elizabethan society" (1971, 69). As Riggs observes:

> the representation of a modern "worthy" aspiring to heroic fortitude generally resembles the most important phenomenon of the late sixteenth century: a rapid rise in social status by an individual who looks to his personal abilities rather than his gentle birth to justify his high worldly station. (63)

The apparent centrality of Tamburlaine's appeal does not, however, make Tamburlaine the kind of "sixteenth-century Everyman" Franklin McCann describes, who "speaks and acts as the average Elizabethan imagined he himself would if he could command an English fighting ship or take the field at the head of English troops" (1952, 198–99). Rather, it is very much to Marlowe's purpose that the "real" aspirations he exploits are not only "highly suspect" with respect to Elizabethan orthodoxies but often antagonistic to the real interests of a large portion of the playgoing public.

There are few plays for which the vexed question of who, in fact, constituted this public is so integral to an understanding of its probable effects as *Tamburlaine*. If, for example, we accept Gurr's determination that "citizens" of London constituted the majority of playgoers in the public playhouses—and if we assume a direct relationship between their practical interests and their imaginative investment in theatrical experience—then we must wonder whether they were threatened or pleasurably aroused by Tamburlaine's "high astounding terms." Surely, they would register the fulfillment of their own material ambitions in Tamburlaine's disdainful disvestiture of his shepherd's "weeds" in I.ii. But having already fulfilled many of their own worldly aims, how would they respond to Tamburlaine's celebration of a program of relentless, unceasing quests for "the ripest fruit of all"? Urged on by Marlowe's mighty line to participate in an enterprise without limits, might they not feel their own well-earned prerogatives threatened? I ask such questions not because I wish to engage in a literal-minded quest for specific analogues and determinate effects, but because Tamburlaine's agenda would seem to appeal most to those who would have the most to gain from a change in the status quo. The clownish Mycetes and his presumptive usurper, Cosroe, may, for example, serve in Part I to represent an imaginatively impoverished social order fit to be opposed by a modern "worthy" assured of his gifts and conscientious in their application. But they may also represent a similarly impoverished political order fit to be transformed by men who are not easily mastered and resist any and all impediment to the sovereignty of their will. Such men would probably find their supporters not among the prosperous citizen playgoers of Elizabethan London, but among those in whom the capacity to fantasize such challenges would be enabled by a restlessness with the status quo that the Tamburlaine plays repeatedly enforce. To the masterless men at the disordered margins of Elizabethan society and "the master spirits of the age" at the unstable peaks of privilege, Tamburlaine's "love to live at liberty" and determination to maintain a "life exempt from servitude" (I.ii.26, 31) may have had an appeal that could be readily acknowledged and imaginatively appropriated.[4] In this respect, it may well be argued that Marlowe's play was less a vehicle of escapism than a medium for bringing the social and generational tensions of Elizabethan England into focus.[5]

The evidence recently assembled by A.L. Beier and others suggests that London in particular "experienced unprecedented social problems in the late Elizabethan period" (1978, 217), and the examples of civil disruptions in the immediate area of London playhouses are too numerous to discount the participation of playgoers. As David Riggs observes, "In the face of such evidence, it is hard to preserve the image of an audience whose capacity for reflection on historical themes could be aroused only by solemn homilies on the miseries of civil dissension and the splendors of hierarchical order" (71). And, as Riggs writes with reference to a particularly violent encounter between self-professed gentlemen and a group of apprentices "nere the Theatre or Curten at the tyme of the Playes" in 1584:

> No one doubts that the apprentices of London had a proper fear of civil war; but that is in a sense what they were engaged in when they chased "my lo ffitzgerold" (who had himself struck the first blow) into the nearest shelter. (71)

While one may quarrel with Riggs's possible overestimation of the significance of this incident, further evidence of the chronic nature of similar disorders—which "usually were the product of class antagonisms"—makes it harder to debate his designation of the playhouses as "a place where social tensions were liable to rise to the fore of their own accord" (70).

It is, nonetheless, often assumed that *Tamburlaine*'s exotic setting, its unusual blend of mocking ironies and bombastic rhetoric, and the status of Tamburlaine and his confederates as "The strangest men that ever nature made," should have served to set Marlowe's drama at some remove from definite social and political applications. David Bevington, for example, contends that Tamburlaine's "appeal to the individual free spirit embraces no specific political analogy. The vision is escapist and dreamlike, asking the spectator to imagine himself mounted on the back of a pagan king, or in some faraway land commanding imperiously, 'Holla, ye pampered jades of Asia!'" (1968, 215). An Elizabethan playgoer, with only a modicum of knowledge of his own country's history, would, however, recognize that Tamburlaine's appeal specifically embraces the political maxim "might makes right," and does so from the proscribed vantage point of an aspiring commoner bent on successive acts of usurpation. Bevington also fails to recognize that what Marlowe presents in "escapist and dreamlike" terms may be appropriated by the interested playgoer in ways that apply specifically to his or her own concerns and preoccupations. What Marlowe establishes on one level of fantasy may, in other words, be re-established by the playgoer on another that embraces a corresponding or, for that matter, competing political or social analogy.

Even within the confines of the play, we may witness the politically specific ways in which individual characters respond to Tamburlaine's appeal. An exemplary case in point is the exchange of loyalty enacted early on in *1 Tamburlaine* when Theridamas—"The chiefest captain of Mycetes' host"—

is summarily transformed by Tamburlaine's "pathetical persuasions" into an ardent member of Tamburlaine's inner circle. Theridamas's conversion from a trusted subordinate in a feudal hierarchy to one among several aspiring minds under the charismatic leadership of Tamburlaine—a self-made man if there ever was one—represents for him at least more than an escape into a dreamlike state. Becoming "the trusty friend of Tamburlaine" involves subordinating such notions as proving "a traitor to my king" to the "strong enchantments" of an ambition that knows no bounds and acknowledges no constraints (I.ii.224–27). It specifically involves the displacement of one clearly delineated set of values and obligations—which Marlowe's audience might well have associated with the duties and obligations enjoined on Elizabethan subjects—by another that can be measured only in terms of enlightened self-interest. In choosing to side with Tamburlaine against Mycetes, Theridamas is certainly doing more than Launcelot Gobbo does when he exchanges his master Shylock for his master Bassanio (though even Gobbo's servile opportunism is based in contemporary Elizabethan realities). He is effectively rewriting the terms of his apprenticeship, breaking the bonds of his indenture, and becoming his own master.

In the immediate context of this transaction, the allegedly unspecific nature of Tamburlaine's appeal specifically opposes itself to official proscriptions against social mobility and political activity. Apprised of Theridamas's betrayal, Mycetes and his remaining subordinate, Meander, construe the "band of brothers" Tamburlaine assembles in terms familiarly employed to describe participants in domestic disturbances and civil insurrections:[6]

> *Mean.*   Suppose they be in number infinite,
> Yet being void of martial discipline,
> All running headlong after greedy spoils:
> And more regarding gain than victory:
> Like to the cruel brothers of the earth,
> Sprung of the teeth of dragons venemous,
> Their careless swords shall lanch their fellows' throats
> And make us triumph in their overthrow.
>
> (II.ii.43–50)

As if to demonstrate the inappropriateness of such estimates of Tamburlaine and his confederates, Marlowe subsequently has Tamburlaine refuse to steal the crown from Mycetes's head when the opportunity presents it-self, a gesture that leads Mycetes to exclaim, "O gods, is this Tamburlaine the thief? / I marvel much he stole it not away" (II.iv.41–42). In the process, Marlowe effectively robs the discourse of masterlessness of its capacity to serve as an accurate index of those who resist subjection.[7]

If we compare such a sequence with others in *2 Henry VI* (c. 1589–1592) and *The Life and Death of Jack Straw* (1594), we find rebels against authority anatomized by their opponents in much the same language but dramati-cally represented in a manner consistent with that language. In *2 Henry VI*, Jack Cade and his cohorts are construed as "a ragged multitude / Of hinds and peasants, rude and merciless" and their supporters as the "rascal peo-ple, thirsting after prey" (IV.iv.31–32; 50). In *Jack Straw* the individual iden-tities of the rebels are dissolved into the familiar image of the "Beast of many heads, / Of misconceiving and misconstruing minds (I.ii.188–89). The pretensions of such characters to be "Lords within ourselves" are in both plays nothing more than pretensions, and are mocked by the play-wright who depicts them and by history alike.[8] In *Tamburlaine*, however, such condescending estimates of the motives and manners of a cast of char-acters who declare, as Jack Straw and Wat Tyler do, that "if the world hold out we shalbe Kings shortly" (*Jack Straw*, II.i.486) are repeatedly counter-manded by actions and words that attest to the grandeur and nobility of the aspirants in question. Moreover, as Mark Burnett observes, the "official view of the masterless man is placed in the mouths of braggarts, fools, and hypocrites" whose claims are repeatedly "discredited and held up for ridi-cule" (1987, 321). As a result, the potential for audience engagement with rebellious figures that is at least authorially discouraged in plays like *Jack Straw* and *2 Henry VI* is sustained in Marlowe's treatment of Tamburlaine and his confederates, which subordinates the official discourse of master-lessness to a theatrically privileged discourse of mastery.

The Discourse of Mastery

When Theridamas first encounters Tamburlaine, and asks with un-disguised arrogance, "Where is this Scythian Tamburlaine?" he approaches him from the same position of aristocratic disdain for the low-born occu-pied by Mycetes and Meander. After Tamburlaine's equally arrogant iden-

tification of himself—"Whom seek'st thou Persian? I am Tamburlaine"—
the following exchange ensues:

> *Ther.*   Tamburlaine?
> A Scythian shepherd, so embellished
> With nature's pride, and richest furniture,
> His looks do menace heaven and dare the gods,
> His fiery eyes are fixed upon the earth,
> As if he now devised some stratagem:
> Or meant to pierce Avernus' darksome vaults,
> Or pull the triple-headed dog from hell.
>
> *Tamb.*   Noble and mild this Persian seems to be,
> If outward habit judge the inward man.
>
> *Tech.*   His deep affections make him passionate.
>
> *Tamb.*   With what a majesty he rears his looks:
> In thee, thou valiant man of Persia,
> I see the folly of thy emperor,
> Art thou but the captain of a thousand horse[?]
>
> (I.ii.154–68)

This largely introspective exchange of first impressions is most notable for
its immediate supercession of the stereotypical attitudes with which it begins. The aristocratic Theridamas quickly discerns a natural nobility in the
low-born Tamburlaine, while Tamburlaine judges Theridamas in terms of
the "majesty" that overarches his present position as "but the captain of a
thousand horse." Each perceives in the other the figure of a master spirit
and the potential for unlimited mastery that a joining of forces will bring.
As the "normative" character in this exchange, whose existence has heretofore been rooted in dutiful service to his king, Theridamas effectively
serves as a surrogate for the audience-at-large. His attribution to Tamburlaine of qualities of mind and manner that any aspiring man must find
desirable and attractive in another brings what is extraordinary about Tamburlaine into a normative frame of reference. For his part, Tamburlaine's
generous capacity to find virtue in a worthy opponent seems meant to con-
vey to the interested playgoer an indirect acknowledgment of his or her
own fantasies of underrewarded merit. And the prospect of what such figures may achieve in concert is framed to appeal directly to the playgoer's
own dream of effortless mastery and command:

> *Tamb.*   Both we will walk upon the lofty clifts,
> And Christian merchants that with Russian stems
> Plow up huge furrows in the Caspian Sea,
> Shall vail to us as lords of all the lake.
>
> (I.ii.193–96)

The larger-than-life vision of worldly dominion Tamburlaine conjures up for himself and Theridamas as "lords of all the lake" is poised to appeal to ambitions and drives that a previously "subjected" Theridamas—in common with similarly subjected playgoers—has had to inhibit. In choosing to term his own estate "mean"—"I call it mean because, being yet obscure, / The nations far removed admire me not" (I.ii.201–2)—Tamburlaine attempts to fill the underemployed Theridamas with the taste and desire for grander exposure, while simultaneously remarking the potential worth of those whose value goes unnoticed and the arbitrariness of prevailing social arrangements. This alliance of like-minded souls, divided only by the circumstances of birth, soon reaches out to embrace the audience-at-large as Tamburlaine and company engage in another shared revery concerning the glories of kingship:

> *Tamb.*   And ride in triumph through Persepolis!
> Is it not brave to be a king, Techelles?
> Usumcasane and Theridamas,
> Is it not passing brave to be a king,
> And ride in triumph through Persepolis?
> *Tech.*   O, my lord, 'tis sweet and full of pomp!
> *Usum.*   To be a king, is half to be a god.
> *Ther.*   A god is not so glorious as a king:
> I think the pleasure they enjoy in heaven,
> Cannot compare with kingly joys in earth;
> . . . .
> *Tamb.*   What says my other friends, will you be kings?
> *Tech.*   I, if I could, with all my heart, my lord.
> *Tamb.*   Why, that's well said, Techelles; so would I.
> And so would you, my masters, would you not?
>
> (II.vi.50–59, 67–70)

Tamburlaine's elaboration of what is no more than a prosaic statement of fact on Cosroe's part demonstrates his capacity to articulate in the most prescient terms the inmost fantasies of his "rapt" confederates who, in turn, serve as dramatic surrogates for the only figures Tamburlaine addresses as his "masters," namely, the offstage audience. As Theridamas extends Usumcasane's conception of king as demigod into a dream of easeful omnipotence—"To wear a crown enchas'd with pearl and gold, / Whose virtues carry with it life and death; / To ask and have, command and be obeyed" (II.vi.60–62)—he gives the audience an occasion to dwell on a fantasy that it is in their power to see realized onstage through the simple act of collective affirmation. In silently affirming that they too would be kings and "lords of all the lake," Marlowe's playgoers license Tamburlaine to take his first step to worldly dominion and revive in themselves the sleeping desire for mastery whose embodiment Tamburlaine becomes.[9]

The sudden resolve Tamburlaine makes at the end of this exchange "To get the Persian kingdom to myself" is thus conceivably undertaken with the imaginative backing of an audience enlisted in a collective quest for self-made sovereignty. It is, consequently, noteworthy that as soon as Cosroe learns of Tamburlaine's plans, Tamburlaine and his cohorts are re-cast in the role of anarchic underlings and monstrous slaves of presumption:

> *Cos.* What means this devilish shepherd, to aspire
> With such a giantly presumption,
> To cast up hills against the face of heaven,
> And dare the force of angry Jupiter?
>
> (II.vi.1–4)

We see here the usual discursive terms employed for representing rebellion recapitulated at a higher pitch, one that accounts for the raised stakes of the encounter. For it is no longer a matter of one "official" aspirant for the crown competing with another. The fraternal rivalry of Cosroe and Mycetes has now been superseded by a transgressive social conflict which the ruling order invests with religious overtones. As Meander states:

> Some powers divine, or else infernal, mixed
> Their angry seeds at his conception;
> For he was never sprung of human race,
> Since with the spirit of his fearful pride,
> He dares so doubtlessly resolve of rule,
> And by profession be ambitious.
>
> (II.vi.9–14)

The presumption of Tamburlaine is here represented as something so unprecedented that it exists outside what passes for purely human understanding in the realm of officially constituted belief. It is particularly Tamburlaine's "doubtless" resolve and his appropriation of ambition into a virtual "profession" that evokes Meander's wonder and indignation. The delegation to Tamburlaine of "unnatural" desires places both his self-assurance and single-minded professionalism on the margins of officially countenanced and comprehensible behavior. Indeed, it places them on a revealing continuum in which the ambitions of latter-day slaves and thieves are identified with the anarchic exertions of mythological Titans, and all aspirants are seen to be engaged in a transgressive struggle against legally constituted orders of authority.

Rather than have Tamburlaine reject the transgressive terms within which his activities are framed by his opponents, Marlowe has Tamburlaine appropriate and embellish them in the famous speech that follows his defeat of Cosroe:

> The thirst of reign and sweetness of a crown,
> That caused the eldest son of heavenly Ops
> To thrust his doting father from his chair,
> And place himself in the imperial heaven,
> Mov'd me to manage arms against thy state.
> What better precedent than mighty Jove?
> Nature, that fram'd us of four elements
> Warring within our breasts for regiment,
> Doth teach us all to have aspiring minds:
>   (II.vii.12–20)

He does so, first, by accepting the example of Jupiter's defeat of Saturn as an apt precedent for his own actions, which significantly involves a potent son's displacement of a "doting father," an action that would have as much a material as mythic resonance for an Elizabethan audience.[10] But more important is Tamburlaine's assertion that Nature "Doth teach us *all* to have aspiring minds" (my emphasis). At stake here is nothing less than a competing estimate of the natural in which Cosroe's essentialist estimate of the unvarying hierarchical structure of worldly power is being challenged by what is arguably yet another essentialist position, but one that is premised on ideas of unvarying conflict and of contentions for sovereignty in which everyone is free to join.

Critics have, of course, often contended that there are contradictions in the position Tamburlaine takes in identifying "the ripest fruit of all" with "The sweet fruition of an earthly crown" and in his odd conceptual mix of ceaseless movement with a determinate goal. But as Anthony Esler notes, while "Modern minds may see 'bathos' in the speech's primary message," members of Marlowe's generation may have seen nothing less than a "merging of the idealistic and materialistic goals of their aspirations." According to Esler, "Marlowe's classic statement of the creed of the aspiring mind, climaxing in the praise of earthly power, illustrates perfectly the emotional and normative equivalence of the material and the ideal realms in the minds of his generation" (1966, 161). There were undoubtedly other members of Marlowe's audience who were as unprepared as some "modern minds" to resolve Tamburlaine's alleged contradictions in an "emotional and normative equivalence." But they also may have found Marlowe's confounding "of the material and ideal realms" less provocative than the social inversion Marlowe is at once dramatizing and programmatizing.

If we pause for a moment over the stage image of the triumphant Tamburlaine preaching his homily of worldly presumption to the stunned embodiment of political authority that is Cosroe, we may better comprehend why similar stage images (e.g., Tamburlaine's use of Bajazeth as his footstool and his harnessing of the "jades of Asia") so profoundly impressed the Elizabethan playgoer. Each image communicates in the starkest terms a comprehensive inversion of prevailing social and political arrangements. Each image also reveals the extent to which the official discourse of masterlessness actually functions as a discourse of subjection, employed by these fallen princes "to keep men in awe." As Tamburlaine assumes control over the bodies and destinies of men who formerly made all other men humble, he effectively breaks the spell of a subjection that speaks the language of prohibitions and limits, and introduces the audience to the pleasures of transgressive unrestraint.

What the Elizabethan audience actually experienced at the prospect of Tamburlaine lording it over the uncomprehending Cosroe may, of course, have been as unsettling as it was enlivening (cf. Belsey 1985, 29–30). As Marlowe presents in the most compelling and realized form the empowerment of characters who transform their subjection to their ordained masters into mastery over the same, he also brings into focus the transgressive status of the playgoer's desire to achieve a corresponding sense of mastery within the prevailing structures of power. He consequently represents the destabilizing potential of such inversions of the social and political order.

The sense of "amoral wonder" allegedly engendered in audiences by such sequences may thus be said to consist of a volatile mixture of anxiety and fascination, fueled by the audience's desire to experience for itself a feeling of empowerment it knows to be radically unsettling.

The Tamburlaine Phenomenon (1)

I have to this point suggested that Marlowe's development of a discourse of mastery was most apt to stir the emotions and fulfill the fantasies of playgoers located at the extreme verges of Elizabethan society, namely, masterless men on the one hand, and "master spirits" on the other. In the process, I have speculated that the citizen playgoer—represented in Elizabethan class terminology as "the middling sort"—may have experienced a more divided response to Tamburlaine, acknowledging that Tamburlaine's assault on the order of inherited privilege and unearned distinction was an exaggerated version of his own social and economic advancement while at the same time feeling the need to defend his hard-won prerogatives against the competing ambitions of new aspirants. Such a class of playgoers would, presumably, have been most apt to respond defensively to Tamburlaine's subjugation of Cosroe and to his ensuing manifesto.

The contemporary perception of *Tamburlaine* was, however, sufficiently broad to support several more historically specific and less easily generalized observations. While the examples of the same that Richard Levin has assembled are many and varied, at least three demonstrate how political and social concerns influence and re-direct some of the broader psychological effects of the Tamburlaine phenomenon. My first example is drawn from an obscure work entitled *Micrologia* (1629) by one "R.M." which offers "Characters or Essayes, Of Persons, Trades and Places between Ludgate and Newgate." The passage cited by Levin specifically refers to the "pampered jades of Asia" speech in *2 Tamburlaine*. According to Levin, R.M. "testifies to the widespread recognition of these words when he praises a new law condemning Bridewell prisoners to be 'yoakt in Carts' which they must 'draw like Horses' as they

> purge the street
> Of noysome Garbage, carry Dirt and Dung;
> The Beadles following with a mighty throng;

> Whilst as they passe the people scoffing say,
> Holla, ye pampred Iades of Asia.
>   (D6v; quoted in Levin, 60–61)

If we decide to trust R.M.'s reportorial accuracy (and not to assign the Tamburlainean scoffs to his invention), the words he attributes to "the people" demonstrate how Marlowe's powerful image of the subjugation of kings by a former commoner could be appropriated by other commoners to ridicule the aspiring minds of now subjugated inferiors. In the context of a London street scene, Tamburlaine's words are appropriated by "scoffing people" who see in the yoked prisoners the degraded image of Tamburlaine's jades. Rather than use Tamburlaine's example to motivate their own aggressive assault on authority, the "scoffing" people employ it to celebrate the limited power they maintain over their inferiors, and identify their own interests with those of the Beadles who play the role of minor Tamburlaines in this scenario, men "so Satyricall, that on the least fault committed they are ready to giue you a Ierke" (D4).

The delegation to the officious Beadles of the dominating role formerly played by Tamburlaine is not the only reversal evident in this example. The collection of prisoners that suffers the "new laws Iudgment" is drawn not from the ranks of the royally presumptuous but from roughly the same ranks of the masterless and defiant with which Tamburlaine is rhetorically associated by his opponents:

> Bold roaring Boyes, base Queenes, and unchast wiues,
> Cutpurses, Canters, Cheaters, Hie-way-standers,
> Bawdes, Bouncing-Megs, Decoyes, Puncks, Pimps, and Panders,
> Sharks, Prigs, Nips, Foysts, that pill and liue by Stealth, . . .

This reversal suggests that in some minds at least the former scourge of God had become capable of functioning as the scourge of civil society, and, hence, had become culturally normalized. In the process, Tamburlaine's volatile associations with "the rascal meinie" have yielded to what appears to have become his stronger association as an agent of social retribution.

Tamburlaine's presumption is again recuperated in the safe confines of what may be termed "citizen-consciousness" towards the end of Dekker's *The Shoemaker's Holiday* as Simon Eyre confidently prepares to meet the king: "Sim Eyre knows how to speak to a pope, to Sultan Soliman, to Tamburlaine an he were here. And shall I melt, shall I droop before my soveraign? No! . . . Firk, frisk about, and about, and about, for the honour of mad Simon Eyre, Lord Mayor of London" (sc. xx, 58–65). What is more noteworthy here than Eyre's testimony to Tamburlaine's awesomeness (see Levin, 56–57) is his implicit identification of the awesomeness of his own standing as Lord Mayor of London with that of Tamburlaine's position as emperor of all the world. It is as if Eyre has learned from the Tamburlaine to whom he knows how to speak that such a man as *he* need not "droop" to such a man as the king. Indeed, Simon Eyre's catchphrase (which he repeats in the presence of the king), "Prince am I none, yet am I princely born!" (xxi, 17; and see vii, 49–50, "Prince am I none, yet am I nobly born, as being the sole son of a shoemaker"), is exactly what one would expect of a presumptuous citizen who has appropriated as his own Tamburlaine's habit of self-glorification.

The potential subversiveness of Tamburlaine's appeal is both realized and contained in this example. It provides a heroic gloss to citizen pretensions to noble standing while restricting its range of reference to an already domesticated domain of citizen influence, one that is beyond the reach of "the meaner sort" and legally subservient to royal authority. A more socially complex rendering of Tamburlaine's standing as a focus for civil dissension is provided in a third example drawn from Levin's collection of allusions. In Samuel Rowlands's verse-history of the Anabaptist rising in Munster, *Hell's Broke Loose* (1605), we find the Anabaptist leader, John of Leyden, alluding to the episode of the captive kings in order to inspire ardor in his soldiers:

> Haue you not heard that *Scythian Tamburlaine*
> Was earst a Sheepheard ere he play'd the King?
> First over Cattell hee began his raigne,
> Then Countries in subiection hee did bring:
> And Fortunes fauours so mayntain'd his side,
> Kings were his Coach-horse, when he pleas'd to ride.
>   (D3v [1880; rep. 1966, 34]; quoted in Levin, 60)

This example comes packed with a range of references that are well worth examining and that work directly against the associations cultivated in *Micrologia*.[11] Rowlands's anachronistic depiction of the German Anabaptist, John of Leyden, alluding during the siege of Munster in 1534–35 to a play produced on the London stage no earlier than 1588, reveals how deeply Tamburlaine's assault against legally constituted authority may have pene-

trated the minds of its beholders, and does much to substantiate C.L. Barber's observation that "It is not such a long way from the Scythian
Shepherd to John of Leyden" (1988, 83). Most interesting for our purposes
is Rowlands's implicit identification of Tamburlaine's lawless presumption
with that of the notoriously presumptuous leader of a popular rebellion, a
man whom Jack Wilton in Nashe's *The Unfortunate Traveller* condescend-
ingly calls "*Iohn Leiden* the Botcher" (McKerrow ed., vol. 2, 1904, 232) in
an account of the Munster rising characterized by "a typical ruling-class
attitude" (Hill 1958, 324). Rowlands underplays the religous and commu-
nitarian aspects of Leyden's revolt and emphasizes, instead, what the events
at Munster share with other popular and populist uprisings, namely, the
common man's unnatural desire to rise in the world. That Rowlands
should choose to read Leyden's revolt through the medium of *Tamburlaine*
indicates that he would also be ready to read *Tamburlaine* itself through
the medium of other insurrections against established authority. Indeed,
Rowlands repeatedly has Leyden speak and act in a broadly allusive manner that makes Tamburlaine himself seem less a Scythian warlord than a
comrade-in-arms of Jack Straw, Wat Tyler, and John Ball.

Marlowe, of course, invites such comparisons even as he insists on Tamburlaine's status as a distinct, inimitable phenomenon. It is very much to
Marlowe's point for Tamburlaine and company to suffer identification
with "the many headed monster" only to demonstrate a nobility that is
every bit as inborn as it is acquired. However, the repeated instances in
which Tamburlaine is described by his royal opponents as a "sturdy felon"
or "base bred thief"—like the "horror stories" told of John of Leyden by
the enemies of the Anabaptists "to make the flesh of heretics creep" (Hill
1958, 324–25)—may well have established in some minds a ruling-class perspective on Tamburlaine that was as difficult to dislodge as the ruling-class
itself. Passages like the following, drawn from the Soldan's speech in the
fourth act of *1 Tamburlaine*, may have too thoroughly reproduced the discourse of masterlessness to be susceptible to erasure or transformation:

> A monster of five hundred thousand heads,
> Compact of rapine, piracy and spoil,
> The scum of men, the hate and scourge of God,
> Raves in Egyptia, and annoyeth us.
> My Lord, it is the bloody Tamburlaine,
> A sturdy felon and a base-bred thief,
> By murder raised to the Persian crown,

That dares control us in our territories.

. . . .

It is a blemish to the majesty
And high estate of mighty emperors,
That such a base usurping vagabond
Should brave a king, or wear a princely crown.

                                    (IV.iii.7–14, 19–22)

The ease with which Tamburlaine topples the Soldan from this imperious perch and wins approval of his honorable treatment of Zenocrate—who is free of "all blot of foul inchastity" (V.ii.424)—should resolve in stage terms what is left unresolved with respect to the social and political ramifications of Tamburlaine's presumption. But though Tamburlaine structures his domestic behavior on orthodox courtly models and exercises his imperial prerogatives with a decorum surpassing that of his predecessors, his presumption—and the emulation it encourages—outlive his stage-existence to prompt Rowlands to make him an inspiration to the long-dead John of Leyden and his followers who, according to Jack Wilton, "thought they knew as much of Gods minde as richer men" (Nashe, *Unfortunate Traveler*, 278).

These intertextual transactions demonstrate the exceptional range of the Tamburlaine phenomenon's class-interested applications. Tamburlaine serves, respectively, as a precedent and rallying cry for commoners reveling in the punishment of criminals; as a subject of comparison for Dekker's Lord Mayor as he celebrates the privileges and accomplishments of London citizens and craftsmen; and for Rowlands as a cautionary example of the potential for civil dissension inherent in all challenges to legal authority mounted by aspiring minds. The use to which Tamburlaine is put in each instance shows the extent to which contemporary responses to Tamburlaine were filtered through a network of opposed social and political interests and assumptions, and suggests how difficult it is to reconstruct a common ground of response to the Tamburlaine phenomenon. There is, however, one area of overlap in each of the preceding examples—namely, that of class consciousness and class conflict—which suggests that far from dissolving social differences by transporting its audience into some remote dreamworld, *Tamburlaine* had the effect of reinforcing class identifications and antagonisms. This is, at least, the impression one gets from the allusions to Tamburlaine we have just examined, all of which approach Tamburlaine at some distance from the conditions that obtain in performance.

A more vivid rendering of audience response to *Tamburlaine* in the immediate give-and-take of performance may be supplied by an example of Levin's drawn from the third Satire of Book One of Joseph Hall's *Virgidemiarum* (1597). Hall envisions an unnamed poet at a drinking session, "higher pitch'd" than his fellow revelers, setting

> his soaring thought
> On crowned kings that Fortune hath low brought:
> Or some vpreared, high-aspiring swaine
> As it might be the Turkish Tamberlaine.
> . . . .
> Such soone, as some braue-minded hungry youth,
> Sees fitly frame to his wide-strained mouth,
> He vaunts his voyce vpon an hyred stage,
> With high-set steps, and princely carriage:
> . . . .
> There if he can with termes Italianate,
> Big-sounding sentences, and words of state,
> Faire patch me vp his pure *Iambick* verse,
> He ravishes the gazing Scaffolders:
> . . . .
> Now, least such frightfull showes of Fortune fall,
> And bloody Tyrants rage, should chance appall
> The dead stroke audience, mids the silent rout
> Comes leaping in a self-misformed lout.
>   (Davenport ed., 1969, 14–15, ll. 9–34;
>   quoted in Levin, 52–53)

Since Hall's is hardly a friendly review of a play he elsewhere calls a "goodly *hoch-poch*" (l. 39) inspired by a "base drink-drowned spright" (l. 13), we should probably not take his depiction of "The dead stroke audience" as an authoritative representation of audience response to *Tamburlaine*. Nevertheless, Hall's condescending critique of *Tamburlaine* has the virtue of channelling his unabashed disgust at what he takes to be the general entrancement of "the gazing Scaffolders" into a graphic rendering of the "ravishing" effects of Tamburlaine's "high-set steps," "princely carriage," "Big-sounding sentences, and words of state." He vividly depicts what Anthony Munday would doubtless recognize as the "webs" of plays that "are so subtilie spun, that there is no man that is once within them, that can avoide them without danger" (*Third Blast*, 142). In so doing, he reminds us that the allusions to *Tamburlaine* we have examined above, although set a distance from the "dead stroke" of audience engagement, all bear traces of playgoers so deeply immersed in theatrical experience that they remain stuck in subtle ways in the web of the Tamburlaine phenomenon. Whether they play street-side Tamburlaines mocking the bad luck of criminals, pompous burghers casually addressing royalty on equal terms, or notorious rebels enjoying the pleasures of power, the figures depicted by "R.M.," Dekker, and Rowlands specifically testify to their portrayers' appreciation of the effects of theatrical engagement.

A series of similarly suggestive echoes of *Tamburlaine* that Levin does not examine and that emphatically demonstrate the applicability of Tamburlaine's appeal to a range of social positions may be found throughout Shakespeare's *2 Henry VI*, a play that was both composed and performed in the shadow of the Tamburlaine plays. From Richard, the Duke of York's claim that he is "far better born than is the King, / More like a king, more kingly in my thoughts" (V.i.28–29) to Jack Cade's vow that "the proudest peer in the realm shall not wear a head / on his shoulders, unless he pay me tribute" (IV.vii.114–15), *2 Henry VI* is virtually saturated in Tamburlainean statements of proud self-assertion. Although York may appear to occupy a position no more unsettling than Cosroe's as he attempts to wrest the crown from the childish-foolish King Henry, his presumption does not stop at his self-serving comparison of aristocratic blood-lines but extends to the belief that performative criteria—"I am . . . / More like a king, more kingly in my thoughts"—may legitimate his planned usurpation of royal authority. For his part, Cade makes significant interventions in the discursive dominance of the ruling class as he turns the rhetoric of masterlessness on its head in his encounter with Stafford—

> *Staf.*   Villain! thy father was a plasterer
> And thou thyself a shearman, art thou not?
> *Cade*.   And Adam was a gardener.
>
> (IV.ii.126–28)

—and chides his retreating supporters for remaining in awe of a nobility that systematically oppresses them:

> you are all recreants and dastards,
> and delight to live in slavery to the nobility.

Let them break your backs with burdens, take your
houses over your heads, ravish your wives and
daughters before your faces.

(IV.viii.27–31)

While Cade ultimately fails even to maintain the support of his onstage
confederates in the face of Clifford's subsequent appeal to the name and
memory of Henry V—"the name of Henrie the Fifth hales them to an
hundred mischiefs, and makes them leave me desolate," says Cade in response to the same (IV.viii.56–58)—his resistance to the social enslavement
in which his former supporters allegedly "delight" is not as singular as he
suggests. It is, instead, diffused throughout the play and appears in instances as disparate as Peter the apprentice's allegations against the treach-
erousness of his master, Horner, in I.iii and in the proud Suffolk's
execution by equally proud pirates who take upon themselves the defense
of the realm in IV.i.

In the latter scene we witness a particularly revealing variation on Tamburlainean practice as the arrogant aristocrat, Suffolk, styles himself in the
very language of Tamburlaine—"Jove sometimes went disguis'd, and why
not I?" (IV.i.48)—while simultaneously addressing his captors in the language of Tamburlaine's princely opponents and detractors:

Obscure and lowly swain, King Henry's blood,
The honorable blood of Lancaster,
Must not be shed by such a jaded groom.
Hast thou not kiss'd thy hand and held my stirrup?
And bare-head plodded by my foot-cloth mule,
And thought thee happy when I shook my head?

(IV.i.50–55)

Rather than intimidating his captors into servile submission, Suffolk's
denigrating comments arouse their casual contempt: "Speak, Captain, shall
I stab the forlorn swain?" (IV.i.65). The refusal of Suffolk's interlocutors
either to accept his estimate of their baseness or to become overawed by
his position is rooted in a competing confidence in their own self-worth
that also bears traces of Tamburlainean presumption. Indeed, their fearless
execution of Suffolk is predictably represented as a "barbarous and bloody
spectacle" by the ransomed gentleman who is charged with bearing
Suffolk's body back to the queen and who, like Cosroe in response to

Tamburlaine's triumph, views their action more as an abridgment of the social hierarchy than as an exercise in rough justice.

Another, less complicated reference to *Tamburlaine the Great* is delegated to Duke Humphrey as he comments on his ambitious wife's fall from fortune:

> Sweet Nell, ill can thy noble mind abrook
> The abject people gazing on thy face,
> With envious looks laughing at thy shame,
> That erst did follow thy proud chariot-wheels
> When thou didst ride in triumph through the streets.
>
> (II.iv.10–14)

Unlike R.M.'s allusion to Tamburlaine's "jades of Asia" speech, Duke Humphrey's statement works within the well-worn *de casibus* tradition and employs the imagery of Tamburlaine's triumphs as an emblem of pride laid low. The Duchess of Gloucester is at once represented as a quondam and would-be Tamburlainean figure who is now reduced to the humiliated proportions of one of Tamburlaine's conquered kings. As she enters "barefoot, in a white sheet, with verses pinned upon her back," mocked by the "abject people," it would appear that Shakespeare seeks exactly the kind of connection between Tamburlainean presumption and its humbling aftermath that Marlowe rejects in both parts of his drama. As is the case in his representation of Suffolk's fall, Shakespeare effectively reads Tamburlaine out of Marlowe's drama of fantasy fulfillments only to re-inscribe him in the drama of moralized history. Yet insofar as Tamburlaine's influence is felt on both sides of its competing social applications—*in* Cade as much as against Cade, *in* Suffolk's captors as much as against Suffolk—one would have to conclude that Shakespeare himself, at the time of *2 Henry VI*'s composition, was too immersed in the Tamburlaine phenomenon to sustain a consistent critical detachment.

The Tamburlaine Phenomenon (2)

The capacity of contemporary playwrights and playgoers from many walks of life to find in Tamburlaine a common focus for socially competitive fantasies of aggression, defiance, and self-aggrandizement exemplifies Marlowe's skill at making Tamburlaine less an Elizabethan Everyman than the theatrical equivalent of a magnetic field attracting everything within reach into its orbit. It also demonstrates Marlowe's success in transforming potential audience resistance to the Tamburlaine phenomenon into realized engagement: a success Marlowe seems to have had no trouble repeating in his sequel to *Tamburlaine the Great* where occasions for resistance more often overlap with occasions for engagement and where Tamburlaine contends with complications that have the potential to deny "the very nature of [his] genius" (Ellis-Fermor 1967, 45). These complications include the death of Zenocrate; the intractability of Tamburlaine's effeminate, eldest son; and the more aggressive exertions of his opponents who generally fail to bow and scrape before the power and pressure of the Tamburlaine phenomenon, and at times present themselves as minor Tamburlaines in their own right. They also include a marked change in Tamburlaine's dramatic status. Tamburlaine formerly represented the small man made large, the son defeating the fathers, the self-reliant commoner fashioning a princely role for himself in the world. In the second play, with the stabilization and institutionalization of his power, Tamburlaine often takes on the appearance of his former opponents. He receives the plaudits and pledges of his own contributory kings, opposes in arms the aspiring son of a defeated enemy, issues claims that he has no capacity to substantiate, and destroys one of his own sons who chafes (with disarming sarcasm) against the imperiousness of his will.

Tamburlaine responds to these changed conditions in a manner that surely tests Freud's formulation regarding "the limits set upon the employment of abnormal characters on the stage." Yet as the popularity of the captive kings sequence demonstrates, Tamburlaine's virulent responses to the changed nature of his dramatic existence appear to have occasioned no change in audience response to the Tamburlaine phenomenon.[12] The original appeal of the small man made large has effectively been re-directed into the theatrical appeal of the large man who makes or keeps others small (note, for example, how this re-directed appeal functions in the passage drawn from *Micrologia*). It is in this sense, among others, that Marlowe fails to sustain anything amounting to a populist political stance. Rather than have Tamburlaine displace a repressive discourse of masterlessness with a politically liberating discourse of popular mastery, Marlowe remains more faithful to a model of behavior in which the achievement of mastery is both premised on and conducive to concomitant acts of subjection. One must, on this account, recall that there is nothing particularly reformist or utopian in Tamburlaine's dramatic orientation, and acknowledge that his appeal largely rests on his capacity to feed his audience's fantasies of self-aggrandizement.

Throughout Marlowe's sequel, Tamburlaine continues to operate as the privileged focus of dramatic discourse, conceiving and subduing the very forces of resistance that would seem to oppose his continuing claim on audience regard. Voices that oppose Tamburlaine's estimate of himself are either literally silenced or dramatically "countermanded." Voices that adopt a recognizably Tamburlainean idiom of their own—as does Callapine's in 2 Tamburlaine—establish themselves as but minor echoes of the major chords Tamburlaine continues to strike even as his command of the stage reduces in compass to the size of a map.[13] All this is not to suggest that Marlowe sets no limits on Tamburlaine's appeal in the context of the second play. In purely performative terms, the freshness and freedom of Tamburlaine's former approach to conquest have become dulled and rigidified. His actions seem undirected and all-consuming, pursued more to fill time and occupy space, to exploit what has already been accomplished in the name of scourge of God, than to lead on to new fruitions as emperor of all the world. Few contemporary playgoers could fail to notice that in applying himself to fit the terms of his self-styled role, Tamburlaine becomes caught in a bind of arbitrary motion in which his very relentlessness demonstrates a need to compensate for his exhaustion of further possibilities and makes him seem but "a desiring machine that produces violence and death" (Greenblatt 1977, 43). But this need of Tamburlaine "to repeat himself in order to be the same character on stage" (50) also becomes for Marlowe (who similarly needs to repeat himself in order to reconstitute his earlier success) a dramatic resource for a more volatile provocation of the audience's capacity for engagement.

Of all the instances of violence and violation in the two parts of *Tamburlaine*, the scene that begins with the "*Governor of Babylon . . . hanging in chains on the walls*" (stage-direction) and ends with the massacre of his fellow Babylonians in the fifth act of 2 *Tamburlaine* has often seemed the hardest to countenance and is, consequently, of crucial importance in the determination of audience response. The inexorable movement from the Governor's appearance on the walls of Babylon to the first shot that wounds him and, then, to the succession of shots that kill him constitutes a precise dwelling on the event that was presumably designed to arouse the playgoer's capacity to enjoy a simultaneous act of mastery and subjection. And the graphic report Techelles subsequently delivers of his offstage fulfillment of Tamburlaine's order to "drown them all, man, woman, and child; / Leave not a Babylonian in the town" (V.i.168–69) seems similarly directed to arouse in the playgoer a combined sense of awe and perverse fascination:

> I have fulfilled your highness' will, my lord.
> Thousands of men, drowned in Asphaltis' lake,
> Have made the water swell above the banks,
> And fishes, fed by human carcasses,
> Amazed, swim up and down upon the waves,
> As when they swallow asafoetida,
> Which makes them fleet aloft and gasp for air.
>
> (V.i.201–7)

That Marlowe chooses (and manages) to make poetry of a high order out of this vision of biological excess and decay indicates that he trusted it to function as yet another in a series of punishing fantasies that seduces as it shocks, as a pointed provocation of his audience's capacity to find pleasure in the charged affective field of transgression.

Marlowe must also have known that playgoers who could walk back and forth over London Bridge on their way to and from the playhouse without becoming disturbed by the sight of the "more than thirty skulls of noble men," which "were stuck on tall stakes" there, could not only countenance Tamburlaine's treatment of the Babylonians but admire—and even vicariously participate in—his daring, as Thomas Platter's observation regarding the self-interested boasts of the noblemen's descendents suggests. William Camden's contemporary report on a celebrated act of official violence offers an even more revealing insight into the psychic disposition of Elizabethan "audiences." Camden's report focuses on the punishment meted out to John Stubbs, author of *The Discovery of a Gaping Gulf Whereinto England Is Like to Be Swallowed* (1579), an anonymously published pamphlet, written to criticize the queen's plans for a French marriage (see Adams 1977, 78–90). In exchange for what Elizabeth herself seems to have termed his "lewde seditious booke" (Adams, 79) and at the queen's express bidding, Stubbs, and his publisher, William Page, suffered the following fate:

> Hereby had Stubbs and Page their right hands cut off with a Cleaver driven thorow the wrist with the force of a beetle [heavy mallet], upon a scaffold in the market place at Westminster. . . . I remember (being present thereat,) that when

> Stubbs, having his right hand cut off, put off his hat with his left, and sayd with a loud voyce, *God save the Queene*; the multitude standing about, was altogether silent, either out of horrour of this new and unwonted punishment, or else out of pitty towards the man being of most honorable and unblameable report, or else out of hatred of the marriage, which most men presaged would be the overthrow of Religion. (Camden, 238–39; quoted in Adams, 83)

Elaborating on Camden's report of the interactive dynamics of this event, Robert P. Adams also emphasizes "the crowd's extraordinary silence," its "sense of horror," and "its mingled sense of pity and fear," but concludes that "All three stimulated this audience to a sense of participation in the experience of tragedy as history ruled by *raison d'état*, even when their most apparent role—like Stubbs's—had become to be "eaten" in the power-games of ruthless princes (86). According to Adams, rather than view Stubbs's punishment with direct reference to their own "most apparent role" as fellow subjects and, hence, as potential victims of a similar fate, the "multitude" appears to behave like an audience at a play, identifying less with Stubbs than with the affective field of the scenario that enfolds him. Whereas Camden specifically attributes the multitude's "horrour" to "this new and unwonted punishment" and suggests that the standers about feel keenly their own subjection in identifying both with Stubbs and his position, Adams effectively theatricalizes Camden's report, making a "dead stroke audience" out of a multitude whose most conspicuous characteristic was also its silence.

As the only surviving remnant of that audience to speak to us, Camden's voice should, perhaps, be preferred to Adams's. But Camden does not, finally, speak from a position which has been mediated by that cultural moment when multitudes became audiences that paid for the pleasure of participating vicariously in events like the one he describes. While Adams may distort "the facts" of Camden's report, he does so in the interest of bringing those facts into contact with the emerging moment of the theater's cultural predominance and with "that historic instant" when "the age's supreme rival myths of power—those of the Christian prince and its allegedly polar opposite, the Machiavellian tyrant— . . . appeared to fuse" (85). What these myths fused into, according to Adams, was a new myth of "the supreme man-of-respect . . . who by whatever means can and does generate supreme fear" (84), a myth (I submit) that finds its apotheosis in the Tamburlaine phenomenon.

The cultural moment of Elizabethan drama and the "historic instant" when it became apparent to English multitudes "standing about" and audiences alike that "political horrors" could be "the deliberate work of legitimate rulers" (85) coalesce in the two parts of *Tamburlaine the Great*, which brought together people from diverse walks of life to countenance and take pleasure in actions that rendered them speechless. The difference between the silence of Camden's multitude and the silence of the dead-stroke audiences described by Adams and Joseph Hall may be measured in terms of the former's presumptive identification with the victim of "political horrors" and the latter's probable experience of an awestruck sense of complicity with purveyors of the same. Indeed, the transfer of sympathy from victim to purveyor of violence operates as an enabling force both in Marlowe's drama and in the plays of many of his contemporaries. Although Marlowe will also prove himself capable of contributing incisive dramatic critiques of the uses and abuses of power, in *Tamburlaine* at least he appears to have made the vicarious empowerment of audiences for whom subjection was a political fact of life too attractive a prospect for playgoers to resist.

4. Banquo's Ghost

In concluding his recent essay on "*Macbeth* and the Politics of Historiography" (1987), David Norbrook offers the following appraisal of Macbeth:

> As a regicide who was condemned equally by [the "democratic theorist" and historian, George] Buchanan and by conservatives, and yet had half-buried associations with constitutionalist traditions, Macbeth was a figure bound to evoke ambivalent responses from a Renaissance humanist. If the audience can sympathize with Macbeth even though he outrages the play's moral order, it may be because vestiges remain of a worldview in which regicide could be a noble rather than an evil act. Shakespeare may have come under pressure from his royal patron to substitute a mystical and legitimist version of Scottish history for the rationalist and constitutionalist viewpoint of the old tutor who haunted his nightmares, but it is impossible to exorcise a ghost without first summoning forth its presence (116).

I quote Norbrook at such length because the conclusion he reaches through an exhaustive discussion of the historiographic underpinnings of *Macbeth* is consistent with the one I arrive at by entirely different means, and because he provides my argument with the kind of historical grounding it otherwise lacks. But I also do so because I, too, want to "summon forth" a ghost, one that will help us to distinguish Norbrook's conception of an audience that could be moved to sympathize with the vestigial nobility of Macbeth's actions from the competing conception of an audience that was more apt to be moved by less easily rationalized inducements for engagement with Macbeth. For Norbrook, the audience and the "Renaissance humanist," who has synthesized his characterization of Macbeth from a variety of sources, share an ambivalence that is both conscious and consciously political. From my perspective, *Macbeth* does more than demonstrate that Shakespeare's "plays retain elements of the attitudes they are rejecting" and that these elements may occasionally be identified with "certain radical currents of thought" (116). In offering so exemplary an occasion for exploring the contradictions between a playtext's apparent aims and a performance's less easily monitored effects, *Macbeth* radically alters the nature of what is retained and what is rejected, allowing the audience to "share" the kind of experience that cannot be reduced to a "current of thought."

Although the play *Macbeth* is framed from the start by the overarching "sponsorship" of maleficent witches, the initial actions of Macbeth himself are framed by his feudal status as the loyal thane of Glamis and delegated position as "Bellona's bridegroom." The violence that "brave Macbeth" is said to visit upon the "merciless Macdonwald" is thus officially sponsored and sanctioned in a way that Tamburlaine's actions are not. "O valiant cousin, worthy gentleman!" says Duncan after hearing that Macbeth, whose "brandish'd steel . . . smok'd with bloody execution," has "unseam'd" this enemy of the state "from the nave to th' chops" (see I.ii. 10–26). However, the ardor with which Macbeth fulfills his charge as defender of Duncan's state is also represented in a manner that could, conceivably, unsettle both his royal sponsor and an offstage audience that thus far can only associate Macbeth's exploits with a name and the plaudits attached to it. In particular, the reported "unseaming" of Macdonwald—which occurs in the unstable confines of a battle whose outcome stood "Doubtful . . . / As two spent swimmers, that do cling together / And choke their art" (I.ii.9–11)—elides the ordered brutality of state-sponsored violence with the altogether more "disjoint" violence of a war that a state sponsors, but cannot reasonably monitor or contain. While the successive reports of Macbeth's executions evoke in their royal auditor unqualified exclamations of approval, they also provoke a response as mingled in pity and fear, fascination and admiration, as the "dead-stroke" silences that reportedly accompanied the resolution of the *Gaping Gulf* affair and performances of *Tamburlaine*.

Macbeth occupies at this early moment of the drama an equivocal position in which a subject's devotion to the state uneasily coexists with a dominating and potentially defiant subjectivity. The official limits within which this subject exercises his devotion are, moreover, already blurred by his success in expressing a dominance that has unsettled the fixity of his own name, giving it the kind of mobility which, as Macbeth himself notes, "Stands not within the prospect of belief" (I.iii.74). Like Tamburlaine's, Macbeth's advancement beyond the prospect of belief comes as a consequence of his own "unnatural" actions and largely in payment for them. That it also "comes" from the words of the witches tends to mystify the source of a social mobility that he initially resists but ultimately craves. And it is, finally, the agency of mystification that also brings the officially unearnable crown within the prospect of belief. In a sense, then, Shakespeare's play forgives Macbeth what it condemns him for. While ambition may be said to become Macbeth's disease, Macbeth's advancement is actually bred out of a "disjoint" frame of civil dissension within which intention and effect are as doubtful to distinguish as "two spent swimmers, that do cling together/And choke their art."

But perhaps the play's most powerful image of equivocation is supplied by the embodiment onstage of Banquo's ghost in the play's third act. Banquo is, of course, the thoroughly undeserving victim of violence "sponsored" by a regicidal king and executed by assassins who are motivated by money and an alleged private complaint rather than by feudal allegiance. As such, his posthumous appearance at Macbeth's banquet would appear to operate entirely outside the bounds of equivocation as a clear-cut sign of Macbeth's responsibility for disjoining "the frame of things." Shakespeare, however, complicates this dramatic design in a manner that affects his play's management of audience reception every bit as profoundly as Marlowe's repeated privileging of Tamburlaine's point of view.

Banquo's Ghost

Audiences, directors, and scholars have long been fascinated by that pivotal moment when the ghost of Banquo takes Macbeth's seat at the banquet table and twice drives him to distraction while the dinner-guests look on, ignorant of what Macbeth sees. The shape our fascination takes is often determined by our own or a given production's response to the staging problem this moment always poses: namely, does one fill Macbeth's chair with an actor portraying the nodding corpse of Banquo, or leave the chair empty since empty it seems to everyone onstage apart from Macbeth?[1] If the ghost of Banquo physically appears onstage, Macbeth's dramatically private vision becomes an experience that is theatrically shared; that is, the offstage audience sees *with* Macbeth what the onstage audience—Lady Macbeth and the dinner-guests—do not and cannot see.[2] If, on the other hand, the chair remains empty, the offstage audience shares the perspective of the onstage audience, and sees Macbeth looking "but on a stool."[3] In this respect, our perspective is analogous to Gertrude's in the closet scene of *Hamlet* when she protests that she sees all there is to see, implying that what she cannot see "is not."

Allowing Macbeth's chair to remain empty may even become equivalent to transforming the tragedy of *Macbeth* into a modern morality play in which the normatively "good" citizens offstage unite with their surrogates onstage to witness the psychological torment justly visited upon an increasingly isolated tyrant. The alternative—presenting Banquo's ghost "in the flesh"—has the opposite effect of sundering the normative ties between on- and off-stage audiences, at least on a cognitive level, thereby making our response to Macbeth a psychologically provocative experience. Although there is nothing terribly original in accepting this alternative as the most "faithful" resolution to the staging problem, my reasons for doing so here differ from those of A.C. Bradley, Kenneth Muir, and others who prefer to view Banquo's ghost as an embodied hallucination.[4] I work from the assumption that the onstage embodiment of Banquo's ghost is the logical product or fruition of a dramatic process initiated by the "fair is foul" refrain of the witches at the beginning of the play and spurred on by Macbeth's murder of Duncan: a process that systematically undermines an ordered world of familiar verities and establishes a disordered world of unfamiliar phenomena in its stead. But what is most significant for our present purpose, I see what happens *dramatically* to the characters onstage as happening *theatrically* to the audience-at-large, as the "first world" from which the play is viewed becomes displaced and enveloped by the prevailing atmosphere of the drama.

Macbeth's success as a play is predicated on this extension of its dramatic range beyond the limits of the stage into the province of the audience. The play achieves dramatic extension by actively engaging its audience from the start in what G. Wilson Knight once described as "a wrestling of destruction with creation" (1953, 153). By means of the concentrated orchestration of incantatory verse and violently strained imagery with a plot constructed to translate the unnatural into the realm of the natural, the play attempts to disarm its audience of the same kind of imaginative constraint that compels Banquo, upon the disappearance of the witches, to ask whether he and Macbeth "have eaten on the insane root, / That takes the reason prisoner" (I.iii.84–85). As first Lady Macbeth—"Come, you Spirits / That tend on mortal thoughts" (I.v.40ff.)—and then Macbeth himself—"Thou sure and firm set earth, / Hear not my steps" (II.i.56ff.)—appropriate the incantatory idiom of the weird sisters and begin to move dreamlike through a world in which "Nature seems dead," the audience is forced to cede its grounding in a reality more "sure and firm set" than that emanating from the stage, and is eventually compelled to add Macbeth's peculiar ontological discovery, "Nothing is but what is not," to its stock of available perceptions. The play, moreover, conditions the audience, entranced and no less "rapt" than Macbeth himself by the strange communion of "fair and foul," to respond sympathetically to Macbeth's ability to give visual substance to the forms of things unknown and to his propensity to translate what is known into other areas of apprehension entirely. In the dagger speech, for instance, the playgoer conceivably both sees (in the mind's eye) and does not see a dagger that is at once both visible and invisible to the playgoer's cognitive surrogate, Macbeth:

> Is this a dagger, which I see before me,
> The handle toward my hand? Come, let me clutch thee:—
> I have thee not, and yet I see thee still.
> Art thou not, fatal vision, sensible
> To feeling, as to sight? or art thou but
> A dagger of the mind, a false creation,
> Proceeding from the heat-oppressed brain?
> . . . .
> Mine eyes are made the fools o'th'other senses,
> Or else worth all the rest:
>
> (II.i.33–39, 44–45)

By leaving the audience alone with Macbeth as he performs this subtle balancing act between the "dagger of the mind" and the more "palpable" dagger he now proceeds to draw, Shakespeare draws the audience inside Macbeth's circuit of mixed perceptions and, in so doing, makes the audience itself increasingly susceptible to the suggestiveness of Macbeth's subjective preoccupations. Although Macbeth himself ultimately succeeds in distinguishing between the false forms that derive from within and the true forms that have their being from without—"There's no such thing. / It is the bloody business which informs / Thus to mine eyes" (II.i.47–49)—the audience is left to ponder at greater length the proposition that Macbeth finally discards, namely, whether the eyes, instead of playing fools to the other senses, are, indeed, "worth all the rest."

In short, Macbeth's manner of approaching the air-drawn dagger both conditions the audience to accept his ability to distinguish between the truth and falseness of appearances in consistency with what the audience itself sees and does not see embodied on the stage, and persuades the audience that in *his* mind's eye at least, Macbeth has seen the floating dagger, has, as it were, conjured up out of himself the form and figure of the deed he intends to commit. Indeed, the presence of "gouts of blood" on this dagger's "blade and dudgeon" places "false creation" and real dagger into so close a relationship that the false article actually anticipates the imminent exploit of the true one.[5] Macbeth's words effectively give substance to the undone deed and "create" a real dagger out of the false one he has so suggestively summoned up. Macbeth himself comes to assume in this scene the shape of a reluctant and haunted conjurer whose role it is to draw both himself and his audience into an apprehension of more than meets the common eye.

Macbeth is, of course, less a conjurer than a character endowed with an extraordinary imaginative capability which, wedded to an equally acute moral sensibility, makes him more conscious than anyone else onstage of the interpenetration of material and immaterial realities. And it is exactly the wide-ranging nature of his consciousness that allows him to comprehend immediately almost all the moral, personal, and social consequences of his murder of Duncan:

> What hands are here? Ha! they pluck out mine eyes.
> Will all great Neptune's ocean wash this blood
> Clean from my hand? No, this my hand will rather
> The multitudinous seas incarnadine,
> Making the green one red.
>
> (II.ii.58–62)

> Had I but died an hour before this chance,
> I had liv'd a blessed time; for, from this instant,
> There's nothing serious in mortality;
> All is but toys: renown, and grace, is dead;
> The wine of life is drawn, and the mere lees
> Is left this vault to brag of.
>
> (II.iii.89–94)

I say "almost all" because in the second quoted passage Macbeth is playing a formal public role and may be speaking more wisely than he intends or knows, and in the first is expressing a figurative truth whose imminent fulfillment will strike him with the shock of first recognition when the green seas become red in the form of Banquo's ghost.[6] For in murdering Duncan, in attempting to "leap the life to come," Macbeth has, quite literally, brought that life down to earth, and has effectively answered Banquo's earlier doubts about the "fantastical" by making it a commonplace in the new order of reality he has spurred into being. The later embodiment onstage of Banquo's ghost is, therefore, nothing less than the visible consequence of Macbeth's every motion to realize the "future in the instant."

Shakespeare, nevertheless, goes to further trouble in the banquet scene to persuade the audience of the reality of Banquo's ghost, to make the audience perceptually intimate with Macbeth at the precise moment when he becomes perceptually estranged from his only confidante, Lady Macbeth. Unlike the audience, Lady Macbeth is unaware of the immediate occasion of Macbeth's distraction, his murder of Banquo. Macbeth has, we recall, kept her "innocent of the knowledge" until she might "applaud the deed." She is not, however, unaware of Macbeth's imaginative and moral acuity. She has heard of the "air-drawn dagger," chided him for dwelling too precisely on the event ("Consider it not so deeply," she responds, to his inability to say "Amen"), and witnessed the defensive intensity that seems now to fill all his days made night and nights made day. But Lady Macbeth is a rationalist, skeptical of Macbeth's penchant for penetrating the superficial trappings of what passes for objective reality. She firmly believes in the capacity of strong-minded men and women to exert rational control over themselves and their environment. "They must lie there!" she commands as the distracted Macbeth returns from the murder, bloody daggers in hand. She is, in short, ignorant of the immaterial realities which increasingly dominate Macbeth and which will later drive *her* to suicide in the closing moments of the play. And it is this same ignorance that prevents her from seeing, in the banquet scene, that all that "is not" is all there is, that the ghost of Banquo is no "dagger of the mind" or "false creation":

> O proper stuff!
> This is the very painting of your fear:
> This is the air-drawn dagger, which, you said,
> Led you to Duncan . . . .
> . . . .
> Why do you make such faces? When all's done,
> You look but on a stool.
>
> (III.iv.59–62;66–67)

By speaking of the dagger and Banquo's ghost as if they were similarly derived phenomena while the stage holds the crucial difference before us,

Lady Macbeth actually forces the audience to distinguish between them, to make, with Macbeth, a distinction that she ("innocent" of such knowledge) is incapable of making for herself:

> the time has been,
> That, when the brains were out, the man would die,
> And there an end; but now, they rise again
> With twenty mortal murthers on their crowns,
> And push us from our stool. This is more strange
> Than such a murther is.
>
> (III.iv.77–82)

The exactness of Macbeth's anatomy of the new world that has supplanted the old constitutes the last step in a dramatic process that negotiates the audience's collective surrender to the powerful illusions cultivated by the play, and that makes the audience, for better or for worse, Macbeth's visionary accomplice.

The Shared Vision

Having provided for the ghost, I would now like to provide for our increasingly hypothetical audience. What, first of all, does the shared vision of Banquo's ghost contribute to an audience's relationship with Macbeth? If Shakespeare succeeds in making the audience Macbeth's visionary accomplice, does this imply that the audience operates as his emotional accomplice as well? Second, what happens to the protected space occupied by the audience if its collective imagination is solidly linked with Macbeth's and alienated from the onstage audience that is alienated from him? Does the audience lose its sense of neutrality, surrender its detachment, and begin to identify its interests with the affective field of transgression Macbeth has so assiduously cultivated?

Even speaking conservatively, it seems clear that when Banquo's ghost takes Macbeth's seat at table, the audience must be moved out of its complacency to attend to an extraordinary event. The moment virtually requires the kind of alienation that is, in Brechtian terms, best depicted as the movement from one perceptual mode to another, although in this instance the Brechtian movement from involvement to detachment must be reversed. The audience is simultaneously compelled to become aware of a choice between Macbeth's and Lady Macbeth's competing estimates of the situation, and to recognize that its own choice has already been made once it has become sufficiently absorbed in the dramatic process that culminates in the ghost's appearance. The reversed process of alienation or estrangement occasioned by the extraordinary event makes the audience shift its ground as the drama itself shifts ground. The audience now finds itself alienated from the normative onstage community that looks "but on a stool" and engaged totally in the vision of Banquo's ghost which it shares with Macbeth. Through this movement between different ways of seeing, the audience gains visible access to what amounts to a fourth dimension of dramatic reality. As the dinner guests and Lady Macbeth look on in wonder and annoyance respectively, the audience's own perspective opens up to embrace a psychically charged theatrical moment which conceivably externalizes its own most suppressed fears and anxieties.

But what really does the audience *see* when it shares Macbeth's vision of Banquo's ghost? What is the substance and what are the consequences of the shared vision? What the audience sees vividly embodied onstage is, to distort slightly Macbeth's own defensive formulation, an "unreal mock'ry" of life that turns all its pretty fictions of permanence and stability to no account, that penetrates what David Willbern terms "the conventional confine of theatrical space" and, in so doing, breaks or, at least, bends the theatrical frame that divides art from life, illusion from reality.[7] As if Shakespeare were offering his audience dubious compensation for his secondhand portrayal of the murder of Duncan, we see "death itself," the "great doom's image," presiding over a world in which every deed has its immediate consequence materially objectified: a world in which "present fear" conjoins with "horrible imagining" to undermine the formal mastery of threatening fantasy material which dramatic art usually expedites. Banquo's ghost is less a cautionary vision of judgment than the material embodiment of Macbeth's desires and, by extension, of the audience's desire to satisfy through Macbeth its own transgressive fantasies. Seeing the ghost does, then, require the audience to surrender its protected space in order to experience with Macbeth what life in this fourth dimension of dramatic reality actually entails. The shared vision serves as a theatrical gate of horn that takes the audience into a frontier of perception where what it experiences has far more staying power than any mere dream or nightmare. However much the audience may resist the terms of its engagement with Macbeth, it is, I believe, committed to exploring the new dimension of dramatic reality Macbeth inhabits, committed to seeing (if not actually feeling) what he and no other character onstage can see and feel. And it is precisely this psychic or perceptual bond the audience establishes with Macbeth that allows it to comprehend what Macbeth himself later comprehends when he stands, as it were, on the far side of existence, looking back on life as he has lived it:

> Life's but a walking shadow; a poor player
> That struts and frets his hour upon the stage,
> And then is heard no more: it is a tale
> Told by an idiot, full of sound and fury,
> Signifying nothing.
>
> (V.v.24–28)

Macbeth's powerful conceptualization of life as "but a walking shadow" is profoundly indebted to his privileged confrontation with Banquo's ghost, the "horrible shadow" that silently departs at his bidding but shapes his final metaphorical persuasion. It is substantiated by his now complete identification with the same shadow-world of "Direness" grown familiar that first loosed the ghost of Banquo upon the stage of his existence. For the audience, an empathetic understanding of the speech becomes contingent on having achieved and maintained the capacity to look on life from Macbeth's perspective of closed possibility, and to do so without flinching. It requires much the same type of psychological freedom that informs Macbeth's tough-minded estimate of a life demystified of its comfortable illusions and comforting fictions. To meet the challenge posed by the speech, the audience must overcome the predictable anxiety inspired by Macbeth's presentation as fact of unnerving conceptions of the human condition.

The audience conceivably negotiates this confrontation with anxiety by drawing strength from the collective nature of its earlier encounter with Banquo's ghost which may be re-created in the following manner. As the vision of Banquo's ghost isolates Macbeth completely from the onstage community that looks on uncomprehendingly, it estranges the offstage audience from that community as well. To say it simply, the audience sees more than the characters onstage do, is aware of more than they can imagine, knows more about what sights the flesh is heir to when it would go beyond what flesh can bear. As Macbeth transcends the normative vision of reality he once superficially shared with the onstage community, he sunders the audience's normative connection with its surrogates onstage. One probable consequence of this theatrical transaction is the breakdown of the audience's individually differentiated responses to what is happening onstage. That is, the shared vision encourages the audience to come together perceptually around a common focus of theatrical discourse; it generates a perceptual consensus out of a pre-existing mass of differentiated responses, transforms a crowd of playgoing subjects into an attentive and engaged community of spectators. In the process, the shared vision reduces the anxiety of remaining a private subject in a company of anonymous "others" by making the source of that anxiety the basis of collective perception.

This theory may be concisely outlined in performative terms. We have all, in attending the theater, experienced that special intensity that takes charge of an audience when a single dramatic moment so actualizes itself that we attend to the play in question as if for the first time. This is usually the moment when the coughs cease, people stop shifting in their chairs and eagerly lean forward, all eyes and ears. The moment may be the storm scene in *King Lear*, the concluding episode of *Doctor Faustus*, or it may be evoked by unusually fine acting in an otherwise forgettable production. At such a moment the play takes complete charge of our senses, indeed, heightens them, makes us so alert to the smallest nuance of speech and gesture that we begin to lose touch with our immediate surroundings. The play may at this point come to define itself in radically different terms; it may suddenly disclose new and striking levels of meaning, or make completely explicit for the first time dramatic possibilities and potentials that had been previously submerged in a pattern of suggestiveness. When such a moment occurs in *Macbeth*—as it arguably does in the space between the first entrance and second exit of Banquo's ghost—it raises the audience's sights above and beyond the limited perceptions of the other characters in the play and focuses them on the revelation of the drama's prevailing concern with Macbeth's own victimization by the very forces he has himself unleashed. When, for example, we see Macbeth raise his cup and hear him say, "I drink to th'general joy o'th'whole table, / And to our dear friend Banquo, whom we miss; / Would he were here" (III.iv.88–90), and see at the same time the silent ghost again make its way to the head of the table, we are given the kind of privileged insight into the ironies of Macbeth's immediate situation that plainly distinguishes our perspective from that of those who cannot see what we see.

The Contemporary Perception of *Macbeth*

My habit of speaking of audiences in general and then speaking even more generally in terms of "we" may give the resisting reader pause, and may make what I have to say about *Macbeth* appear inapplicable to the range of perceptions likely to be available to the Jacobean playgoer. The only first-hand record we possess of a contemporary response to *Macbeth* is Simon Forman's account of a production of the play at the Globe on Saturday, 20 April 1611. Although Forman can hardly be considered an exemplary or representative playgoer, his account has the virtue of demonstrating the capacity of a contemporary playgoer to entertain a variety of competing perceptions of what the playtext of *Macbeth* appears to present. Forman offers a notably prosaic rendering of the appearance of Banquo's ghost that is not in any way consistent with the claims regarding audience response I have advanced:

> . . . being at supper with his noblemen whom he bid to a feast to the which Banquo should have come, [Macbeth] began to speak of noble Banquo, and to wish that he were there. And as he thus did, standing up to drink a carouse to him, the ghost of Banquo came and sat down in his chair behind him. And he turning about to sit down again saw the ghost of Banquo, which fronted him so, that he fell into a great passion of fear and fury, uttering many words about his murder, by which, when they heard Banquo was murdered they suspected Macbeth. (modernized spelling, in Salgado 1975, 31–32)

For Forman, the banquet scene serves only to advance the plot of the play. It is how the other characters onstage learn of Banquo's death and Macbeth's guilt, and it also precipitates, in the chronology of Forman's recounting, the flight of Macduff and the consolidation of Macbeth's enemies ("Then Macduff fled to England to the king's son, and so they raised an army, . . .").

Rather than dismiss this plot-oriented reading of the banquet scene by a man also capable of reducing the role of Autolycus in *The Winter's Tale* to a cautionary tag—"Beware of trusting feigned beggars or fawning fellows," are the words with which Forman concludes his account of that play—I am happy to concede that the banquet scene is at least partially designed to fulfill the purpose Forman delegates to it. However, I would also submit that Forman's earlier reproduction of II.ii, the scene in which Macbeth returns to Lady Macbeth after the murder of Duncan, demonstrates the same kind of response to a highly charged theatrical moment that the banquet scene is capable of eliciting. Forman writes that "when Macbeth had murdered the king, the blood on his hands could not be washed off by any means, nor from his wife's hands, which handled the bloody daggers in hiding them, by which means they became both much amazed and affronted" (Salgado, 31). Peter Thomson believes that Forman's observation "suggests that there was some detailed work on stage business here," implying that Forman may be contributing an insight into Jacobean stage practice that could alter our estimate of the authority of the folio text of *Macbeth* (1983, 139). I believe that Forman is, instead, demonstrating the imaginative consequences of theatrical engagement in taking for a fact what is actually a powerful image powerfully cultivated by Macbeth:

> Will all great Neptune's ocean wash this blood
> Clean from my hand? No, this my hand will rather
> The multitudinous seas incarnadine,
> Making the green one red.
>
> (II.ii.59–62)

Forman's confusion of metaphor for fact is symptomatic of his susceptibility to Shakespeare's privileging of Macbeth's imaginative persuasion which, in this instance, appears to have swallowed up entirely Lady Macbeth's statement, "A little water clears us of this deed" (II.ii.66), and the act of washing that follows hard upon it.

Forman demonstrates a similar responsiveness to the play's subtextual import in compressing Banquo's eloquent request that the witches also speak to him (I.iii.52-61) to the peremptory demand, "What all to Macbeth, and nothing to me?" (Salgado, 31). Whereas Thomson detects no textual basis for "Banquo's impetuously self-interested questioning of the witches" and seeks to attribute Forman's observation to "a culling from Holinshed" (1983, 139), Forman's apparent distortion of the text of *Macbeth* that has passed down to us is more likely the product of a "reading" of *Macbeth* in performance that quite simply eludes Thomson's interpretive grasp. It is, moreover, a reading consistent with the doubts some scholars have harbored regarding Banquo's delegated status as the noble source of the royal line of James I. As David Norbrook writes:

Shakespeare could, had he chosen, have made Banquo a less shadowy and ambiguous figure, and thus made the dynastic compliment more direct. Why does
he cooperate with Macbeth even after Duncan's murder? If Macbeth's ambition
to found a dynasty is evil, is it so very different from Banquo's "hope"? (1987,
94)

Forman's account also fails to support arguments advanced by scholars
who take their lead from Henry N. Paul (1950) and read *Macbeth* either as
a "royal play" deliberately designed to flatter James I or as a politically
topical play that draws heavily on the Gowrie Conspiracy and Gunpowder
Plot. While Forman admittedly viewed *Macbeth* some years after its probable original production date (1606), hence, at some temporal remove from
the play's topical moment, his failure to show any interest in the play's
political dimensions and his attribution to Macbeth of the position of
"Prince of Northumberland" suggests that for some playgoers at least,
Macbeth was as much an English play as it was a Scottish play, in any event
limited to the dramatic world Shakespeare cultivated on the stage.

This is not at all to submit that *Macbeth* lacks political applications of an
historically specific variety. But as some of the best recent commentators
on the play have noted, while Shakespeare may have "simplified the outlines of [his source in Holinshed] to create a structure of clear antitheses"
(Stallybrass 1982, 193), "the political 'lessons' and characterization of *Macbeth*" are presented with a great deal of ambiguity (Hawkins 1982, 185). As
Steven Mullaney observes:

> In *Macbeth*, Shakespeare develops an unsettling affiliation between treason's
> spectacle and its audience. To engage treason's motions is to participate in them,
> threatening the otherwise clear antithesis that would seem to hold between rule
> and misrule and revealing the latter to be less the antithesis of rule than its alter-
> nating current, its overextension and in a sense its consequence. (1988, 125)

Mullaney also notes that even if we assume that James I "occupies the position of authority" as the primary audience to whom the royal play of
Macbeth is directed, the king nevertheless constitutes "a passive audience,
'subjected' to . . . a drama more ambivalent . . . than the one James had
fashioned out of the seditious desires of Guy Fawkes and his fellow con-
spirators" (133). Mullaney's remarks on the play's ambivalence and on the
"affiliation between treason's spectacle and its audience" do much to substantiate Jonathan Goldberg's assertion that "Resemblance, not difference,
dominates the text" of *Macbeth* (1987, 250). *Macbeth*'s capacity to blur the

outlines between rule and misrule, between "treason's spectacle" and the specular mirroring of the audience's transgressive desires, and to transform into resemblance so apparent a difference between characters as the one that presumably distinguishes Banquo from Macbeth, becomes increasingly obvious when this text is performatively realized in a manner that encourages its audience to experience a sense of imaginative "affiliation" with Macbeth. If, or when, this occurs, the audience may continue to register the self-deluding and socially destructive aspects of Macbeth's transgressive career, but may no longer consider transgression to be a terribly exceptional aspect of political behavior.

Illusion-Breakers

But for how long after the shared vision of Banquo's ghost does the audience remain imaginatively affiliated with Macbeth? Why should the play's plot, especially as Forman reproduces it, encourage the audience to remain complicit with Macbeth at the same time that it encourages Macbeth's onstage audience to prepare to effect Macbeth's imminent defeat and destruction? To begin with, Shakespeare goes to great lengths after the banquet scene to discredit Macbeth and to disengage the audience from sympathy with him, visionary or otherwise. He not only attempts to establish a moral opposition to Macbeth that is decidedly associated with all that is great and good in the daytime world of men, but also deploys a series of what David Kranz has called "illusion-breakers" in order to subvert the systematic entrancement of the audience by Macbeth.[8] The first of these illusion-breakers is, appropriately enough, the textually disreputable and generally discredited Hecate scene (III.v) which immediately follows the exit of the Macbeths in III.iv.[9] In this scene a new variable obtrudes upon the drama in the person of Hecate, who enters with the three witches in tow ostensibly to inform the audience that she and her confederates are going to give Macbeth a very hard time of it in the near future. She promises, in brief, to so manipulate Macbeth by means of strong illusions that "he shall spurn fate, scorn death, and bear / His hopes 'bove wisdom, grace, and fear" (III.v.30–31). In so doing, she implicitly alerts the audience to the danger of maintaining Macbeth as its imaginative surrogate by giving the audience ample forewarning of Macbeth's imminent misreadings of the messages of the three apparitions. As the audience subsequently witnesses Macbeth selectively accept what he deems good news and deny whatever seems implausible, impossible, or just plain unpleasant, the audience may be apt to withdraw into its protected space and, in withdrawing, to recognize that Macbeth's boldness is indistinguishable from the foolishness that is mortal to all such playthings of the gods. The audience may be apt, moreover, especially when the series of apparitions culminates in the reappearance of Banquo's ghost, to revise its earlier estimate of that ghost as an independent embodiment of the dark forces Macbeth himself has unleashed, and to reinterpret the ghost as a deliberate "plant," placed in Macbeth's chair by the witches to taunt and terrorize him. Indeed, a close retrospective look at the timing of the ghost's two entrances and exits may well indicate the insidious working of supernatural agents whose puppet the ghost may be. By having the ghost appear at the precise moment that Macbeth summons up remembrance of Banquo and observes his absence, and by having it twice depart when Macbeth demands its departure, these supernatural agents may, in short, be seducing Macbeth into a mistaken belief in his continued capacity to dominate his dramatic environment.

Now it may surely be argued that Shakespeare is, in the Hecate scene and throughout the fourth and fifth acts, doing no more than fulfilling his own preconceived dramatic design for the play as a whole and, for that matter, is doing so in deference either to moral imperatives in which (we have good reason to believe) he believed fervently or to political expedience. But I would qualify such an argument by suggesting that Shakespeare is retreating with discernible reluctance from the provocative alliance between the audience and Macbeth that he has cultivated. He is specifically reluctant at this point in the drama—the much disputed interval between III.iv and IV.i—to allow Macbeth's second interview with the witches to occur without some fairly obvious form of dramatic mediation, unsure, perhaps, of the audience's capacity to recognize Macbeth's misguided reading of the apparitions' pronouncements without first being placed in a position of critical detachment from Macbeth. This mediation may have been initially provided by the questionable Hecate episode (a very stiff piece of dramatic construction and obtrusive signpost, whatever its origin), or it may have been negotiated by the more artfully ironic Lenox scene (III.vi), the second of the playtext's illusion-breakers, which some scholars would, however, place after, not before, IV.i (see Muir 1980, xxxi–xxxii). Although the exact origin and placement of each of these scenes remains uncertain, both clearly serve the same dramatic purposes: to disengage the audience from and to discredit Macbeth; to alert the audience to the moral and intellectual dangers of maintaining Macbeth as its surrogate; and to impede or block the dramatic momentum which has, heretofore, made some measure of audience engagement with Macbeth unavoidable.[10] In presenting the audience with its bitterly sarcastic and completely demystified version of Macbeth's murderous career, the more textually reputable Lenox scene additionally serves to reintroduce that influential strain of choric authority which has been comparatively silent since the brief dialogue between Rosse and the anonymous old man at the beginning of II.iv. Lenox begins to sound this note in the following persuasive manner:

> The gracious Duncan
> Was pitied of Macbeth:—marry, he was dead:—
> And the right-valiant Banquo walk'd too late;
> Whom, you may say (if't please you) Fleance killed,
> For Fleance fled. Men must not walk too late.
> It was for Malcolm, and for Donalbain,
> To kill their gracious father? damned fact!
> How it did grieve Macbeth! did he not straight,
> In pious rage, the two delinquents tear,
> That were the slaves of drink, and thralls of sleep?
> Was not that nobly done? Ay, and wisely too;
> For 'twould have anger'd any heart alive
> To hear the men deny't.
>   (III.vi.3–16)

In their ensuing conversation, Lenox and the anonymous lord who is his companion directly refer to Macbeth as a tyrant while speaking in laudatory and reverential terms of the redemptive force embodied by Macbeth's opposite, "the most pious Edward" of England, "the holy King" whose work is ratified by "Him above." They thus encourage the audience to readjust its attitude towards Macbeth, to bring to conscious awareness a set of moral assumptions it needed, consciously or otherwise, to block or suppress entirely in order to allow its fantasies free rein.

The problem in all this is that Shakespeare's attempt at mediating his audience's relationship with Macbeth works against the very effects the playwright has elicited in the recently concluded banquet scene. If audience alienation from Macbeth immediately supersedes the most crucial stage in its process of engagement with Macbeth, the only purpose that can have been served in facilitating audience engagement in the first place must, in the words of Simon O. Lesser, be the "cautionary" one of vividly reminding the audience of "the terrible price the gratification" of forbidden delights always exacts (1976, 172). Although Lesser is certainly attuned to the play's psychic drift, I would like to propose another approach to the problem-at-hand.

As noted above, the insertion of either the Hecate or the Lenox scene at this point in the drama can be plausibly attributed to Shakespeare's anxiety about the effects of audience engagement with Macbeth and with the powerful fantasies cultivated in every episode of Macbeth's history of transgression. Lesser himself acknowledges that Shakespeare possibly "let things well up from the unconscious to an exceptional degree while writing *Macbeth*" (152). If Lesser's "guess" is correct, what wells up must, according to Freud's model of psychic economy, eventually be inhibited or resisted. Viewed from this perspective, Shakespeare's anxiety becomes at least one of the sources of the formal pattern of defenses he establishes at the end of the third act and elaborates in the last two. Shakespeare's ambivalence about his overall dramatic project makes itself felt in the very attempt to manage or control the psychologically (and politically) provocative interactions between play and audience generated by the shared vision of Banquo's ghost. Since Shakespeare's defensive pattern effectively requires the play to assume a moralized approach to its subject that makes clear distinctions between good and bad, right and wrong, the audience will, presumably, register the play's conspicuous departure from a prevailing dramatic persuasion that has refused to make such distinctions, premised as it has been on the image of nights that are "Almost at odds with morning, which is which." The purposed transformation of the audience's potentially dangerous and unseemly alliance with Macbeth into a safer detachment may become so obvious to engaged playgoers that they may resist the attempt to manipulate their sympathies, especially given their continued responsiveness to "the memory" of earlier moments in the play "when [the audience's] unconscious wishes were granted more room to exercise."[11]

It may, of course, be objected that however palpable Shakespeare's designs may seem, they are consistent with the capacity of theatrical representation—and of literary art generally—to transform the pleasures of vicarious fantasy fulfillment into the pleasures of protection from the anxieties aroused by a fantasy fulfilled. Norman Holland describes this transaction in the following manner:

... the key to the most successful literary works (in my experience, anyway) is that their very defenses give me pleasure.

The reason seems to be that pleasure from defenses has a peculiarly powerful effect. . . . In life, defenses stand off and modify drives and so cut down the amount of pleasure we get even if the drives are gratified. If, however, the defense itself gives pleasure, there is a net increase in pleasure, and that increase in pleasure (according to Freud) buys a permit for "a still greater pleasure arising from deeper psychical sources," the gratification from the drive (or, in literature, unconscious content). Thus even the pleasure from satisfying the drive becomes greater. (1975, 131–32)

At first glance, Holland seems to provide the perfect solution to our interpretive dilemma, especially since his psychological paradigm corresponds closely to the overall dramatic structure of *Macbeth*. But I am not, in the end, persuaded that Shakespeare managed his dramatic mediation so effectively that his formal defenses do, in fact, yield the kind of pleasure Holland has in mind, much less protect the audience from continued immersion in the Macbeth phenomenon. In the context of dramatic performance, a play's fantasy-content usually proves more powerful than the defenses set up against it, the theatrical appeal of audience engagement more perdurable than the superimposition of an orthodox moral or political dimension upon it. And in terms of theatrical appeal alone, neither the scenes centering on Hecate and Lenox, nor those that follow can summarily counteract the profound impact of the banquet scene and what has led up to it. Nor can they summarily moralize or, for that matter, politicize audience response to a character whose appeal to his audience has already been defined in moral and political terms.

Shakespeare's preoccupation with the moral and political aspects of Macbeth's theatrical appeal characterizes his next challenge to the audience's continued imaginative affiliation with Macbeth. This challenge is advanced by the integration of such obvious illusion-breakers as the Hecate and Lenox scenes into the drama's increasingly dominant concern with the gathering momentum of Macbeth's opponents (especially Malcolm and Macduff), the domestic tragedies of Scotland (localized in the sad case of Lady Macduff), and the redemptive potential associated with England. With the establishment of this countermovement in the drama, Shakespeare effectively doubles the focus of audience attention. He reinvokes dramatically the morally normative and politically orthodox society whose prescribed values and customs Macbeth has transgressed; and he places that society in critical juxtaposition with the morally defiant and politically impoverished world Macbeth has spurred into being.[12] In more broadly psychological terms, Shakespeare begins to focus his play's energies on a climactic competition between unmanageable fantasy-material and what Holland would call "meaning as defense." In so doing, he makes the peculiar tension between the otherwise proscribed or generally unavailable gratifications of fantasy fulfillment and the satisfactions and safety of a more normative persuasion as sustained a focus of audience attention as the downward incline of Macbeth's fortunes.

The Macbeth Phenomenon

Shakespeare cultivates an analogous field of competing provocations in the course of *Richard III*. He will, for example, allow Richard of Gloucester to work his audience mercilessly until he has it eating out of his crooked hand, only to shift gears upon Richard's ascension to the throne and encourage the audience to identify its interests with the moral and political orthodoxies associated with the performatively unappealing Richmond. Although this presumptive shift in audience affiliation is in its way as complicated as the one Shakespeare may seek to elicit in *Macbeth*, it has a better chance of succeeding onstage largely because Richard's own performance appeal diminishes considerably in the closing movement of the earlier play.[13] Indeed, Richard's appeal to the audience never really operates on the same level of intensity as does Macbeth's. Richard is at once a more theatrical creature and a more expressly political agent than is Macbeth. He presents himself directly as a mediator between the stage and the audience and also as a mediator between the past and present of English political life. He is theatrically specific in his joint cultivation of the qualities of a morality Vice and a Machiavellian villain, and politically specific in a manner that *Macbeth* can only approximate when viewed from the perspective of James I.

Macbeth neither appeals to his audience through sheer intellectual wizardry and performative guile (as does Richard), nor by dint of pure theatrical energy (as does Barabas in *The Jew of Malta*). Rather, his appeal has its most accessible basis in the same fantasy of daring ambition and aggression that motivates Tamburlaine, although its deeper source must be sought in the more proscribed channels of parricidal rumination.[14] Unlike Tamburlaine, Macbeth does not operate in a moral vacuum. Macbeth pulls the audience towards him through a series of humanly comprehensible conflicts which not only engage its interest, but arouse its anxieties and speak to its own psychic preoccupations. His attempt to transcend the normative order of ordinary men is, from his perspective at least, a comparatively private affair that does not achieve the unconditional fulfillment Tamburlaine experiences. It leads, instead, to sleepless nights, haunted days, and terrifying confrontations with Banquo's ghost. Although, as Janet Adelman notes, after "punishing Macbeth for his participation in a fantasy of escape from the maternal matrix, [the play] nonetheless allows the audience the partial satisfaction of a dramatic equivalent to it" in the form of the "motherless" Macduff's eventual triumph (1985, 103), Macbeth himself never promises the audience that any fruitions will follow from his pursuit of an earthly crown.

As a consequence of Macbeth's dubious status as mediator of the audience's desire for vicarious mastery or empowerment, the prevailing tension between performance appeal and normative persuasion is raised to a critical level in the scenes that follow the shared vision of Banquo's ghost. The audience must conceivably decide whether or not to forsake its alliance with Macbeth, and to accept in its stead the more pedestrian pleasures of psychic detachment. But Shakespeare undermines the audience's capacity to choose between clear-cut alternatives by engaging it with a protagonist who has already confronted and resolved his own struggle between fantasy fulfillment and moral restraint. Consequently, when Shakespeare dramatically reinvokes a morally and politically normative society in the last two acts of the play, he does so at the expense of summarily reducing Macbeth to the more manageable proportions of a morally bankrupt Richard of Gloucester. To mediate the psychologically volatile alliance that obtains between Macbeth and the audience, he at once attempts to reduce the compass of Macbeth's theatrical appeal and to disprize Macbeth's far from negligible moral consciousness of his own position by showing Macbeth to poor advantage beside his morally and politically self-righteous opposition. He attempts, in other words, to distort his uncompromisingly complete dramatic conception of Macbeth in order to protect the audience not only from Macbeth, but from itself, from the psychologically problematic position it has occupied since the shared vision of Banquo's ghost. And, as with the Hecate and Lenox scenes, the attempt, in my opinion, fails. Shakespeare's anxiety about his own creation never develops sufficient dramatic power and integrity to measure up to (much less overwhelm) the power and integrity of his earlier achievement.

It is, for instance, striking that almost every effort by a character in the last movement of the play to portray Macbeth as a bloodthirsty monster, or to reduce him to the lowly proportions of a coward is ultimately countered by strong evidence to the contrary. One such moment is provided by the conversation of Macbeth's enemies in V.ii concerning Macbeth's present state of mind which immediately prefaces his next appearance onstage and consequently seems to have been intended to condition the audience's reception of him. In response to Cathness's comparatively even-handed treatment of Macbeth—"Some say he's mad; others, that lesser hate him, / Do call it valiant fury: but, for certain, / He cannot buckle his distemper'd cause / Within the belt of rule" (V.ii.13–16)—Angus delivers the following subjectively charged commentary on the present state of Macbeth's soul:

> Now does he feel
> His secret murthers sticking on his hands;
> Now minutely revolts upbraid his faith-breach:
> Those he commands move only in command,
> Nothing in love: now does he feel his title
> Hang loose about him, like a giant's robe
> Upon a dwarfish thief.
> (V.ii.16–22)

Angus's rhetorical strategy of reiterating the adverb "now" has the indirect, theatrical goal of sundering the audience's attachment to a conception of Macbeth that existed "then," in the less-immediate past of the play when that attachment was first negotiated. It has its dramatic virtue in the fact that some of what he says—namely, that "Those [Macbeth] commands move only in command, / Nothing in love"—will soon be verified by none other than Macbeth himself in one of the most affecting passages he utters:

> And that which should accompany old age,
> As honour, love, obedience, troops of friends,
> I must not look to have; but in their stead,
> Curses, not loud, but deep, mouth-honour, breath,
> Which the poor heart would fain deny, and dare not.
> (V.iii.24–28)

But when Angus likens Macbeth to "a dwarfish thief," he runs afoul of his own occupational need to reduce to manageable proportions the far from dwarfish stature of the still commanding character of Macbeth who, in the above passage, demonstrates a profounder understanding of his own situation than does Angus and, in the face of his wife's disintegration, can imperiously say, "Throw physic to the dogs; I'll none of it" (V.iii.47).

Macbeth is, of course, throughout V.iii artificially puffed up by his absolute trust in his mistranslation of the witches' prophecies. But even before V.v, immediately before he says that he begins "To doubt th'equivocation of the fiend," Macbeth stands well beyond the moral and rhetorical pale within which his enemies (and, perhaps, Shakespeare himself) attempt to confine him:

> I have almost forgot the taste of fears.
> The time has been, my senses would have cool'd
> To hear a night-shriek; and my fell of hair
> Would at a dismal treatise rouse, and stir,
> As life were in't. I have supped full with horrors:
> Direness, familiar to my slaughterous thoughts,
> Cannot once start me.
>
> (V.v.9–15)

This is clearly not the speech of a mere tyrant or monster incapable of recognizing the difference between good and evil. Rather, it is the speech of a man isolated in the full consciousness of his own irreversible alienation from the world of ordinary men, who nostalgically recalls (as we recall with him) a time when he was less courageous than he must be now in order to contend with the terrors of the quotidian. Although Macbeth suffers a temporary lapse in courage when he finally encounters Macduff in V.viii, he recovers sufficiently to again raise his stature to the performative level of his original transgression and to supply an embodied denial of Macduff's understandable but uninformed accusation of cowardice:

> Though Birnam wood be come to Dunsinane,
> And thou oppos'd, being of no woman born,
> Yet I will try the last: before my body
> I throw my warlike shield: lay on, Macduff;
> And damn'd be him that first cries, 'Hold, enough.'
>
> (V.viii.30–34)

Indeed, the sharp, incisive heroic couplet that closes off Macbeth's dramatic existence once and for all may well represent the resurgent attempt of the play's fantasy content to achieve gratification at the cost of the anxiety provoked upon its final brutal suppression by Macduff, who re-enters in the play's last scene carrying what he calls "Th'usurper's cursed head" and announcing that "the time is free" (V.ix.21; cf. Egan 1978, 342–43).

I would argue from this evidence that Shakespeare's continued devotion to the transgressive power of his own dramatic conception is so clearly discernible in the misrepresentations of Macbeth's character advanced by Macbeth's enemies, and so generally suffused throughout the last two acts of the play, that he fails really to provide a morally normative alternative to Macbeth that is either dramatically convincing or theatrically appealing. Although Shakespeare expends a great deal of effort in developing his conditioning apparatus, the alternatives to Macbeth never fully come to represent characters with whom an audience (of contemporary Jacobeans or otherwise) can easily ally itself, or even accept as representatives of a social order that stands in decided contradistinction to Macbeth. Malcolm, for example, as Robert Egan has noted, "gives evidence of a far subtler and more politic performance" of royal prerogative than Macbeth, revealing a profoundly suspicious and suspect nature as he puts Macduff through his deliberately ambiguous paces in the first part of of IV.iii (1978, 345). His relentlessly insensitive attempt to exploit Macduff's sorrow for his own political ends after Macduff learns of the slaughter of his family also bears an uncannily apt resemblance to Lady Macbeth's earlier inquisitorial manipulation of Macbeth. So apt that one wonders whether Shakespeare consciously planned it this way—and if so, to what purpose?—or was unconsciously compelled to work within the same pattern established in the prior episode. Indeed, when Macduff responds to Malcolm's injunction to "Dispute it like a man" by saying "I shall do so; / But I must also feel it like a man" (IV.iii.22–21), an unmistakable sense of repetition obtains that would seem to undercut Shakespeare's alleged effort "to create a structure of clear antitheses" (Stallybrass 1982, 193), and that is, moreover, soon compounded by Malcolm's speech at the end of the play which closely echoes Duncan's remarks in the play's first act.[15] Even the sympathetic appeal of the ostensibly more straightforward Lady Macduff murder scene is compromised by reason of the scene's obvious status as a conditioning device, and because both Macduff's and Macbeth's distance from the scene of the crime ultimately casts as much doubt on the former's wisdom and judiciousness as certainty of the latter's cruelty.[16] In short, it seems as if Shakespeare's anxiety about Macbeth is actually an anxiety about political agency in general and that, try as he might in composing the closing movement of the play, he could not escape remaining absorbed in the most disturbing aspects of his own dramatic creation.

Nor could he escape the fact that the theater (as Brecht writes) "theatres it all down," measures mainly in performative terms anything a playwright may present that lacks sufficient performance appeal. Shakespeare's failure to neutralize completely the provocative impact of the shared vision of Banquo's ghost may consequently be viewed as an inevitable concession to the psychological power of theatrical experience; his failure to protect the audience from continued engagement with the Macbeth phenomenon as dramatic evidence of his own play's capacity to penetrate that invisible frame which conventionally separates the audience from the stage. In attempting to distract his audience from, and otherwise to discredit, Macbeth by turning his sights on the comparatively decent but performatively unappealing men who are his antagonists, Shakespeare finally succeeds in making Macbeth the only complete embodiment of the prevailing tensions and energies of his drama. When the play ends Macbeth consequently succeeds Banquo's ghost as the primary focus of a vision the members of the audience continue to share with each other, whether they separate in the black of night or light of day.

Part III

A Poetics of Demystification

5. King Edward's Body

To this point, I have attempted to demonstrate that, whether by authorial intention or through the theatrical translation of intention into apparently unintended effect, audience engagement in the Elizabethan playhouse was often elicited in a manner that encouraged resistance to authority and vicarious participation in the enactment of transgressive fantasies. In the two succeeding chapters, I will be additionally concerned with the ways in which Marlowe and Shakespeare make playgoers receptive to positions that effectively demystify established structures of meaning and belief. In the case of Marlowe, such efforts at demystification are specifically designed to undermine the playgoer's complacency about the naturalness of prevailing social and political arrangements. In the particular case of *Edward II*, they are undertaken in a manner that renders suspect the satisfactions of more conventional representations of the ennoblement of the tragic subject, such as we find in Shakespeare's *Richard II*. Rather than pursue a connection between the two plays that is, in fact, more of a disjunction (insofar as Shakespeare repeatedly inflates in *Richard II* what Marlowe chooses to *de*flate in *Edward II*), I prefer to place Marlowe's play in the context of Shakespeare's comparable participation in the "enterprise of demystification" (Macherey 1978, 133). In the chapter that follows this one, I will consequently consider the extent to which Shakespeare's plays could elicit resistance to their own elaborately rendered inducements to submit to the authority of orthodox positions and pronouncements. What draws the work of the two playwrights together is its common grounding in a poetics of demystification whose nominal theorist was Machiavelli.

The Machiavellian Playwright

Machiavellism, as it was popularly understood and as Marlowe chose to understand it in his plays and offstage pronouncements, seems to have functioned as a particularly enabling source of theatrical energy for

Marlowe. In the plays that followed *1 and 2 Tamburlaine*, it provided a sustained focus for him in his position as a master fabricator and purveyor of fantasies for the Elizabethan public theater. Marlowe was responsive not only to the theatrical possibilities of the Machiavellian character-type—with which he works overtly in *Edward II*, *The Jew of Malta*, and *The Massacre at Paris*—but also to the seductive potential of a Machiavellian approach to his audience, which he realized by making the manipulation of audience response a virtual policy of playmaking. Marlowe was also acutely responsive to the destabilizing appeal of Machiavelli's ideas.[1] His indebtedness to Machiavelli can be detected both in the style and content of his plays, each of which presents political and religious contention in terms of the self-interested pursuit of power, and treats the exercise of power as the most desirable of activities for the "aspiring mind." It is discernible as well in the notorious Baines deposition where we gain privileged insight into Marlowe's habit of entertaining the kinds of thoughts his contemporaries chose to attribute to marginal figures in their midst.[2]

A revealing pattern emerges from Marlowe's appropriation of Machiavelli's penchant for demystification in the Baines deposition. In one item, for example, Marlowe remarks Moses' ability as a subtle, educated man to manipulate "a rude and grosse people," while in another he identifies religion as a means of social control by contending, "That the first beginning of Religioun was only to keep men in awe." He thus expresses an ambivalent attitude towards the lawgiver, successively identifying himself as an unawed analyst of the mysteries of power, as an admirer of the cultivater of mysteries, and as a skeptical degrader of Moses himself. In affirming, in Baines's words, "that Moyses was but a Jugler & that one Heriots being Sir W Raleighs man Can do more than he," Marlowe attempts to deny Moses' claim to authority while expressing his own pleasure in the prospect of the gifted scholar's ability to master and manipulate a culture's belief system. If Baines's words be credited, Marlowe represents here his capacity at once to anatomize and celebrate the workings of power.

In *Doctor Faustus*, his most celebrated achievement, we again find Marlowe casting about in seemingly opposed directions at one and the same time. At one moment, he has Mephistophilis offer a metaphysical portrayal of hell which is at odds with the anachronistic infernal machines he elsewhere introduces into the play. His protagonist, Faustus, mouths opinions that resemble those attributed to Marlowe in the Baines deposition, but is nonetheless presented as a misguided soul whose mistakes would be worthy of ridicule were they not so fatally consequential. Faustus is himself a mystified demystifier, and his damnation recuperates the very world-view Marlowe is alleged to have repeatedly mocked in his offstage conversations (cf. Greenblatt 1977, 53). Yet, to further complicate matters, this recuperation of what Wilbur Sanders calls "the old scholastic cosmos" (1968, 229) may spring from the same fascination with power and the powerful, and lack of sympathy for the powerless, that we witness in the Baines deposition and throughout the Tamburlaine plays, and not, as others have argued, from some obscurely orthodox religious motivation.

From this brief inventory we can isolate some frequently perceived characteristics of Marlowe's writing, namely, his lack of human(e) sympathy; his preoccupation with power and the powerful; his chronic or, more precisely, compulsive heterodoxy; and the apparent contradictions between his intellectual radicalism and the orthodox endings of several of his plays. The former characteristics are apparent in his fascination with the manipulation of belief systems and in his lack of interest in the effects of their manipulation on those he revealingly calls a "rude and grosse people." The contradictions are discernible in his tendency to demystify one embodiment of authority only to identify with another.

The Power of Pleasure

The intricacy of Marlowe's approach to received ideas and the structures of power is especially evident in the opening and closing movements of *Edward II* where his compulsion to demystify runs squarely against the expectations aroused by his cultivation of what appear to be morally exemplary set pieces. In the first scene of the play Marlowe pits the insidious attractions of Gaveston against the more modest ambitions for employment of three poor men. The lines of sympathy appear clearly drawn here, especially given the scene's formal consistency with those sequences in *Doctor Faustus* and earlier moralities in which characters discredit themselves in the eyes of the audience by pursuing selfish or deceptive designs at the expense either of their souls or of the common good. However, in this instance, as elsewhere in his work, Marlowe subordinates moral expectation to the pragmatics of self-interest, and valorizes his transvaluation by giving Gaveston privileged access to an audience that might otherwise be repulsed by his behavior.

Dramatically positioned in the role of the play's Presenter, Gaveston be-

gins by establishing a tone of amorous negligence that privileges the exclusive pleasures of a personal relationship with royalty:

> The sight of London to my exiled eyes
> Is as Elysium to a new-come soul;
> Not that I love the city or the men,
> But that it harbors him I hold so dear,
> The king, upon whose bosom let me die,
> And with the world be still at enmity.
>
> (I.i.10–15)

The extended egotism of Gaveston's romantic conceit is licensed by the
freedom from subservience to others Gaveston imagines his alliance with
the king will allow him to enjoy:

> Farewell base stooping to the lordly peers.
> My knee shall bow to none but to the king.
> As for the multitude that are but sparks,
> Raked up in embers of their poverty—
> *Tanti*; I'll fawn first on the wind
> That glanceth at my lips and flieth away.
>
> (I.i.18–23)

The confidently derisive manner in which Gaveston expresses his contempt
for rich and poor alike seems designed less to alienate his audience than to
solicit its responsive investment in his fantasy of self-enrichment. As if to
test the appeal of this suspect but aspiring gentleman to an audience otherwise apt to censure so mercenary a sensibility, Marlowe again draws on
the contemporary phenomenon of masterless men in the entrance of three
supplicants for Gaveston's favor:

> *Gaveston.*   But how now, what are these?
>
> *Enter three Poor Men.*
>
> *Poor Men.*   Such as desire your worship's service.
> *Gaveston.*   What canst thou do?
> *First Poor Man.*   I can ride.
> *Gaveston.*   But I have no horses. What art thou?
> *Second Poor Man.*   A traveler.

Gaveston.   Let me see—thou wouldst do well
   To wait at my trencher and tell me lies at dinner time,
   And as I like your discoursing, I'll have you.
   And what art thou?
Third Poor Man.   A soldier, that hath served against the Scot.
Gaveston.   Why, there are hospitals for such as you.
   I have no war, and therefore, sir, be gone.
Third Poor Man.   Farewell, and perish by a soldier's hand,
   That wouldst reward them with an hospital.
Gaveston.   Ay, ay, these words of his move me as much
   As if a goose should play the porpentine
   And dart her plumes, thinking to pierce my breast.
             (I.i.24–41)

Gaveston playfully adopts attitudes towards the lower orders that were characteristic of a ruling class with little patience either for the indolent poor or for the indolence enforced upon those whose capacity for service had been exhausted ("there are hospitals for such as you"). Setting himself up as a parodic version of a contemporary gentleman who enlists servants "to tell [him] lies at dinner time," Gaveston both focuses and deflects the rampant hostility of the Elizabethan poor toward the gentry. He simultaneously reveals and revels in the haughtiness of the high born, eliding the fact that to the "the lordly peers" he is, himself, nothing more than a more sophisticated species of masterless man. In so doing, he carves out an ambiguous but appealing position for himself as someone who aspires to more than any poor man could appreciate or any aristocrat could countenance.[3]

While Gaveston ultimately chooses to disguise his contempt for the common man by "flattering" his servitors and "mak[ing] them live in hope," as he reveals in a subsequent aside, he is far more candid with the audience to whom he confides his true designs in the speech that succeeds the poor men's exit:

Poor Men.   We will wait here about the court.

                   Exeunt

Gaveston.   Do. These are not men for me,
   I must have wanton poets, pleasant wits,
   Musicians, that with touching of a string
   May draw the pliant king which way I please.

Music and poetry is his delight,
Therefore I'll have Italian masks by night,
Sweet speeches, comedies, and pleasing shows,
And in the day, when he shall walk abroad,
Like sylvan nymphs my pages shall be clad,
My men, like satyrs grazing on the lawns,
Shall with their goat-feet dance an antic hay.
Sometime a lovely boy in Dian's shape,
With hair that gilds the water as it glides,
Crownets of pearle about his naked arms,
And in his sportful hands an olive tree,
To hide those parts which men delight to see,
Shall bathe him in a spring; and there hard by,
One like Actaeon peeping through the grove,
Shall by the angry goddess be transformed,
And running in the likeness of an hart,
By yelping hounds pulled down, and seem to die—
Such things as these best please his majesty.

                                        (I.i.49–71)

What Marlowe aims at here is less a subversion of the conventional preference for the normative than a normalizing of the attractions of the devi-
ant or unusual. He proceeds by making Gaveston the eloquent champion
of desires and pleasures that are decidedly more "curious" than the mundane needs of three poor men. In offering a splendidly imagined representation of what life may resemble when the marginal becomes mainstream,
Gaveston effectively depicts the normative as the product of a limited and
limiting consciousness of life's possibilities: as something that may surely
satisfy the desires of those who identify with his would-be servants, but
that cannot satisfy men like him.

There are, of course, any number of ways for an audience to respond to
this speech, but only one that Marlowe would probably endorse. On the
one hand, the playgoer may feel that Gaveston's attitudes toward his suitors and Edward alike are both morally and politically reprehensible. From
this perspective, Gaveston appears poised to plunder both the body-politic
of England and the king's body that should otherwise preside over the
commonwealth and commonweal. On the other hand, the playgoer may
find Gaveston's flawlessly designed plans so seductive that consideration
of their practical consequences becomes submerged in the anticipation

of their realization. There is, I would submit, something alluringly decadent in Gaveston's conceit which (like many decadent things) plays upon the deepest springs of our responses, co-habiting, as it were, with our most studied and settled repressions. And what is more, Gaveston (or, more correctly, Marlowe) seems to know this. Gaveston audaciously registers the implicit consent of the audience in his depiction of the artful striptease performed by "a lovely boy in Dian's shape" who holds "in his sportful hands an olive tree, / To hide those parts which men delight to see." It is, of course, the homoeroticism of this imagined masque that constitutes its primary challenge to the audience since (sexual prejudices being what they were—and are) if a lovely girl were substituted for the lovely boy, the scenario would not be considered decadent at all but merely lascivious, conforming as it would to the less intricate delights of "The Passionate Shepherd." One cannot respond fully to Gaveston's images and the lyrical swing with which they are described without implicitly associating oneself with the men (not just *some* men, but, as Gaveston has it, simply "men") who "delight to see" the boy-Dian's private parts. For a playgoer can hardly register satisfaction with Gaveston's proposed masque without also sanctioning what its realization involves: namely, an inversion of the normative heterosexual order. If Gaveston succeeds in making accomplices of playgoers who are psychologically responsive to his suggestions, then he succeeds as well in at least temporarily restructuring their moral and sexual priorities, which restructuring can only occur in concert with the demystification of their starting positions.[4]

Like Shakespeare's Edmund or Iago, Gaveston is, of course, the reigning demon of his dramatic world who, in attempting to seduce the audience into identifying with his designs, is presumably meant to stimulate its resistance as well. But Marlowe's work in this kind may be distinguished from Shakespeare's on the ground that where Shakespeare generally attempts to recuperate the subversions of the moral and political order he dramatizes, Marlowe generally seeks to enforce them. In *Edward II*, for instance, when the play-proper begins and Gaveston withdraws to the margins of the stage, his seemingly marginal fantasy of an eroticized court life maintains its theatrical appeal in the face of the fierce but decidedly stiff aggression of the peers. In rendering the lords their aesthetic due in brief, pointed asides, Gaveston deflates their moral self-righteousness and makes the patriotic positions they assume seem what Marlowe shows them to be in the course of the play, namely, defenses of their own prerogatives and preoccupations:

> *Mort. jun.*   Mine uncle here, this earl, and I myself
> Were sworn to your father at his death,
> That he should ne'er return into the realm.
> And know, my lord, ere I will break my oath,
> This sword of mine, that should offend your foes,
> Shall sleep within the scabbard at thy need,
> And underneath thy banners march who will,
> For Mortimer will hang his armor up.
> *Gavest. Mort Dieu*! [Aside.]
>
> (I.i.82–90)

Gaveston's dramatic status, in respect to such moments, has often been critically misconstrued because the values he ridicules are superficially akin to those Marlowe celebrates in the *Tamburlaine* plays—-masculine pride, martial fervor, etc. In fact, the peers' values are only poor and petty shadows of Tamburlaine's ethic of omnipotence, and the peers themselves actually more closely resemble the vaunting Bajazeth and his confederates who brag and bluster themselves into prominence, than they do Tamburlaine himself. It takes also only an elementary comparison of Mortimers senior and junior with their more noble likenesses in *Richard II*—Bolingbroke and John of Gaunt, for example—to conclude that Marlowe did not, like Shakespeare, intend to censure his weak king's party by immediate reference to representatives of superior values.⁵ This early exchange between Edward and his nobles provides, then, a second instance of Marlowe's inversion of the dramatic import of the exemplary set-piece, in this case one that has its analogues in the meetings between an unwise king and his virtuous ministers. And it too appears to be indebted to a Machiavellian habit of mind that schematizes such contentions not in terms of moral polarities but in terms of the struggle of two parties competing for power.

I am careful to add this last observation because I believe that the critical application of moral distinctions to Marlowe's plays is frequently misplaced, especially given the extent to which Marlowe's thinking appears to be influenced by the materialist bias of Machiavellian political analysis. A morally oriented criticism is also disabled by its incapacity to offer authoritative evaluations of contentions that Marlowe characteristically resolves in terms of their competing theatrical appeal. The scene under scrutiny, for example, resolves itself in a manner that most commentators find disturbing, with Gaveston running into Edward's embrace; summarily being "created" Lord High Chamberlain, secretary of state, Earl of Cornwall, and

King and Lord of Man; and mightily abusing the Bishop of Coventry. But in theatrical terms, the long-postponed (and recently forbidden) reunion of Edward and Gaveston energetically opposes itself to the pompous puritanism of the lords; the creation of the base-born Gaveston as a veritable lord of misrule subverts the lords' emphasis on the exclusivity of their power and position; and Gaveston's abuse of the bishop is licensed both by its sheer audacity and by an anticlerical pronouncement that would surely have found a responsive auditory in the anti-papist environment of the 1590s: "What should a priest do with so fair a house? / A prison may beseem his holiness" (1.2.206–7).

In short, Marlowe carnivalizes Edward's and Gaveston's deviations from orthodox social and political behavior. By making the king himself and his base-born favorite the agents of antiauthoritarian misrule, he establishes a provocative alliance between royalty and presumption, united in an erotically charged assault on the constraints imposed on both by an aggressive peerage and an entrenched church. Mortimer and his confederates are cast as counter-fantasists in this theatrical transaction, as the puritanical enemies of pleasure who aim to suppress violently any deviation from their colorless and self-interested rule. The prospect of a carnivalized court presided over by a sexually "ambiguous" lord of misrule whose intentions and interests are, moreover, antipopulist in the extreme may not, admittedly, have warmed the heart of an Elizabethan playgoer who saw any possibility of the same being realized in fact. But "fact" is neither the province of the drama itself, nor the point of reference for audience reception or receptivity. And although the playgoer's capacity for engagement is at least partly rooted in the facts of his or her life and preoccupations, it is how the dramatist reconstructs those facts to fit the forms of the playgoer's fantasy that will largely dictate the nature of audience response.

The common critical view that the audience of *Edward II* will, for example, identify with the three poor men whom Gaveston rejects and ridicules assumes that the "average" Elizabethan playgoer will operate imaginatively in accord with a normative Christian or humanist imperative grounded in compassion, while the comparatively unprivileged playgoer will respond in a class-interested manner to Gaveston's provocation. Such an assumption not only assigns specific moral and political profiles to playgoers who may have made their judgments on more self-interested or psychological grounds; it assigns the same profile to Marlowe as well whose capacity to treat such schematic material in unorthodox ways and to construct unorthodox positions for the audience to inhabit is retrospectively inhibited and repressed. Marlowe may actually have intended the three poor men to arouse the revulsion of an audience distanced by their own privileges or their desire for psychic relief from scenes of social misery in which they might otherwise find themselves implicated: a possibility that "facts" about Elizabethan playwrights and playgoers drawn from the domain of professed or prescribed cultural practices and beliefs cannot provide for. Such facts exclude the fantasy life of Marlowe's audience to which the unachieved ambitions and unrealized dreams of Gaveston appear to be addressed. If, however, fantasies are accorded the same phenomenal status as facts, then we may contend that it is the audience's presumed eagerness to raise its own station in life and desire to have its difference from such poor specimens of humanity confirmed that Gaveston and Marlowe play upon here. As Gaveston turns from his supplicants and says, "These are not men for me," he may well be suggesting that braver spirits are likelier to be found in the audience, among those who aspire to conditions where what they are in fact may give place to what they are or would be in fantasy.[6]

Of course, both here and in the scenes that focus on Edward and Gaveston's conflict with the peerage, Marlowe cultivates the possibility of an opposing point of view, one grounded either in the audience's conceivable resistance to the homoerotic union of king and minion or in a more consciously political preference for the position of the nobles. Nevertheless, Marlowe's disposition of dramatic energy clearly favors the theatrically appealing interchange of love and power focused on Edward and Gaveston, and later extended to include Spencer and Baldock, a pair of masterless men in whom a decidedly Machiavellian opportunism takes precedence over the fawning servility of the three poor men. And it is, finally, Marlowe's privileging of the erotic and political conjunction of king and aspiring commoner in each instance that similarly takes precedence in helping to situate the possibly resistant playgoer in a corresponding position.

The Pleasures of Power

Marlowe's decision to privilege Edward's and Gaveston's iconoclastic contestation of the nobility's claim to superiority is generically consistent with his treatment of Tamburlaine's and Faustus's respective approaches to the structures of secular and religious power. But it has, perhaps, an even stronger autobiographical component. Whereas Tamburlaine and Faustus embody fantasies Marlowe presumably shared with a great many of his contemporaries, Gaveston and his successors, Spencer and Baldock, are marginal figures with whom we may identify the marginalized preoccupations of Marlowe's abbreviated life. In addition to an alleged taste for young boys, Gaveston shares with Marlowe the desire to make a place for himself in the world through his creative resources. Cynical and clever, unawed by the mystifications that restrict the imaginative range of their contemporaries, both Gaveston and Marlowe conceive and invent "pleasing shows" of the erotically charged Ovidian variety. They share an antipopulist contempt for the common man, and aspire to an antihumanist position of power unmediated either by conscience or concern for the commonweal.[7] Marlowe's other apparent preference for a behind-the-scenes role in the exercise of power is possibly expressed in his introduction of Spencer Junior and Baldock in II.i, where Spencer defines the qualifications required of the self-made courtier in stage-Machiavellian terms: "You must be proud, bold, pleasant, resolute, / And now and then stab, as occasion serves" (II.i.42–43). For his part, Baldock plays an even more proximate role in relation to Marlowe's offstage career as scholar and spy when he speaks of the "formal toys" that disguise the pedant's preference for intrigue and the licentious life of the court. In this instance, we may well be witnessing the former Cambridge scholar's inscription of his own aspirations into the only play in the language that makes the life and loves of a conspicuously homosexual king the object of sustained dramatic scrutiny.[8]

For Marlowe, Edward's weakness as a king does not derive simply from an extreme self-indulgence. It is exacerbated by a jealous and homophobic peerage that repeatedly oversteps the bounds of accepted feudal behavior, motivated more by class animosity and personal insecurity than by a concern for good government. Marlowe makes this peerage unsympathetic both in terms of its rhetorical self-display and its actions. Edward's love for Gaveston is, for example, flatteringly contrasted with Mortimer's equally exploitative but romantically lackluster liaison with Isabella; Gaveston's mistreatment of the bishop of Coventry is greatly overmatched by his vicious murder at the hands of the treacherous Warwick; and Edward's various transgressions are obscured by the relentlessly sadistic ministrations of Mortimer's henchmen.

Whereas Marlowe discredits the peers at every turn—making Mortimer one of the stiffest, least theatrical Elizabethan stage-villains on record—his compulsion to demystify self-justifying behavior is often withheld with respect to Edward, whose claim to power is seldom dramatically disputed so long as he is capable of sustaining it. I add this qualification because Marlowe shifts his dramatic point of view when Edward no longer provides him with the pleasure and security the playwright appears to have enjoyed in allying himself with the agents and executors of secular power. Once Edward surrenders the prerogatives of power to Mortimer, the king's body becomes a site both for the power of the usurper to play itself out upon and for Marlowe to anatomize and demystify.

The body of the king—"upon whose bosom" Gaveston is content to die and upon whose senses Gaveston desires to play—is subjected, in the closing movement of *Edward II*, to indignities that rival and, ultimately, exceed those visited upon Queen Elizabeth's victims in the *Gaping Gulf* affair and upon Tamburlaine's opponents. And while Edward elicits considerably more sympathy than does the Governor of Babylon, the completeness of his subjection to Mortimer and his henchmen also elicits from Marlowe yet another shift in perspective in the direction of those who now "mak[e] Fortune's wheel turn as [they] please" (V.ii.53). Most prominent among the temptations that Marlowe indulges in the scenes of Edward's suffering is his refusal to mystify the harsh facts he found in his sources and, hence, make the physical reduction of a king any more momentous than that of other victims of state-sponsored violence.

Licensed by Mortimer to "amplify" Edward's grief by whatever means they can devise, Matrevis, Gurney, and, later, Lightborn operate on Edward's presumably sovereign body with the same freedom from constraint that Gaveston enjoys as he "frolics" with Edward's private body and preys on the body-politic of England. The subjection of King Edward's body to what could either be construed as competing or complementary forms of violation thus serves to demystify the sovereign's claim to exemption from a common humanity and *to make common* otherwise extraordinary acts of transgression. This effort at demystification helps to explain Marlowe's selective divergences from his source in Stow where Edward's sufferings are in some sense dignified by his Christ-like endurance of a crown of hay and his poignant provision of tears in place of warm water for his shaving.[9] In Marlowe's play, Edward's abasement is presented with a gruff, mocking economy of word and gesture:

> *King Edward.*   O, water, gentle friends, to cool my thirst
>   And clear my body from foul excrements.
> *Matrevis.*   Here's channel water, as our charge is given.
>   Sit down, for we'll be barbers to your grace.

King Edward.   Traitors, away! What, will you murder me,
          Or choke your sovereign with puddle water?
Gurney.   No, but wash your face and shave away your beard,
          Lest you be known and so rescued.
Matrevis.   Why strive you thus? Your labor is in vain.
King Edward.   The wren may strive against the lion's strength,
          But all in vain; so vainly do I strive
          To seek for mercy at a tyrant's hand.
              They wash him with puddle water, and shave his beard away.
                              (V.iii.25–36)

While the forced shaving of Edward "with puddle water" surely must arouse the sympathy of most playgoers, the sympathy that a playgoer feels must be extended to a king whose majesty is now sufficiently sullied to make him indistinguishable from his own most abject subjects. Subjecting Edward to the meanest, most debasing ministrations, Matrevis and Gurney dramatically enact the kind of "deconsecration of sovereignty" that Franco Moretti positions historically as the enabling medium of a "real" king's eventual decapitation. But what Moretti sees as a long-term historical process that has its roots in the development of English tragic form and its culmination in the execution of Charles I in 1649, Marlowe presents in the concentrated span of five acts and in a manner even more threatening to the residual claims of absolute sovereignty.[10]

In preparing and performing Edward's execution, Mortimer's henchman, Lightborn, orchestrates a violently literal version of Gaveston's erotic fantasy. As an informed manipulator of men and situations in the typical stage-Machiavellian mode, Lightborn not only knows how "to draw the pliant king which way" he chooses, but knows also what it is men most fear and desire. His refinement of brutality (under the sponsorship of the state) is, in its way, the consummation of Gaveston's pornographic refinement of eroticism, and, indeed, contains a marked erotic element with the king, as Actaeon, being seduced into a death that is not simply apparent. Lightborn's craft also insidiously recalls the craft of the playwright himself, as does his goal, which involves not only the violation of the king's body but the demystification of the royal prerogatives that made that body appear kingly. When, for example, Edward enjoins Lightborn, "Tell Isabel the Queen, I looked not thus, / When for her sake I ran at tilt in France, / And there unhorsed the duke of Clermont" (V.v.67–69) and then attempts to bribe Lightborn with the present of his last jewel, the audience is compelled to register the utter irrelevance of royal presumption when royalty is rendered powerless. And, as playgoers watch Edward acquiesce to Lightborn's ministrations like a child trying to overcome his fear of the dark, they are compelled to register also the utter arbitrariness of social distinctions in the face of the only prerogatives that matter in the end, namely, the prerogatives of power. They are also encouraged to participate to some extent in Lightborn's own interest in the proceedings, which involves manipulating Edward, in an ostensibly sympathetic manner, into assuming a position most conducive to the planned mode of execution: "O speak no more, my lord; this breaks my heart. / Lie on this bed, and rest yourself awhile" (V.v.70–71).[11]

Apart from Edward's passivity and the insidiousness of the proceedings, the most striking aspects of the murder scene are the speed, specificity, and professional detachment of Lightborn as he goes about his business. The brutal economy with which he finally identifies his mission; his indifference to anything other than Edward's body as he executes his designs; and the pride with which he practices his craft conspicuously call attention to themselves, and further mediate our sympathetic involvement with Edward's sufferings. Indeed, Marlowe seems to want us to admire the precision of the execution almost more than he wants to shock us with the terrible logic of its composition. When Lightborn turns to his onstage auditors, Matrevis and Gurney (who will soon murder *him* with the same professional detachment, though without his theatrical flair), and says, "Tell me sirs, was it not bravely done?" (V.vi.115), he does not simply express his perverse pleasure in the deed he has done, but challenges the offstage audience to acknowledge its complicity in his performance.[12]

Compared to the closing movement of *Edward II*, the murder of Clarence in *Richard III* and of the king in *Richard II* are humanist fantasies. The stripped-down image Marlowe draws of the weak, enfeebled king, lying prone and submissive on his bed, while his murderers move purposefully about the room to execute a murder that is also a rape, even exceeds in horror—and daring—Shakespeare's depiction of Gloucester's blinding in *King Lear*. And as is the case in the latter scene, the playwright situates the spectating subject in a position of affiliated agency with the transgressive actor and action. As Lightborn efficiently lulls Edward into submission, has a table placed over his body to contain his cries and movements, and drives a hot poker into Edward's anus to leave no noticeable mark of violence upon his body, the conventional separation between audience and stage is temporarily suspended: theater assumes the immediacy and materiality of an actual event. The audience's presumptive sympathy for Edward and censure of Lightborn become bound up with the respective success each has in commanding his theatrical properties. Voluntary witnesses at the scene of royalty's abjection and sovereignty's deconsecration, Marlowe's audience may well have experienced feelings of transgressive release and excitation at Lightborn's professional command of these proceedings: feelings that would be inconsistent with a normatively prescribed sympathy for the royal victim of violence sponsored by a precipitately constructed state. Indeed, I would submit that in his studied failure to provide (as Shakespeare is careful to provide in *Richard III* and *Richard II*) any mention of repentance or mark of indecision on the part of his assassins, much less any act of intervention as Shakespeare supplies in *Lear*, Marlowe encourages his audience to *will* Edward's murder, to participate vicariously in the climactic act of demystification it observes.[13]

In this respect, we may be reminded of the end of *Doctor Faustus* where Marlowe abruptly shifts our attention from Faustus' status as tragic victim to the orthodox Christian commentary on his fall and damnation provided by the unforgiving Chorus. There is discernible, in both instances, a studied withdrawal of the playwright from the very space of human suffering he has so assiduously cultivated and a simultaneous identification with the exacting symmetry of punishments that close the door on character and play alike. This pattern recurs in a generally farcical vein at the end of *The Jew of Malta* as Barabas boils in his cauldron while Ferneze gives thanks to the Christian God, and at the close of *The Massacre at Paris* where the dying Guise is treated as a species of papist obscenity by the triumphant Protestants. That the same scenario does not occur in either of the two parts of *Tamburlaine* may be attributed to Marlowe's unqualified commitment to a protagonist who, as a self-styled scourge of God, exists to render others powerless and is, until his understated death, never rendered powerless by anyone.

6. Radical Shakespeare

In the generally one-sided comparatist debate about Marlowe and Shakespeare, "radical" usually modifies Marlowe, not Shakespeare. I employ the word now in relation to Shakespeare not to reverse the terms of the debate, or to elide the very real differences between Marlowe and Shakespeare. Nor do I wish to contribute a new argument for Shakespeare's uniqueness and transcendence of his own culture, one that might provide a contemporary basis for validating the Shakespeare myth. What I consider radical about Shakespeare has as much to do with the effects engendered by the theatrical realization of his plays as it does with what I take to be his intentions for them. In this respect, Shakespeare may be construed as circumstantially radical, though I do not, finally, believe that there is anything fortuitous about his more incisive dramatic interventions.

In a comparatist turn of his own, John D. Cox has recently contended that "Marlowe demystifies the power he craves but cannot obtain," whereas "Shakespeare's skepticism functions as political analysis rather than a projection of social striving" (1989, 98). The terms with which Cox frames his distinction suggest something altogether more energetic and emotionally charged in Marlowe's efforts at demystification than in Shakespeare's. Personally detached from Marlowe's "social striving," Shakespeare anatomizes and dissects the contradictions that inspire and unsettle Marlowe. While I suggest something of the same with respect to Marlowe in the preceding chapter, I am not persuaded that Shakespeare was quite as free of what amounts to an ideological investment in his productions as Cox suggests. The difference between the two playwrights has, I believe, more to do with how such contradictions are assembled and represented in their plays, and with the generally more dialogic nature of Shakespearean dramaturgy. Except for *Doctor Faustus*, which in each of its versions is traversed by several competing and, occasionally, contradictory voices, Marlowe's plays are decidedly monologic. They speak to their audiences from a single privileged point of view and construct correspondingly singular, though occasionally shifting, positions for the playgoer to inhabit.

Shakespearean dramaturgy opens itself up to radical perspectives by putting them into play in immediate relation to more orthodox points of view. While Shakespeare tends to privilege the latter at the expense of the former, he often stages his interventions with an incisiveness that blurs the difference between intention and apparently unintended effect. In this kind of transaction, Shakespeare's capacity to employ his skepticism in the interests of comparatively radical political analysis is affirmed at the same time as it is identified as only one component of an author-function that is otherwise committed to a mystification of its own interventions.

Ideology, Subversion, and the Shakespearean Set Speech

In the first chapter of *Radical Tragedy* (1984), Jonathan Dollimore makes a distinction regarding Montaigne that can just as profitably be applied to Shakespeare as to Marlowe. Contending that "We need to recognise . . . how a writer can be intellectually radical without necessarily being politically so" (10), Dollimore broaches a proposition that is seldom acknowledged by Shakespeareans who assume that the playwright's apparent political conservatism is firmly rooted in his identification with the received ideas of his time, conveniently summarized in the still influential model of the Elizabethan world picture. Thanks to a new generation of Renaissance scholars, we are now able to recognize that this model itself may need drastic revision, indeed, that it may well constitute a unitary myth of our own century's making, and therefore an extremely reductive view of an age that was actually engaged in an intensive interrogation of its received ideas.[1] It would be equally reductive to assign to Shakespeare a role in his age's revisionist projects that overestimates his intellectual radicalism, that substitutes, for example, a figure of subversiveness in place of that of the wise embodiment of moderation or, at worst, the apologist for Tudor absolutism. As Felix Raab has suggested in his survey of Machiavelli's reception in Tudor England, though the providentialist assumptions of the past were clearly being threatened throughout the last half of the sixteenth century and "the outlines of the traditional structure were blurring quickly" (1964, 70), few Elizabethans were capable of applying anything as systematic as "a Machiavellian critique to the English political scene" (48). But as Raab also suggests, and as Stephen Greenblatt (1981) has recently illustrated, a number of Shakespeare's contemporaries had become capable of adopting a predominantly "secular approach to political affairs" (Raab, 76), one that compelled the more adventurous among them to recognize that a given system of beliefs could be manipulated to reveal the porousness of its claims to universal validity.[2] Marlowe was, in this respect, only the most prominent of Shakespeare's contemporaries to foster an awareness of the mystifying effects of prevailing cultural practices.

In the body of this chapter, I intend to explore how similar recognitions inform Shakespeare's treatment of ostensibly orthodox dramatic pronouncements in three plays whose approach to dominant political and religious ideologies is at least contestatory, if not, at times, authentically subversive. I would, with Dollimore, like to stress from the start that "what makes an idea subversive is not so much what is intrinsic to it or the mere thinking of it, but the context of its articulation—to whom, and to how many and in what circumstances it is said or written" (1984, 10).[3] This context of articulation is, for our purposes, not only the Elizabethan playhouse itself with its complex of social variables and economic prerogatives, but the play proper which, in Shakespeare's case, is often engaged in staging a competition of positions and ideas whose appeal must ultimately be reconstructed and evaluated in theatrical terms. In order to do justice to the performative framework within which the subversive sometimes makes itself felt, I take for my immediate subject three (of many) moments in Shakespearean drama when a leading character appears to step forward, leaving temporarily that level of dramatic expression Brecht classifies as "plain speech," to address an issue that has both specific relevance to the play in question and clear extradramatic implications for the audience-at-large (Willett 1964, 44–45). Such moments are not limited to the plays I plan to discuss, as a brief glance at set speeches in any number of Shakespeare's plays would indicate. What makes Henry V's speech on ceremony, Ulysses' speech on degree, and Portia's on mercy of particular critical interest is their foregrounding of orthodox ideological content in dramatic contexts that reveal the speakers' self-investment in the positions they advance and consequently undermine the authority of their pronouncements.

The Shakespearean set speech is especially ripe for re-examination from a theatrical perspective since it has for so long supplied the focal point for the now widely disputed prioritizing of theme in literary criticism. As an extremely stylized mode of expression that tends to address subjects that presumably mean as much to its auditors as to its speaker—the wounds of civil war, the nationhood of England, the obligations of royalty, just to mention a few examples from the first and second tetralogies—the set speech occupies a privileged place in the theatrical economy of many of

Shakespeare's productions. It frequently assumes a decisive role in the interactive dynamics of a given performance, providing the pivot around which audience responses are elicited and assembled. The prominence of the set speech has, however, occasioned a chronic critical oversimplification of its actual effects on audiences that is directly related to a corresponding oversimplification of Shakespeare's intellectual proclivities. The very formality of the set speech, its rigorous and unusually symmetrical organization, has served to fix or circumscribe its content in more ways than one, making it appear to be the vehicle both of the play's overall meaning or message and of the author's ideological point of view. It is this supposed convergence of formalization, theme, and ideology that I would like to investigate, taking my cue from Terry Eagleton's illuminating summary of Pierre Macherey's discussion of text and ideology in *A Theory of Literary Production* (1978).[4] Eagleton writes (and I now ask the reader to substitute "the Shakespearean set speech" for Eagleton's "literary text"):

> What Macherey means . . . is that the literary text throws ideology into disarray *by* fixing it. By endowing the ideological with a precise, specific configuration, it gives it a certain "foregrounding," but thereby also begins to foreground its limits and lacunae, that of which it cannot at any cost speak, those significations that necessarily evade (but also covertly invade) it. By "formalizing" ideology, the text begins to highlight its absences, expose its essential incompleteness, articulate the ghostly penumbra of absent signs that lurk within its pronouncements.
>
> (1980, 160)[5]

If we perform the substitution I have requested, we gain access to what may occur when John of Gaunt, for example, issues his remarkably moving but just as remarkably porous sermon on English nationalism in *Richard II* ("Methinks I am a prophet new inspir'd," II.i.31–68). As Gaunt raises compelling image after image in his eulogistic paean to "this sceptred isle," he simultaneously reveals the nostalgic basis of his position and the subjective nature of his investment in the glories of an idealized past, hence the illusory foundation upon which his (and our own if we are English) patriotic fervor is built. Surely partisan audiences will respond with an answering fervor to his prophetic intensity when his speech reaches its climax—"[This England] . . . Is now leas'd out—I die pronouncing it— / Like to a tenement or pelting farm" (59–60)—but many playgoers will just as surely share at least a little of Richard's answering cynicism—"Can sick men play so nicely with their names?" (84)—whose *in*formality tends to "expose" further the "essential incompleteness" of Gaunt's position.

In short, although both Eagleton and Macherey share a textually, as opposed to a performatively, oriented point of view, I believe I can make a case for their position's relevance to a re-examination of the Shakespearean set speech without unduly stretching either the reader's credulity or Shakespeare's range of reference. I can, at the very least, promise that a kind of rough justice will be done to what Eagleton, in the same essay, terms "the *cunning* of the ideological" (1980, 153).

Ceremony

In his essay on tragic form, Franco Moretti states that the purpose of the soliloquy—one of a variety of set speeches I intend to discuss—is "not of promoting the action [of a play] or establishing its implications, but rather of retarding it and making its implications ungraspable." For Moretti, the soliloquy is essentially a "self-referential" form of "poetry" that is "born from the disjunction of idea and reality" and "can be 'spoken' only by one who has lived through an analogous disjunction in his own person—by the sovereign who is unable to unite history and transcendence, action and value, passion and reason." Moretti is speaking here of soliloquies delivered by tragic characters in tragic circumstances, by characters "whose fall," in his words, "epitomizes the collapse of an entire civilization" (1981, 32–33). But I would like to apply his formulation, first, to a different variety of set speech in order to demonstrate the similar self-referentiality of equally stylized but more superficially thematic forms of expression.

I begin with a speech from *Henry V* that has been considered sufficiently broad in its range of reference to represent "the thematic climax of the entire tetralogy" of which *Henry V* comprises the last part. According to this school of thought, Shakespeare, in Henry's speech on ceremony (IV.i.227–81), is "showing us that at last we have a king free of the crippling disabilities of his predecessors and wise in what the [other three] plays have been teaching" (Rabkin 1981, 47).[6] When Henry addresses ceremony as an "idol," equivalent to "place, degree, and form" in "Creating awe and fear in other men," he is (the argument goes) specifically distinguishing himself from the tragically divided Richard II, who confused ceremony with reality and whose reign shattered upon their disjunction. From this point of view, Henry becomes the thinking man's king, fully aware of the political fictions that have made him what he is, but decisive enough to shoulder his lonely burden and get on with being kingly, the artificiality of his culture's social

constructions notwithstanding. Opponents of this rather optimistic estimate of Henry's character have employed the same speech to substantiate
their view of a peevish, condescending king, seemingly as incapable as
Measure for Measure's Duke Vincentio of seeing criticism as anything other
than slander, and as insensitive as Coriolanus in acknowledging the validity
of the competing complaints of common men. From this perspective,
Henry becomes more the manipulative Machiavellian than the meditative
mirror of English kings.

Rather than attempt to reconcile here what Norman Rabkin has aptly
described as the irreconcilability of these two positions (1981, 60), I would
prefer to take a more circuitous approach to the speech on ceremony in
order to uncover the distinctly ideological dimensions of what presents
itself as a personal meditation. There is, to begin with, an oddly insular and
dissociated quality to Henry's reasoning in this speech that reveals a closer
resemblance to Richard II than has generally been observed, and marks a
crucial departure from the Machiavellian character-type (e.g., Richard III)
who, with the wink of an eye or a cunning aside, manages to bridge his
own alienation by bringing himself into contact with an audience outside
himself. What usually makes a soliloquy self-referential, in Moretti's terms,
is its enforced quality; characters like Hamlet and Macbeth have no choice
but to speak their bitterness into their hands, isolated as they are by exclu-
sions from normative social exchanges that are sufficiently sustained as to
appear permanent. Henry's insularity, like Richard II's, derives, on the
other hand, from a habitual embeddedness in the prerogatives of kingship
that limits the range of his speculations to the ascriptive pale of royalist
ideology. It is also akin to the insularity of Shakespeare's Ulysses, who can
speak volumes on "degree" or on the social basis of reputation but is oddly
constrained in the realm of self-awareness, and incapable (or at least made
to seem incapable) of plucking out the heart of his own mystery.[7] Henry's
estrangement from the common soldiers of whom he speaks in his soliloquy is, for example, generated by a prevailing sense of exclusivity that privileges his claim to collective responsibility at the same time that it restricts
the introspective range of his thoughts:

> Upon the King! Let us our lives, our souls,
> Our debts, our careful wives,
> Our children, and our sins lay on the King.
> We must bear all. O hard condition,
> Twin-born with greatness, subject to the breath

Of every fool, whose sense no more can feel
But his own wringing!
                                        (IV.i.227–33)

He is, in other words, buffered by his complete absorption in his royal
prerogatives from anything approaching a more flexible or less officious
response to his dramatic situation.

I place Henry in such company because even in his most private moments he seems naturally to gravitate towards ideological constructs as a
means of imaging his condition, of making graspable what would otherwise remain ungraspable. This habit of mind allows him the freedom to
demystify the role played by ceremony in "Creating awe and fear in other
men" without having also to acknowledge, much less contend with, the
subversive implications of having done so.[8] Indeed, it would appear that
Henry sets ceremony apart as a "proud dream" only to reaffirm his difference from ordinary men and dramatize the burdens of his own distinction:

'Tis not the balm, the scepter, and the ball,
The sword, the mace, the crown imperial.
. . . .
No, not all these, thrice-gorgeous ceremony,
Not all these, laid in bed majestical,
Can sleep so soundly as the wretched slave,
Who, with a body fill'd and vacant mind,
Gets him to rest, cramm'd with distressful bread.
                                        (IV.i.257–58, 263–67)

In the process of drawing this distinction between royalty and commons
which—"but for ceremony"—endows the latter with "the forehand and
vantage of a king," Henry stretches his own position to the breaking point,
foregrounds what must appear the unlikeliest argument on behalf of the
structures of power to those members of the audience "cramm'd" likewise
with the "distressful bread" of their own earning. Instead of serving to
cancel or, at least, qualify the artificial divisions between men enforced by
the false idol, ceremony, Henry's speech eventuates in the king's reconsecration of the same hierarchical ideology to which, he would lead us to
believe, he is himself royally subjected. If Henry, in his first body, sees
ceremony as a mere fiction, he sees it, in his second body, as an undeniable
fact of life. By the close of the speech, he has become so oblivious to his

soldiers' objections, which stimulated this bout of conscience in the first place, that he has also begun to lose touch with the series of consciously political choices that have led to his present predicament:

> The slave, a member of the country's peace,
> Enjoys it; but in gross brain little wots
> What watch the King keeps to maintain the peace,
> Whose hours the peasant best advantages.
>
> (IV.i.278–81)

Henry speaks here of a peace that no longer exists for the slave to enjoy, of a peace that he has himself canceled instead of maintaining, and of gross brains that already have demonstrated their capacity to penetrate the trappings of ceremony (see, e.g., the words of Bates and Williams in IV.i.120ff). In so doing, he turns a potential exercise in self-examination and demystification into an occasion for self-advancement and delusion. But, we must ask, to what effect?

Strictly speaking, the soliloquy is not designed to produce the same effects that are produced by a set speech addressed in a public dramatic context that takes more than the isolate self for its theme. It is, instead, designed to bring the solitary speaking character into private and privileged contact with an audience that is led to expect something candid and altogether "unofficial" by the distinctiveness of the dramatic moment. Such contact is, however, never really effected by the speech on ceremony whose presentational style ultimately has more in common with the public set speech than with the soliloquy.

This slippage of an essentially private form of discourse into the style and structure of public address should, perhaps, be expected in "a remarkably public play" which, as Larry S. Champion observes, "utilizes the soliloquy and the aside to a smaller degree than any other work in Shakespeare's canon" (1980, 151). In *Henry V*, the set speech generally functions as an affective instrument, as a vehicle of bravado or outright propaganda, employed by the Chorus to work the audience up to a leap of the imagination and employed by Henry to work his men up (see, e.g., the "St. Crispin's" and "Once more unto the breach" speeches) to a pitch of uniquely English heroism. In most instances, it does much to substantiate Stephen Greenblatt's contention that "theatricality . . . is one of power's essential modes" (1981, 56), although it does so in a more obvious and direct manner than Greenblatt has in mind. How, then, can so potent a medium of theatrical persuasion be considered conducive to subversion?

Clearly, it would be difficult to identify what Greenblatt terms "the possible presence of genuinely subversive elements" (1981, 42) in texts whose express function is to smother surmise in a welter of enthusiasm and bravado.⁹ The ceremony speech is, however, a text different in kind and function from Henry's other set speeches, which tend to collaborate with, rather than compete against, the high standard of achievement set by the Chorus's effusions. Although, in its guise as soliloquy, the speech seems designed to give body and form to the "little touch of Harry in the night" that the Chorus, at its most maudlin, promises, it operates in the immediate context of a dramatic intervention that has the potential to subvert the ideological consensus promoted by the play as a whole. This intervention is advanced by the powerful objections the common soldiers, Bates and Williams, raise against Henry's attempt to mystify the justice and honor of the king's "quarrel" against France (IV.i.85ff). Few playgoers of any class-standing could fail to appreciate the irreverence of Bates's wish that the king "were here alone" so that he might "be ransom'd, and a many poor men's lives sav'd" (IV.i.120–22), which speaks a plain truth that all who are not royal would have to acknowledge. This effort to draw the audience into a feeling of common cause in the face of their shared subjection to royal prerogatives is intensified when Williams offers his vision of a dismembered body politic in which Henry's earlier injunction to "close the wall up with our English dead" is stripped of its glamor and bravado:

> But if the cause be not good, the King himself
> hath a heavy reckoning to make, when all those
> legs and arms and heads, chopp'd off in a battle,
> shall join together at the latter day
> and cry all, "We died at such a place"—some
> swearing, some crying for a surgeon, some upon
> their wives left poor behind them, some upon the
> debts they owe, some upon their children rawly left.
>
> (IV.i.133–40)

Williams's speech effectively contests the terms of engagement the Chorus has been at pains to establish between Henry and the audience by lodging a competing image of the fortunes of war in the mind's eye of the audience. In comparison, Henry's superficially heterodox soliloquy seems ill-equipped to neutralize the impact of Williams's eloquently lurid anatomy of the king's "heavy reckoning."

Henry's emphasis on ceremony as the sole basis of distinction between himself and ordinary men initially promises an ideological breakthrough that will disarm Williams's grievance of its affective power by giving substance to Henry's earlier "disguised" comment that "the King is but a man, as I am" (IV.i.101). It soon becomes apparent, however, that Henry's heterodoxy is a purely rhetorical impulse that mirrors the emptiness of the king's first body; his speech is a text only the king's second body can write, its perspective one that only a king who is nothing but king can share. When Henry refers at all to Williams's vision of the dismembered body politic, he does so by bequeathing it the dreamless sleep of fools, wretches, slaves, lackeys, and peasants—a king's idea of an Elysium for commoners in exchange for their "profitable labor." In short, Henry responds to his soldiers' concern for their own welfare and salvation, first, by privileging the weight of his own royal burdens and, then, by reducing the soldiers to a state of bestial oblivion. He questions the ideological basis of his own condition only to redefine it, generally shorn now of its mythical trappings, in its starkest and most rigid outlines. The feudal relationship between sovereign and subject (elsewhere described by Henry in fraternal terms) is suddenly made equivalent to the relationship between master and slave, indeed, becomes identified with the same insofar as the ground of its being is made plain.

It would appear, then, that far from salving the wound in the body politic of the playhouse, dramatically opened during Henry's interview with his soldiers, the speech on ceremony should serve to widen the breach between subject and sovereign by demystifying the basis of their feudal relationship. I say "should serve" because while Henry's speech casts his actual ideological position in such sharp relief that it threatens to reveal, in Eagleton's words, "that of which [the ideological] cannot at any cost speak," this threat may only have been fully registered and appreciated by those auditors capable of standing at a critical distance from the complete context of the speech's articulation, which significantly includes the erasure of social dissonance Henry's subsequent prayer to the "God of Battles" seeks to effect. For a contemporary audience, as invested as Henry is in the *forms*, if not the prerogatives, of sovereignty, the effect of this rupturing of the feudal contract was probably as limited as the time that elapses between the ceremony speech's conclusion and the beginning of Henry's prayer (IV.i.286ff).

For his part, Henry appears far more comfortable addressing his words to an unseen Other in a plea that effectively submerges the earlier, potentially subversive moment in a moving strain of nostalgia for that lost relationship between subject and sovereign decried in the ceremony speech:

> O God of Battles! Steel my soldiers' hearts,
> Possess them not with fear! Take from them now
> The sense of reck'ning, if th' opposed numbers
> Pluck their hearts from them. Not today, O Lord,
> O, not today, think not upon the fault
> My father made in compassing the crown!
>
> (IV.i.286–91)

This speech seems intended to make as great an emotional claim on its audience as it does on Henry himself by invoking a ceremony of repentant innocence that rhetorically clears Henry of blame for King Richard's death at the same time that it makes him—in a queer subversion of history itself—the ideological heir-apparent of Richard's previously subverted belief in divine right. In the dramatic economy of the play, the potential subversiveness of Williams's vision of the dismembered body politic and Henry's consequent reduction of his subjects to the status of slaves is counteracted *ceremonially* by Henry's reversion to a religious idiom and a providentialist approach to political affairs that effectively subsume and transcend competing secular perspectives.[10] The speech on ceremony initiates this reconsecration of sovereignty by privileging the disjunct relationship between the king's two bodies at the expense of the ruptured relationship between sovereign and subject, making Henry appear subject to his own sovereignty, the reluctant victim of what he perceives to be a palpable but necessary fiction. The second soliloquy, cast as a prayer, sanctions this transaction by ritualizing Henry's attempt to submerge himself in a divinely appointed role. In the process, "place, degree, and form" are recuperated on the heels of their own demystification. The imaginary subsumes the real because, in this play's reconstitution of the operations of feudal society, the ceremony of pious speech exerts a disproportionate hold over the minds of men and because it is the nostalgic recreation of a hero-king, not what Louis Althusser terms "the real relations which govern the existence of individuals" (1971, 165), that is finally at stake.

Degree

The same cannot be said of *Troilus and Cressida*, a play about which it is difficult to say anything for certain except that it is anti-nostalgic in the extreme. Ulysses' speech on degree (I.iii.75–137) does, however, resemble Henry's speech on a number of fronts and is similarly motivated by the apparent failure of a dominant ideology to maintain its adhesive hold on the "hollow factions" that have neglected the "specialty of rule."[11] The speech on degree provides the quintessential example of the variety of Shakespearean set speech we may classify under the rubric "orthodox expression," and the commentary it has provoked epitomizes both the oldest and newest strains of Shakespeare criticism. For Tillyard and his disciples, Ulysses' speech operates as the thematic center of *Troilus*. What Ulysses remarks as "neglected" is, the argument goes, what informed Elizabethans would remark as well; what Ulysses bewails, they would bewail. The more contemporary critic would emphasize the conspicuously Machiavellian slant in Ulysses' position, observing, for example, that Ulysses' argument is mediated by his consciousness of the utility of ideology in manipulating the behavior of men and women. Ulysses becomes, in this reading, less the conservator of traditional values than the conservative manipulator of political fictions, the official propagandist of a ruling class ideology. In each instance, the speech functions as a referential construct, with the (mis)behavior of Achilles serving as its most immediate referent: in the former as an example of what happens when degree is "vizarded"; in the latter as a force of subversion that must be contained in order to restore to Ulysses' own faction the priority it claims.

I would, however, like to consider the self-referential aspects of Ulysses' discourse in order to measure the extent of his personal investment in the social dimensions of the seemingly purposive address he delivers: "To end a tale of length, / Troy in our weakness stands, not in her strength" (I.iii.136–37). My point is not that Ulysses is *wrong* in his diagnosis of the situation of the Greek army, but that it may be misdirected to extrapolate wholesale thematic applications from so local an anatomy of the "pale and bloodless emulation" that besets the Greek project. Such a formulation may be misdirected because, to reverse an earlier interpretive procedure, Ulysses' speech may be a species of soliloquy in masquerade. What generically differentiates it from a soliloquy is, first, its status as a public pronouncement addressed to attentive auditors and, second, the implication that a "remedy" will be forthcoming, hence, that the discourse as a whole is geared to advance some action and is not, therefore, limited to the realm of abstract speculation. But what, one may ask, does Ulysses' speech aim to advance? The answer is usually discovered in the vicinity of Achilles whom, Ulysses says, "opinion crowns / The sinew and forehand of our host" but who "Grows dainty of his worth, and in his tent / Lies mocking our designs" (I.iii.142–46). It is not made plain, however, until the end of the scene in question when Ulysses delegates Ajax in Achilles' place to engage Hector in single combat.

Apparently, then, the speech does function in consistency with its presentational style. Depending on one's critical persuasion, it serves either to deflate or foreshorten the thematic career of a political construct, or to demonstrate the accuracy of Ulysses' analysis of a world eaten up by the "universal wolf" he identifies as "appetite." But I would suggest that the speech does more than advance the mechanisms of plot or theme, and that Ulysses' ostensible promotion of purposive activity provides a crucial clue to Shakespeare's dramatic aims. Throughout the play—which provides the broadest context of this speech's articulation—Shakespeare repeatedly calls attention to Ulysses' insularity and sobriety, to his apparent freedom from the undirected self-indulgence that characterizes the behavior of Achilles and Patroclus, hence, to his personal investment in a symbolic code based on degree. Viewed from this vantage point, Ulysses' speech can be construed as a ceremonial act of self-concealment, as an efficacious rhetorical disguise employed less to conceal a Machiavellian motivation than to submerge his own subjectivity in a language of transcendental signifiers, a bureaucratized discourse of mastery.[12]

If I am at all correct in my reading of Ulysses' personal submersion in the values articulated in the speech on degree, we may well need to revise our estimate of the role played by the set speech in the dramatic economy of Shakespeare's productions. Does such a speech really serve —in plays as distinct as *Henry V*, *Troilus*, and *The Merchant of Venice*—as the ideological center of gravity, or central thematic pronouncement of the production in question? Or is Shakespeare himself sufficiently detached from the ideological projections of his characters to effect their dramatic deconstruction—sufficiently complex in his thinking about the structures of power and their relation to the structures of speech to make such stylized and settled pronouncements objects of sustained dramatic scrutiny?

As my earlier approach to the speech on ceremony should suggest, I believe Shakespeare was less devoted than are many of his characters to the priority of the word in legislating an accurate appraisal of "the real relations which govern the existence of individuals" and societies. I would further contend that it is particularly in the stylized domain of the set speech that he aims to make us skeptical of the referentiality of words, of their claim to represent an objectively verifiable reality outside themselves. And it is especially in the public set speech that we witness a character's attempt to escape into a pre-defined ideological position as a means of transcending the disjunctions between idea and reality he has encountered in the less easily definable world of informal dramatic interactions. A perfect example of such a psychologically strategic escape into ideology is supplied at the close of *Othello* when the Moor dramatically reaffirms his dedication to the Venetian state to the complete exclusion of anything that threatens his imaginary conception of his situation (V.ii.347–65). But perhaps I had better explain more clearly the understanding of ideology with which I am working. According to a thesis advanced some years ago by Louis Althusser:

> it is not their real conditions of existence, their real world, that men "represent to themselves" in ideology, but above all it is their relation to those conditions of existence which is represented to them there. It is this relation which is at the centre of every ideological, i.e., imaginary, representation of the real world. It is this relation that contains the "cause" which has to explain the imaginary distortion of the ideological representation of the real world. Or rather, . . . it is the *imaginary nature of this relation* which underlies all the imaginary distortion that we can observe (if we do not live in its truth) in all ideology. (1971, 164)[13]

Returning now to the example of Ulysses, a character who styles even his most casual pronouncements in the idiom of the public set speech, we may observe that his notion (presented as *our* notion) of a cosmic order based on degree is premised on a projection of himself into a position of priority in a power structure he perceives to be threatened by Achilles and Patroclus who "tax our policy, and call it cowardice" (I.iii.197). What he represents both to himself and to his auditors, on stage and off, as a condition of nature is, in other words, an "ideological, i.e., imaginary, representation of the real world" in whose distortions he is completely invested. Ulysses' investment in this ideology—and his inability to think himself clear of it— are, moreover, linked dramatically with the psychological investment Shakespeare has him make in a projection of selfhood that is cool and rational, as stable and as constant as the sun "In noble eminence enthron'd and spher'd / Amidst the other . . . " (I.iii.90–91), a phrase that Ulysses appears to linger over in a self-reflexive manner.

It is, of course, Ulysses' characteristic position that he is not subject to the imaginary in the way other men are. And his position would seem to be legitimated by his genuine detachment from Achilles' ethic of martial prowess and from Troilus' disillusionment at discovering the power of beauty to transform honesty from what it is to a bawd. But in the latter instance, Ulysses' bewildered response to Troilus' incredulity at Cressida's betrayal—"Let it not be believ'd for womanhood! / Think, we had mothers"—is particularly revealing: "What hath she done, Prince, that can soil our mothers?" (V.ii.132–33; 138). Ulysses' incapacity either to comprehend or countenance Troilus' emotionally charged association of one woman with all women reveals the completeness of Ulysses' submersion in the ideology of degree, measures the extent to which his detachment from one imaginary representation holds him captive to the limitations of another. What makes *Troilus* so rich a text and so provocative a play is its commitment to a habit of subversion that enables the demystification of each of the drama's competing ideologies (Trojan as well as Greek), which are revealed, in the end, to be equally imaginary, equally self-serving and self-referential. Even the possibly choric voice of Thersites, which serves *Troilus*'s most explicitly subversive interests—"All the argument is a whore and a cuckold, a good quarrel to draw emulous factions and bleed to death upon" (II.ii.71–73)—can be construed as a self-referential construct that subverts its own authority by means of its unstinting commitment to a self-serving ethic of misanthropy.

I would conclude from these examples of self-submersion in the imaginary that Shakespeare's enduring preoccupation with the tension between appearance and reality was not so inhibited by his own probable submersion in the power structures of his time as to preclude his awareness of their distortions of the actual. I would also conclude, after Stephen Greenblatt (1980, 253–54), that the traditional attribution to Shakespeare of sentiments far more orthodox in orientation than those attributed to Marlowe has as strong a basis in the subtlety of Shakespeare's subversions as it does in the conservatism of his critics. Shakespearean villains commonly appropriate orthodox positions to advance their own interests; Richard of Gloucester is a notable case in point. In most instances, however, these misappropriations can easily be dramatically discredited or, at least, placed squarely in the context of moral transgression since such characters tend to operate well outside normative structures of behavior. Free as Richard, Edmund, and Iago are of the constraints of political or religious orthodoxy, the orthodoxy in question is likewise free of them. Far from being threatened by the theatrical Machiavellism of Richard of Gloucester, belief in the "naturalness" of a right that is divinely or providentially ordered may ultimately be enhanced in *Richard III* or, at the very least, be made to seem more stable and dependable than its opposite. It is, consequently, a more volatile matter when expressly orthodox characters like Henry V and Ulysses betray the essentially imaginary basis of their relationships to the world by insulating themselves within ideologically soundproof constructions. The fine-tuned use of value-charged language becomes in such instances symptomatic of the difficulties such characters have in coming to terms with the disjunctions between "history and transcendence, action and value, passion and reason" that obtain in their respective dramatic environments. Their personal investment in their own aesthetic productions— "How could . . . / The primogeneity and due of birth, / Prerogative of age, crowns, scepters, laurels, / But by degree stand in authentic place?" (I.iii.103–08), imperiously asserts a clearly self-interested Ulysses—demonstrates the extent to which their very appropriation of the set speech form resolves the problem of self-expression and functions in the service "of inventing imaginary or formal 'solutions' to unresolvable social contradictions" (Jameson 1981, 79)

By having ideologically pure characters like Henry and Ulysses make so apparent the dependence of an entire range of customs and beliefs (in which the audience itself was presumably invested, though not, certainly, to the extent their rulers had to be) on such transparently fragile constructs as ceremony and degree, Shakespeare effectively alerts his audience to the possibility that its own best interests may not be served by the ideology in question. Indeed, Ulysses' insistence on "primogeneity and due of birth" would have warmed the hearts of few Elizabethan second sons had they had the opportunity to witness a performance of this possibly unproduced playtext.[14] Perhaps more importantly, Shakespeare also alerts his presumptive audience to the possibility that the ideology itself may be nothing more than an artificial construction, consciously crafted to create "awe and fear in other men." It is, in short, through their unacknowledged investment in the formal properties and proprieties of the set speech that Shakespeare calls attention to the ideological status of his characters' speech acts and thus implicitly subverts the transcendental claims of their pronouncements.

Mercy

Frank Whigham has recently remarked similar acts of submersion into formal pronouncements in *The Merchant of Venice*, especially in relation to Bassanio's apparent lack of self-consciousness as he delivers his set speech in the casket scene (III.ii.73–107):

> Maybe Bassanio is so unreflective as to be unaware of the irony of his words; even his meditations may be so rhetorically ordered to preclude self-consciousness. . . . He may be unconcerned with the tension between the artful form of his meditation and its moral content; aesthetic and moral perspectives often seem askew from one another in this play. Perhaps some such compartmentalization, and the instrumental utility it implies, are part of Shakespeare's point here. (1979, 101)

Whigham is specifically concerned with Bassanio's mastery of the courtier ideology of disinterestedness, and how such mastery guarantees success in his quest for Portia. My concern with the passage is twofold. I am interested in the connection Whigham draws between Bassanio's un-self-consciousness and the artful ordering of his words, on the one hand, and in the tension Whigham discerns between form and content, on the other. And I am interested in the applicability of Whigham's notions of "compartmentalization" and "instrumental utility" to an understanding of the "point" of the Shakespearean set speech.

The potential for subversiveness in the set speeches I have already discussed is enhanced by the same lack of self-consciousness that Whigham remarks in Bassanio, the performative ease with which each speaker slips into a stylized rhetorical mode that foregrounds a set of abstract values, but simultaneously embodies the speaker's most personal projections. In these instances, it is not only the incompleteness of the ideological position that risks exposure, but also the incompleteness of the speaker, who has submerged his imaginative freedom so fully in the restrictions of a specific symbolic order that he has effectively distanced himself from the consideration of alternative positions. For Brecht in our own time, a set speech (or "set song") occasions the alienation of both actor and audience by explicitly illustrating the actor's movement from his role as character to his role as commentator or spokesperson, and by conjoining this movement to the play's corresponding shift from presentation to proselytizing. For Shakespeare, who operates on a "dramatic" as opposed to an "epic" level, the alienation of the actor proceeds *in character*, as a revelation to the audience of the proselytizing quality of his presentation, hence, of the peculiar *lack* of tension between form and content. And this occurs most often when the character in question shows no awareness of what Moretti terms a "disjunction in his own person," and thus applies most directly to the set speeches of Henry, Ulysses, and, I would now add, Portia, which are addressed well outside the pale of a conventional tragic paradigm.

When Whigham turns his attention to Portia, he adjusts his approach somewhat, making her appear more conscious than Bassanio of the "instrumental utility" of the "compartmentalization" of values. He contends that "Portia's speech on mercy functions precisely as an ideological weapon" and that it "is specifically presented as a *compulsion*" (109–10). Although, like Whigham, I am far from viewing the speech on mercy in a traditionally thematic manner (even in the now traditionally inverted thematic manner, as a document for the defense of Shylock), I would stop short of attributing the motive of willful manipulation to Portia for the very reason that I find Whigham's anatomy of Bassanio's behavior so apt. Just as Bassanio is, so to speak, "innocent" of whatever disparity may obtain between the form and content of his speech, so too is Portia innocent of consciously employing the mercy speech as an ideological weapon against Shylock. She *is* guilty, however, of her unacknowledged submersion in the idiom of a dominant ideological discourse that serves to suppress the claim to validity of any alternative discourse that dares to dispute its prerogatives.

It is no coincidence that the mercy speech has for centuries been removed from its specific dramatic context to serve as a recitation for schoolchildren, presumably in the interests of improving their skills in oral interpretation, but also in the interests of promoting an ideological position which, taken in isolation, could be disputed only by the most ardent proponent of capital punishment. In short, the mercy speech is an unanswerable proposition that gilds its speaker in the trappings of all things bright and beautiful, and allows her to climb to the highest reaches of moral purity, only to cast shadow and suspicion on any deviation from its abstract rule. To say that Portia knows this would be equivalent to saying that she also knows that what she is doing is either wrong, improperly motivated, or, at best, purely instrumental. That she knows no such thing but instead is invested totally in the abstract righteousness of her position and, for that matter, her role (which embodies a gender displacement motivated by her subjection to masculine structures of power) becomes especially apparent toward the close of the trial scene when she blithely places the power to grant a now severely watered-down version of mercy in the hands of the Duke who, in turn, proclaims to Shylock that he shall presently "see the difference of our spirit" (IV.i.366).

The fact that both parties to the controversy are equally wedded to the priority of law over mercy is casually overlooked both by the Duke and Portia who are similarly captive to an ideology which is itself, as Pierre Macherey writes, "a captive of its own limits," an "enclosed, finite" structure of beliefs that "mistakenly proclaims itself to be unlimited (having an answer for everything) within its limits" (1978, 131). Within the specific bounds of the speech on mercy, Portia plainly demonstrates the extent to which her imagination has been colonized by what Althusser calls "the imaginary," which, in Portia's case, takes shape as a religious discourse that purports to transcend seemingly "unresolvable social contradictions" and the existing political arrangements it serves to validate:

> But mercy is above this sceptred sway;
> It is enthroned in the hearts of kings;
> It is an attribute to God himself;
> And earthly power doth then show likest God's
> When mercy seasons justice. Therefore, Jew,
> Though justice be thy plea, consider this, . . .
>   (IV.i.191–96)

I include in this passage Portia's movement away from the pristine horizons of the set speech proper and into the mode of direct address ("Therefore, Jew") to call attention to the clearly demarcated ideological boundary that divides the Christian-woman-become-Christian-man, who has the very power to make mercy season justice that she ascribes to God and king, from the Jew who, despite Shylock's protestations to the contrary, is never anything but Jew in the eyes of the law and Portia alike. Portia's request to have Shylock "consider . . . / That, in the course of justice, none of us / Should see salvation" (IV.i.196–98) proceeds from the same self-enclosed perspective that has already rendered Shylock incapable of deciphering a linguistic code premised on rights, privileges, and ways of thinking from which he is definitionally excluded. Shylock's predictably negative response to this injunction is itself predicated on his own embeddedness in an equally insular ideology which enforces his inflexible allegiance to his only form of social protection, the Venetian law. But Shylock's response is, ultimately, of less immediate concern to Portia than is her own high-minded identification with an unanswerable moral proposition that allows her to submerge humane considerations by becoming their spokesperson.

By summoning up, during a moment of extreme dramatic tension, the image of so transcendent and all reconciling a value as mercy—"it is twice blest: / It blesseth him that gives and him that takes"—Portia opens up a theatrical vista that promises to cancel that tragic disjunction between idea and reality from which both the soliloquy *and ideology* are born. Her speech presents itself in the likeness of a signifier seeking its signified in a world the speech claims to reflect, or, in a more psychological vein, in the guise of a private fantasy seeking fulfillment in the ministrations of others. Once Shylock utters his refusal to cooperate, the bright prospects of mercy are irrevocably withdrawn, and Shylock becomes the scapegoat for the failure of the entire company to transcend the letter of laws that dehumanize the relationships between citizens and subjects in Venetian society (see Girard 1978, 108–19). His assigned status as scapegoat, however, retrospectively reveals the pivotal role played by the mercy speech in the scapegoating process. For Shylock suffers the fate of failing to provide a referent for an ideological construct that is actually being employed in a purely rhetorical or self-referential manner. He becomes the ritual victim for the failure of mercy itself to function in any way other than as a self-sustaining poetic artifact, as a facade of the imaginary that distorts the real conditions of existence as the action of the play depicts them. Sufficiently attentive spectators are, of course, just as likely to "read" the speech on mercy in the context of Portia's ensuing "mercifixion" of Shylock, to see it as referring in an ironic fashion to actions that subvert or contradict the authority of Portia's pronouncements and, hence, make Portia, not Shylock, the true villain of the production.[15] Such a procedure may well be consistent with Shakespeare's own dramatic design which is, in its way, every bit as critical of Christian presumption as is Marlowe's in *The Jew of Malta*.[16] But in this instance Shakespeare is making another, more subversive point about the ungraspable nature of the mercy speech's implications that has little to do with the critical competition between villains and heroes, and that makes Portia as much a victim as Shylock of her rhetorical formulation. Although Shakespeare's contemporary audience was probably too invested in the disparity between Christian theory and secular practice, and in the caricatured difference in spirit of Christian and Jew, to draw such a conclusion for itself, the full context of the mercy speech's articulation makes Portia's unacknowledged submersion in the imaginary the dramatic mirror of its own. Portia's initial insistence on mercy resonates with the mercilessness of her ensuing treatment of Shylock in a manner that renders the very concept indeterminate and her unqualified hold on its validity tragic, insofar as it radically distorts her consciousness of things as they are.

But indeterminate for whom and for how long? Tragic in what sense of the term? No observation regarding the darker implications of the trial scene can be confidently made without at least attempting to account for the way in which "the aristocratic fantasy of Act V" seeks "to obliterate the memory of what has preceded" (Cohen 1982, 777). Walter Cohen is certainly correct in viewing Shakespeare's reversion to the idiom of romantic comedy in the fifth act as a "formal effort" intended to reconcile "the socially irreconcilable" (777). But he is wrong to make the Venetian ideological project appear indistinguishable from Shakespeare's considerably more complex enterprise. Shakespeare's attempt to erect formal defenses against the Christian, aristocratic ideology's "qualification by the alternative and partly oppositional conduct and values of other social classes" (781) strongly suggests his acknowledgment of the dominant ideology's attachment to the forms and functions of artifice, and casts his reluctant service on its behalf in sharp relief. Moreover, the oft-noted porousness of the fifth act's graceful but strained effort to suburbanize an essentially urban conflict testifies to the play's inability to contain or control the subversive energies released in the trial scene: energies that compel Shakespeare not only to approach what Cohen terms "the formal and ideological limits of Renaissance romantic comedy" (782) but to break through them to a consideration of their social limitations. Although we may feel, as Dollimore has observed, that such an effort at containment and closure "was a kind of condition for subversive thought to be foregrounded at all . . . , we should recognize too that such a condition cannot control what it permits: closure could never retrospectively guarantee ideological erasure of what, for a while, existed prior to and so independently of it" (1984, 60). It is for this reason, among others, that the mercilessly degraded figure of Shylock so often shadows the admittedly seductive revels in Belmont both in readings and productions of the play, and probably did the same in the Elizabethan playhouse where, like Marlowe's Barabas, he may well have served to focus the anti-aristocratic contempt of similarly excluded playgoers instead of simply serving as the focus of their anti-Semitism.

The Cunning of the Ideological

Although it has been argued that no form of articulate speech is free of the impress of some ideology, that there is, in short, no escape from ideology, the preceding discussion should demonstrate Shakespeare's consciousness of and detachment from the varieties of self-submersion pursued by a cast of characters whose characteristic eloquence is, not insignificantly, an endowment shared by their playwright-creator. One need not be innocent of ideology to anatomize its working in others, as our latter-day Marxist and anti-Marxist critics repeatedly remind us. And, in a strictly formal vein, Shakespeare was as incapable as Othello of telling a "round unvarnish'd tale" in a plain, unvarnished manner. I would, in any event, claim that Shakespeare inhabits the near side of a middle ground between detachment and submersion in terms of his ideological position. And I would add that his detachment has its closest Renaissance analogues in the habit of demystification and in the immunity against the power of appearances Machiavelli, Montaigne, and Marlowe appear to have enjoyed. This middle ground, and Shakespeare's place within it, are outlined by Macherey in a formulation that addresses the relationship between ideology and literary works in general:

> A work is established against an ideology as much as it is from an ideology. Implicitly, the work contributes to an exposure of ideology, or at least to a definition of it; thus the absurdity of all attempts to "demystify" literary works, which are defined precisely by their enterprise of demystification. (1978, 133)

It is especially important in the present context to note Macherey's emphasis on the engagement of literary works themselves in an "enterprise of demystification" since it both restores an interpretive priority to the primary text which much contemporary criticism would deny and redresses the traditional underestimation of a given text's subversive potential. Macherey's formulation also articulates a point I have been at pains to make throughout this chapter: namely that in the most obviously orthodox pronouncements of its set speakers, Shakespearean drama challenges dominant ideological structures in the very act of using them, indeed, in the very act of *being used* by them.[17] By placing these speeches and their speakers in dramatic contexts that variously contest, subvert, and even radically define the positions being advanced, Shakespeare makes the ideological as sustained a subject of dramatic interest as he elsewhere makes Hamlet's inde-cisiveness, Macbeth's ambition, and Timon's liberality. That he also makes himself the servant of the very structures he sets out to subvert, that he is often used by his own use of ideological formations to advance the posi-tions he exposes, is a consequence both of the cunning of the ideological itself and of Shakespeare's commitment to a "most potent art" whose for-mal devices necessarily resemble those of the dominant discourses it at-tempts to represent.[18]

Part IV

Corrupt Texts

7. Machiavel's Ghost

In this and in the succeeding chapter on *Timon of Athens*, I would like to return to one of this book's starting premises regarding the capacity of a theatrically oriented criticism to operate as a corrective to readerly defined habits of taste and judgment. My choice of plays is specifically dictated by the long-standing critical dissatisfaction with two playtexts that make un-usual claims on readers and audiences alike and have, for that reason among others, often been deemed "corrupt." It is, I should add, the man-ner in which critical disaffection has been expressed, and not merely the allegation of textual corruption, that has led to my selection of these works. Had I wished to address the current controversies regarding multiple texts and editing procedures, I would undoubtedly have chosen to discuss the competing versions of *King Lear* and *Doctor Faustus*.[1] I have, in fact, delib-erately avoided a sustained discussion of *Faustus* in particular, largely be-cause it has received compelling treatment elsewhere (see, e.g., Goldman 1977 and Snow 1977), but also because in repeated attempts to address the multiple playtexts of *Faustus* I count myself defeated.

My difficulties with *Doctor Faustus* have much in common with the dif-ficulties other scholars have had in coming to terms with *The Jew of Malta*. These difficulties may be reduced to a problem of tone and structure, as I suggest below, but they also derive from the kinds of formulations scholars have applied to "Marlovian rebels and skeptics." As Greenblatt writes:

> If Marlowe questions the notion of literature as cautionary tale, if his very use of admonitory fictions subverts them, he cannot dismiss the immense power of the social system in which such fictions play their part. Indeed the attempts to chal-lenge this system—Tamburlaine's world conquests, Barabas's Machiavellianism, Edward's homosexuality, and Faustus's skepticism—are subjected to relentless probing and exposed as unwitting tributes to that social construction of identity against which they struggle. (1980, 209)

For Greenblatt, it makes no great difference whether one approaches one's culture as "rebel or blasphemer" or as "dutiful servant" (see 1980, 253; and

p. 219 n. 18 below). Like the interventions Shakespeare stages in *Henry V* and elsewhere, the resistance of Marlowe's protagonists to Renaissance orthodoxies is doomed from the start by their subjection to cultural constructions that effectively define and contain their resistance. However compelling one may find this formulation, it casts Marlowe's protagonists in roles that have more to do with an abstract critical construction of resistance than with dramas that are materially realized in theaters where the "social construction of identity" must necessarily yield to the more provisional identifications that are negotiated by playgoers. The measure of Marlowe's protagonists may well be taken by anyone who has a mind to it, but the protagonists themselves operate in a domain where their identities are quite literally constructed by the audiences that interact with them. Faustus eludes my own interpretive grasp because for me he remains embedded in the world-historical stage Greenblatt has sketched out for him. Barabas, however, seems to me to elude Greenblatt's categorization precisely because, however accommodated he may be "to an abstract, anti-Semitic fantasy" of subjection (209), he ultimately becomes the occasion for the cultivation of other fantasies that are not as easily defined or contained by Renaissance orthodoxies as Greenblatt suggests. Barabas's capacity to outpace his subjection is, in turn, enabled by Marlowe's attempt to effect a departure of his own from conventional dramatic construction: one that specifically relies on the active participation of playgoers and seems specifically designed to disappoint the expectations of critics.

Breaking Form

Because the last three acts of *The Jew of Malta* are devoted to seemingly arbitrary exercises in sensationalism, and because they fail to sustain the promise of seriousness allegedly established in the first two acts of the play, they have often been critically singled out to testify to the artistic failure or textual corruption of the original play Marlowe wrote.[2] Taking my own critical precedent from scholars whose readings of *The Jew* have been influenced by T.S. Eliot's groundbreaking description of the play as "savage farce," I would submit that efforts to discredit Marlowe's artistic achievement or to question his play's textual authority are often based on a specific misreading of the play's first movement and on a more general failure to appreciate the play's peculiar approach to theatrical representation.[3] While the playtext may well seem corrupt in terms of a textual economy premised on unity of tone and content—and the play it maps may well seem corrupting insofar as it offers abundant "examples of imitation" for the criminally inclined or heterodox playgoer—*The Jew* is remarkably faithful to a theatrical economy premised on the pleasures of audience engagement.

In *The Jew of Malta*, Marlowe offers a free-form approach to theatrical representation which encourages the audience's unqualified engagement with the fantasies of power, play, and moral abandon he cultivates. Most plays, of course, employ the stage as a privileged area that liberates both actor and audience from the constraints of everyday life. But most plays also impose strict limits on the enjoyment of such liberation by means of a formal organization that prevents actor and audience from "going too far," that defends against the possibility of a collective fantasy getting out of hand. Although Marlowe furnishes the path to audience engagement with Barabas with a series of ambiguous cues and directives, he ultimately provokes only minimal resistance to the enjoyment of fantasy fulfillment his play affords. This is the case largely because the compositional basis for such resistance—namely, a formal structure that encourages imaginative and moral restraint—is a conspicuously missing link in the play's dramatic design. In *The Jew* Marlowe does not commit himself to the dramatic economy of checks and balances described by Freud. Instead, he develops a more flexible structure that effectively neutralizes the potential for audience resistance and that fails to identify or sustain an unequivocal source of moral gravity or authority that would serve to inhibit audience engagement.[4] The insistently shifting ground of the play works in concert with Marlowe's demystifying approach to the rhetoric of secular and religious authority to disarm the audience of its ties to defined structures of reception and belief. In exchange, Marlowe offers his audience the prospect of licensed play without engendering in that audience the fear of having its collective hand slapped, or of having its range of engagement confined to the margins of theatrical experience.

In brief, *The Jew of Malta* works within—indeed, establishes for itself—a theatrical mode that encourages and facilitates the informal interplay of fantasy, instead of the formal imitation of an action. It defines itself in opposition to standards of dramatic decorum that require a clearly delineated separation between audience and play by making the stage less an outpost of dramatically privileged activity than a medium for the communication of a sense of shared make-believe. The working premises of this admittedly extreme version of "non-illusory theatre" are fluidity of form and content;

flexibility of movement and perspective; and an approach to characterization that is audience, as opposed to stage, centered.[5]

The fractured logic of Marlowe's theatrical enterprise requires the audience-oriented critic to be particularly sensitive to the desire to develop a "normalized" reading of audience response. In order to meet *The Jew* on its own terms, we must ride the play as we ride an unfamiliar rapids, adjusting our position to fit the contours of its protean shape and texture. Marlowe negotiates his audience's passage to informed engagement by inducing it to surrender any preconceived notions about dramatic consistency it may harbor and to suspend its culturally prescribed prejudices against his play's eponymous protagonist and his ghostly sponsor, Machiavel. He proceeds by means of an opening series of false starts which produce corresponding shifts in dramatic perspective. This shifting of perspective generates, in turn, corresponding shifts in audience response that effectively prevent the playgoer from narrowly defining, and thereby limiting, the play's theatrical range and interests.

Marlowe's interest in the manipulation of plot for specific theatrical—as opposed to dramatic—ends is especially obvious in the first movement of the play. This first movement—roughly consisting of Machiavel's prologue, the establishment of Barabas's mercantile aspirations, and the demonstration of Ferneze's politic hypocrisy, followed by Barabas's resolute response—comprises a series of false starts that determines the theatrical orientation of the play as a whole. The opening scenes establish a pattern of discontinuity which disarms the audience of any expectation of strictly logical development and accommodates it to the acquired freedom of the play's evolving theatrical mode. The first phase of this process of mutual de-centering is appropriately delegated to the agency of Machiavel, whose capacity to unsettle received ideas Marlowe intends to exploit in his own effort to unsettle his audience.

Machiavel's Ghost

Machiavel appears onstage to establish relations between the play and its audience, to set a prevailing tone and supply a point of interpretive contact. Like the insidiously attractive Gaveston, Machiavel brings to bear on play and audience alike a particular style and set of associations which resonate throughout the production and influence our response to it. There is, to begin with, something casually disarming, even "ingratiating" about his first remarks and the manner in which he broaches them, "a suggestion of private knowledge shared by the few who happen to be in the theatre":[6]

> Albeit the world think Machiavel is dead,
> Yet was his soul but flown beyond the Alps,
> And, now the Guise is dead, is come from France
> To view this land and frolic with his friends.
> To some perhaps my name is odious,
> But such as love me guard me from their tongues,
> And let them know that I am Machiavel,
> And weigh not men, and therefore not men's words.
>
> (Prologue, 1–8)

Machiavel's ingratiating style virtually requires the instinctive admission of shared assumptions by pragmatic men who know the way the world works and revel in their respective disclosures. Cutting right to the heart of what often disguises men's hidden desires and doubts, he challenges the audience to declare its freedom from its observance of custom, form, and superstition in order to "frolic" with him in an intellectually licensed release from moral and religious restraint:

> Admired I am of those that hate me most.
> Though some speak openly against my books,
> Yet will they read me and thereby attain
> To Peter's chair; and, when they cast me off,
> Are poisoned by my climbing followers.
> I count religion but a childish toy
> And hold there is no sin but ignorance.
> Birds of the air will tell of murders past;
> I am ashamed to hear such fooleries.
>
> (Prologue, 9–17)

At the same time, the vision of the world Machiavel offers the audience is palpably sensational. When he says, for instance, that lapsed Machiavellians, upon casting him off, "Are poisoned by my climbing followers," Machiavel presents a cynically pragmatic picture of man as a small but ambitious backstabber, an opportunistic competitor for the highest anthill of power, that may have more currency in popular estimates of Medicean intrigue than in commonly perceived political fact. He thus reminds the audience that his status as an indifferent arbiter of reality, who turns all pretty fictions about honor and privilege to critical account, is coextensive with the distorting sensationalism of his theatrical self-presentation. The avowedly authoritative manner in which he demystifies religion and super-stition is, in other words, as much a theatrical style as it is a philosophic position. And, ultimately, it is Machiavel's style more than his position which induces the audience to suspend its own practical discriminations between fact and fantasy, and to enter more fully into the spirit of the proceedings.[7]

This becomes increasingly obvious when Machiavel intensifies his attack on cultural shibboleths in his analysis of the relation between power and the right to govern:

> Many will talk of title to a crown:
> What right had Caesar to the empery?
> Might first made kings, and laws were then most sure
> When, like the Draco's, they were writ in blood.
> Hence comes it that a strong built citadel
> Commands much more than letters can import;
> Which maxim had Phalaris observed,
> H'had never bellowed in a brazen bull
> Of great one's envy. O' the poor petty wights
> Let me be envied and not pitied.
>
> (Prologue, 18–27)

It is Machiavel's knowing insistence on his position that brings his message across to his audience, the incisive and unanswerable manner in which he frames it that persuades the audience to accede imaginatively to its cynical truth. Machiavel's (and Marlowe's) method here can be construed as an aggressive brand of seduction. Marlowe intimidates the audience into let-ting down its normative guards of repression and restraint by exploiting the attraction of Machiavel's appeal to its desire to feel fashionably up-to-date and worldly. Whatever one's normative persuasion, no one wishes to be thought a child playing with toys, or guilty of the sin of ignorance; nor would an interested playgoer wish to feel out of touch with the sense of common conspiracy that informs the prologue throughout and, to a great extent, the play. In generating this sense of conspiracy, Machiavel encour-ages all members of the audience—from professionals who recognize their own cynical practices in Machiavel's speech, to apprentices who may only be able to fantasize their release from social and religious constraints—to participate vicariously in the most sensational forms of forbidden behavior under the auspices of a worldly authority who sanctions their participation with the blessing of common sense.

Like Tamburlaine, Machiavel speaks in the compelling idiom of a discourse of mastery to an auditory apt, by its very presence in the theater, to prove reponsive to it. Unlike Tamburlaine, Machiavel does not use this discourse to mystify the structures of power or to intoxicate the playgoer with the promise of worldly advancement. He supplies a different kind of enabling medium through which playgoers may feel themselves empowered. The mastery he holds out for the playgoer to grasp has more to do with omniscience than it does with omnipotence. Machiavel invites the playgoer to experience the pleasure of release from moral and intellectual constraints, to entertain the feeling that he or she is bound by none of the illusions that bind more slavish spirits. He addresses the playgoer as one master-spirit might address another; he comes "to frolic with his friends."

In the final turn of the prologue, Machiavel pulls his "lecture" up short in order to establish a more problematic connection between himself and the nominal hero of the "tragedy" he is here to introduce:

> But whither am I bound? I come not, I,
> To read a lecture here in Britain,
> But to present the tragedy of a Jew
> Who smiles to see how full his bags are crammed,
> Which money was not got without my means.
> I crave but this: grace him as he deserves,
> And let him not be entertained the worse
> Because he favors me.
>
> (Prologue, 28–35)

Although Barabas does, in the course of the play, make bold statements and perform nefarious deeds which could be construed as Machiavellian in spirit, neither his words nor his deeds are consistent with the intellectual content and rather clinical perspective—in short, the "letter"—of Machiavel's lecture. Indeed, Barabas is first and foremost the victim of the Machiavellian policy of Ferneze (who is himself not a terribly adept Machiavellian, as critics have often observed). The chief indication that Barabas "favors" Machiavel as the prologue represents him is the sensational style with which Barabas pursues his vendetta against Ferneze, and the ruthless and resourceful manner in which he recovers and consolidates his wealth. The disparities that obtain between what Machiavel says and what Barabas does—between Machiavel's theory and Barabas's practice— are, in the end, symptomatic of Marlowe's attempt, first, to establish and, then, to divert into other channels the tendentiousness of the Machiavel- lian letter, while turning the sensationalism of the Machiavellian spirit to continuing theatrical account through the agency of Barabas. They are also symptomatic of Marlowe's effort to condition his audience to the discon- tinuities and fractured logic, the ironies and ambiguities, of the kind of play he is writing.

Marlowe's intentions may be discerned in the studied ambiguity of Ma- chiavel's statement that he comes "But to present the tragedy of a Jew / Who smiles to see how full his bags are crammed." Few playgoers at even the earliest stages of theatrical sophistication could fail to register this pal- pable image of pride going before the fall, or to notice that Machiavel's superficially partisan appeal on behalf of Barabas involves an element of disarming and casual indifference. In such a context, Machiavel's closing request—"And let him not be entertained the worse / Because he favors me"—may be taken as a rather insidious piece of irony in which sympathy is solicited for Barabas by a character whose attachments are notoriously suspect and whose pronouncements are proverbially misleading.

The spirit of irony and ambiguity established by Machiavel is sustained in the early scenes of the play-proper where Marlowe's working logic re- quires Barabas to be placed in a comparatively normative setting before he is sent off to pursue his abnormative exploits. Machiavel sets the tone by ambiguously claiming Barabas as a disciple and Marlowe elaborates on it by superimposing a comic exterior (Barabas's prominent "bottle-nose") on the more sober front of a no-nonsense merchant prince. The audience, which has been led to expect a recognizably Machiavellian intriguer, seems to get, as Alfred Harbage has noted, a relative innocent in his stead (1954, 55–58). Far more interested in the poetry of acquisition than in the prosaic shifts of power, Barabas presents himself as a supremely competent man of means who, from his island base in Malta, commands much of the trade and profit of the Mediterranean:

> Give me the merchants of the Indian mines
> That trade in metal of the purest mold,
> The wealthy Moor that in the eastern rocks
> Without control can pick his riches up

And in his house heap pearl like pebble-stones,
Receive them free and sell them by the weight.
Bags of fiery opals, sapphires, amethysts,
Jacinths, hard topaz, grass-green emeralds,
Beauteous rubies, sparkling diamonds,
And seld-seen costly stones of so great price
As one of them, indifferently rated
And of a carat of this quantity,
May serve in peril of calamity
To ransom great kings from captivity—
This is the ware wherein consists my wealth.

(I.i.19–33)

What is "normative" here is less the extent of Barabas's wealth and his connoisseurial approach to it than the fact that what animates Barabas is what animates "all the world," namely, "Desire for gold." Not only do Barabas's interests here seem infinitely removed from the competitive political infighting portrayed in Machiavel's lecture, but Barabas himself seems (rhetorically, if not physically) far above the roguish proportions of the character who will later poison a bevy of nuns and strangle a priest. As Barabas becomes caught up in describing the glittering inventory of his wealth, the effect is like that elicited by Tamburlaine's hypnotic contemplation of the glories of sovereignty and the Passionate Shepherd's depiction of an exquisite garden of delights. The difference is that in this instance Marlowe is setting his hero up for a fall as pronounced as that presumably suffered by the shepherd upon receipt of the nymph's reply. Marlowe is also setting up his audience by offering it the false scent of Tamburlainean rhetoric, the exciting prospect of "infinite riches," within a dramatic context that will soon transform Barabas's "little room" and everything it represents into the mere backdrop for Barabas's free-form pursuit of theatrical enormity. True to the emerging form of the drama, Marlowe first introduces the audience to a Machiavellian atmosphere of criminal complicity, then establishes a counter-climate of mercantile idealism for Barabas to inhabit, only to subject both to further shifts in perspective.

Once the play is put in motion, the peculiar nature and direction of its theatrical energy become more apparent. The movement of messengers into and out of Barabas's counting house and Barabas's subsequent encounter with his fellow Jews frame Barabas's first arguably Machiavellian pronouncement and lead to his first direct confrontation with Ferneze.

Prior to this encounter with Ferneze, Barabas addresses himself to the audience in a manner that seems designed at once to provoke and disarm its hostility to Jews:

> What more may heaven do for earthly man
> Than thus to pour our plenty in their laps,
> Ripping the bowels of the earth for them,
> Making the sea[s] their servants, and the winds
> To drive their substance with successful blasts?
> Who hateth me but for my happiness?
> Or who is honour'd now but for his wealth?
> Rather had I, a Jew, be hated thus,
> Than pitied in a Christian poverty:
> For I can see no fruits in all their faith,
> But malice, falsehood, and excessive pride,
> Which methinks fits not their profession.
> Haply some hapless man hath conscience,
> And for his conscience lives in beggary.
> They say we are a scatter'd nation:
> I cannot tell; but we have scambled up
> More wealth by far than those that brag of faith:
>   (I.i.105–21)

Barabas draws a sharp, if clearly self-interested, distinction here between Christian professions and the prevailing ways of a world that is itself largely Christian but dominated by purely material standards of value ("who is honour'd now but for his wealth?"). Identifying himself completely with those who make "the sea[s] their servants," Barabas plays on the audience's professed and unprofessed desire for a share of the world's bounty and of the happiness he possesses at the same time as he conceivably arouses its defensiveness at not being willing to endure the "beggary" that a life lived according to conscience promises. In so doing, he lays bare that disparity between Christian theory and practice which will claim him as a victim of his own conscientious presumption in his later interview with Ferneze. But he also lays claim to the position Machiavel has cultivated as a privileged demystifier of cultural pretensions and as a medium of audience engagement. Like Gaveston, Barabas approaches the audience from a position—in this case, that of the "bottle-nosed" Jew—that would appear marginal to its shared interests and preoccupations, but appeals to it in a way that "normalizes" its "suspect" fantasies and aspirations.

The reversal Barabas suffers at the hands of Ferneze in the play's second scene unsettles this tentative alliance of protagonist and playgoer by making the ambiguity of the play's treatment of Machiavellism keenly felt:

> *Bara.* Will you then steal my goods?
> Is theft the ground of your religion?
> *Fern.* No, Jew. We take particularly thine
> To save the ruin of a multitude,
> And better one want for a common good
> Than many perish for a private man.
> Yet, Barabas, we will not banish thee,
> But here in Malta, where thou gott'st thy wealth,
> Live still, and if thou canst, get more.
> (I.ii.95–103)

This exchange with Ferneze should check any residual determination an audience might have to come to terms with the play in a straightforward manner. Conditioned by the prologue to expect Barabas's Machiavellian manipulation of others, the audience is presented, instead, with his own manipulation at the hands of another stand-in Machiavel. This turn of events is apt to make playgoers feel that they are undergoing some kind of test in applied policy. Despite Machiavel's earlier endorsement of Barabas (and perhaps because of it if the endorsement is, in fact, ironic), it may seem that identifying or sympathizing with Barabas is not really the best policy to pursue. Gracing Barabas "as he deserves" may prove to be as ill-advised a pursuit as the statement is ambiguous. Since it is Ferneze, not Barabas, who seems at first (and proves to be in the end) the master Machiavellian, perhaps the audience is really meant to adopt *his* perspective in order to pass the test in applied policy.[8] On the other hand, the audience's recognition of the palpable hypocrisy of Ferneze's pronouncements may combine with a corresponding appreciation of Barabas's spirited and incisive indictment of Ferneze's Christian profession to disarm it of the impulse to identify with the master Machiavellian. To sustain this alternative, Marlowe evokes through Barabas a genuinely moving sense of outrage at his gross victimization by the powers-that-be, though Marlowe does not, admittedly, seek to maintain it for very long.

By encouraging several competing interpretations and authorizing none of them, Marlowe keeps his audience off balance and prevents it from making confident judgments or coming to anything other than provisional conclusions. He tests the audience by providing a dramatic analogue to the subversively appealing pronouncements of the prologue which is apparently meant to separate the dispassionate men from the compassionate boys. But he complicates the test by having it superficially redound against the credit of the nominal hero of the piece, whom we were previously enjoined to favor and with whom we are subsequently encouraged to identify.

The indeterminacy of this situation soon yields to the commanding momentum of Barabas's resolve to revenge his wrongs, a resolve undertaken in a manner that clearly links Barabas to other Marlovian protagonists who are impatient with the status quo and eager to assert their mastery over others. Calling his acquiescent fellow Jews "base slaves" and contending that "Barabas is born to better chance, / And fram'd of finer mould than common men" (I.ii.219–20), Barabas soon makes himself the primary focus of audience attention and the unquestioned medium of audience engagement as he "rouses" himself to action:

> And since you leave me in the ocean thus
> To sink or swim and put me to my shifts,
> I'll rouse my senses and awake myself.
> Daughter, I have it. Thou perceiv'st the plight
> Wherein these Christians have oppressed me.
> Be ruled by me, for in extremity
> We ought to make bar of no policy.
>
> (I.ii.266–73)

What J.B. Steane calls "the Machiavellian key-word," policy, initially seems to identify and encapsulate Barabas's decision to match ruthlessness with ruthlessness (1964, 183). But his adoption of the word and its association with premeditated and purposive activity does not summarily transform Barabas into a card-carrying Machiavellian, either in terms of the philosophic position of the prologue or of the applied philosophy of Ferneze. Barabas only superficially appropriates this term which, if taken too literally, distorts what he is actually about; he conveniently adopts the Machiavellian discourse without ever betraying any theoretical interest in the Machiavellian letter as it is represented in the prologue and applied by Ferneze. He is, however, clearly interested in exploiting the spirit of moral abandon commonly associated with Machiavelli to effect his own, far from philosophic ends and will, from this point forward, transform the exercise of policy into a complicated theatrical game, played for the sheer pleasure it brings in making fantastic pastime of the freedom of the stage.

Barabas's first act upon coming to resolution is, predictably, as comic as it is purposeful, as are most of the activities he subsequently pursues. As he hugs the bags of gold his daughter, Abigail, has secreted from their house, Barabas lacks completely the philosophic calm that would characterize any self-respecting Machiavellian on his way home from a privy poisoning or similarly felonious outing: "O girl! O gold! O beauty! O my bliss!" (II.i.54). The scene as a whole draws out to comically expansive proportions that pompous note of Machiavellian sophistication sounded in the prologue by reducing the scope of intrigue to the backstreet siege of a floorboard in a nunnery.[9] As such, it serves to draw the audience into complicity with the figure who operates so resourcefully in this shifting dramatic terrain. Barabas's earlier "innocence" also yields ground as Barabas compares himself, perversely mothering his bags of gold, to a lark mothering her young and sings a brief hymn to wealth that is, this time, more reminiscent of Volpone than of Tamburlaine:

> Now, Phoebus, ope the eyelids of the day,
> And for the raven wake the morning lark,
> That I may hover with her in the air,
> Singing o'er these as she does her young.
> *Hermoso placer de los dineros.*
>
> (II.i.60–64)

The sheer playfulness of these proceedings seems designed to disarm the audience of the temptation to view Barabas's behavior as symptomatic of the predictable changes wrought in an otherwise serious character by his gross victimization. Barabas emerges here as a protean character who can only be defined in terms of what he does and, hence, invites successive (and successively provisional) redefinition as he moves from one position to another. His dramatic identity exists in a state of continuing process indistinguishable from the fluid process that is the play.

Barabas's resourcefulness in pursuit of his vengeful designs against Ferneze and his exuberance in reveling in his exploits beyond the immediate needs of respective situations encourage the audience also to subordinate its collective identity to an equally "radical will to play" (Greenblatt 1978,

302). The false starts of the play's first movement stimulate the audience's active engagement in this interplay of fantasy by repeatedly denying the audience what Norman Holland calls the "conscious, intellecting" satisfactions of art of a conspicuously serious Apollinian persuasion (1968, 92). Once this denial is accomplished—that is, once the play persuades the audience of its freedom from the formal dramatic constraints that encourage resistance—the audience is effectively freed to pursue its "most primitive method of gratification" which is equivalent, in Holland's terms to a regression into fantasy (74). Since this structural denial coincides with the dramatic reduction of Ferneze—the play's only identifiable representative of secular and, potentially, moral authority—to the same level over which he presumes to preside, both play and audience are rendered independent of anything (short of dramatic closure) that might constrain or confine the imaginative commerce between them. In this manner Marlowe offers his audience the opportunity to play out on a grand scale both waking and unconscious fantasies whose range of expression is usually more limited.

Demystifying the Stage

The fantasy-gratifications that the play-proper encourages its audience to indulge are extensions of those that underlay the appeal of Machiavel's prologue: namely, the urge towards self-aggrandizement and the humbling of all opposition; the desire to feel secretly all-knowing, to gain power by withholding; the desire to role-play, to change shape at will, and, hence, to escape the confining (and legally enforced) self-definition of everyday life; the urge to release pent-up aggression against traditional sources of surveillance and repression (like the Church); and, more generally, to experience the sheer freedom of moral abandon. While the audience's capacity to find gratification in Barabas's fulfillment of such fantasies is initially enabled by their gradual indoctrination into Marlowe's seductive theatrical economy, it is enforced by Marlowe's broadly irreverent approach to established structures of meaning and belief, which is itself rooted in a genuinely Machiavellian detachment from their emotional sub-structure. As in *Edward II*, we find Marlowe curiously indifferent to the scenes of suffering Barabas's actions generate, and consistently committed to presenting such moments from the point of view of those who plot or execute them. Readerly oriented critics have often attempted to fill the spaces left vacant by Marlowe's emotional indifference either by demonizing him or by attributing to him the kind of normalizing intentions they associate with morally focused art. We would do better to note that Marlowe's indifference to suffering and his preference for villainy that is, in the words of Ithamore, "neatly plotted" and "well perform'd" (III.iii.2) work in concert to license the audience's participation in a theatricalized discourse of mastery that is neither particularly demonic nor angelic.

A fine example of how Marlowe's irreverence enforces his audience's "regression" into gratifying fantasy is provided in IV.i where "two religious Caterpillars" attempt to blackmail Barabas. The scene begins with Barabas effectively countering every opening the friars attempt and moving into even more effective dissembling when it becomes obvious that his guilt is known:

> *Bara.* I am a Jew, and therefore am I lost.
>   Would penance serve for this my sin,
>   I could afford to whip myself to death.
> *Itha.* And so could I; but penance will not serve.
> *Bara.* To fast, to pray, and wear a shirt of hair,
>   And on my knees creep to Jerusalem.
>   Cellars of wine, and sollars full of wheat,
>   Warehouses stuff'd with spices and with drugs,
>   Whole chests of gold, in bullion, and in coin,
>   Besides, I know not how much weight in pearl,
>   Orient and round, have I within my house;
>   . . . .
>   All this I'll give to some religious house,
>   So I may be baptiz'd, and live therein.
>   (IV.i.60–70;78–79)

Each of Barabas's lines implies a gesture, glance, or vocal modulation which makes his dissimulation obvious to an audience apt to revel in his hoodwinking of friars who have already given ample notice of a degeneracy that lacks Barabas's theatrical appeal and élan. The rhetorical movement of Barabas's central speech, with its abrupt juxtaposition of ascetic imagery and the compelling shapes of wealthy abundance, demonstrates Barabas's awareness of the friars' greedy motivations and his confidence that their false show of piety will soon be translated into blatant opportunism. The fervor and immediacy of the friars' response, voiced in the idiom of

schoolboys who have forgotten all their fine resolves, perfectly focuses
Marlowe's satirically liberating exposition of normative hypocrisy:

> Friar Jac.   O good Barabas, come to our house!
> Friar Barn.   O no, good Barabas, come to our house!
> (IV.i.80–81)

How the audience responds to the less obviously comedic murder of Friar
Barnardine that soon follows is dramatically premised on this subjection of
both friars to the status of greedy agents of competing religious institutions. Barnardine initially presents himself as a character with some claim
on our fellow feeling:

> Friar Barn.   What, will you have my life?
> Bara.   Pull hard, I say. You would have had my goods.
> Itha.   Ay, and our lives too: therefore pull amain.
> [They strangle him
> (IV.ii.20–22)

But he also represents the corrupt embodiment of an institution whose
constraining hold on the Elizabethan audience has already been deconse-
crated and cast off and is, psychologically speaking, being vividly degraded
once more. He thus serves as a perfectly appropriate object of the audience's desire to experience vicariously (and safely) the pleasure of transgression against a representative of religious authority:

> Bara.   Take him up.
> Itha.   Nay, master, be ruled by me a little. So, let him
>   lean upon his staff; excellent! he stands as if he
>   were begging of bacon.
> Bara.   Who would not think but that this friar liv'd?
> (IV.ii.24–28)

The resourceful stage-management of Ithamore transforms Barnardine
from a warm body that might evoke pity to the comic likeness of a scare-
crow or dummy. It serves as a tension-breaker that allows the audience
freer access to its own fantasies of aggression. If a playgoer is, nevertheless,
moved to commiserate with the friar as he is being murdered by Ithamore
and Barabas, he or she can hardly maintain such a position in the face of

Barnardine's posthumous victimization by his religious competitor, Friar Jacomo:

Bara.	Why, how now, Jacomo! What hast thou done?
Friar Jac.	Why, stricken him that would have struck at me.
Bara.	Who is it? Barnardine! now, out, alas, he is slain.
Itha.	Ay, master, he's slain; look how his brains drop out on's nose.

(IV.iii.14–18)

Ithamore's graphic observation foregrounds Jacomo's brutality at the same time as it helps frame it in the context of Barabas's broader function as the Machiavellian equivalent of a scourge of God. As the scene draws to a close, we find Barabas parodically mouthing the same kind of pious cant that was used to sanction his earlier victimization by Ferneze:

Friar Jac.	Villains, I am a sacred person, touch me not.
Bara.	The law shall touch you; we'll but lead you, we:
	'Las I could weep at your calamity!—
	Take in the staff too, for that must be shown:
	Law wills that each particular be known.

(IV.iii.40–44)

In assuming the legalistic tone of Ferneze, Barabas employs the law itself as an enabling medium for the expression of aggressive energies. In so doing, he not only demystifies the scene of his own victimization; he also demonstrates the range of freedom afforded to those who "hold there is no sin but ignorance." That he does so with no hint of the tendentiousness with which this remark is earlier made by Machiavel demonstrates the extent to which Barabas has translated the Machiavellian letter into the licensing agent of moral and theatrical abandon.

Barabas's command of theatrical resources is both challenged and confirmed in his response to the counter-intrigues of the gutter-Machiavellians, Pilia Borza and Bellamira, and in the grand design he pursues after his "comic resurrection" in the play's final movement (see Greenblatt 1978, 302–3). When Barabas is thrown over the walls of the city only to "spring up full of scheming energy," the play records yet another shift in dramatic perspective. "At this moment," Greenblatt writes, "the audience waits expectantly for Barabas' recovery, *wills* his continued existence, and hence identifies with him" (302–3). J.L. Simmons's reconstruction of the possible staging of this sequence provides a remarkably supportive framework for Greenblatt's observation. According to Simmons, we can reasonably assume that Barabas's "discovery" of himself may have occurred beyond the bounds of the platform stage, in the Yard which also accommodated members of the audience:

> The difficulty posed by the staging vanishes when one considers that the Yard could be occasionally employed as playing area and as an additional resource for spectacular effects involving entrances and exits. The Governor's satisfied "So" follows an easily achieved and theatrically effective representation of his command, the bodily ejection of Barabas from the platform stage into the Yard below. (1971, 96)

If Barabas is, in fact, thrown off the stage and into the lap of the audience, then his subsequent resolve to mount an all-out charge against his Christian tormentors may be said to be undertaken under the auspices of the playgoers who command the area in which he is resurrected:

> I'll be reveng'd on this accursed town;
> For by my means Calymath shall enter in:
> I'll help to slay their children and their wives,
> To fire the churches, pull their houses down,
> Take my goods too, and seize upon my lands.
> I hope to see the governor a slave,
> And, rowing in a galley, whipt to death.
>   (V.i.62–68)

Barabas's promise to turn the world upside down is likely to have had much the same appeal that Tamburlaine offered his audience, with the important difference that Barabas makes his resolve (if Simmons is right) from within the domain of the much-abused groundlings, whose sense of dispossession may be energized in a manner that differentiates them from the rest of the auditory that looks on (and down at them).[10]

If we choose not to make such distinctions regarding what is, after all, only a hypothetical audience operating in response to an hypothesis, then we may at least observe that the immediate juxtaposition of Barabas's fall and resurrection would have the effect of dissolving the conventional separation of stage and audience and of making the audience accomplices in what amounts to a siege of the stage. With the physical barriers between stage and audience temporarily withdrawn, the stage-space itself is demystified and the audience is invited to participate in a fantasy of action that is no longer confined to an enclosed and exclusive play-world. The functional "truss" of the stage becomes equivalent to the walls of Malta over which Barabas is thrown and through which Barabas burrows in order to re-enter the town as the leader of a band of Turks. According to Simmons, we have also to assume the probable existence of a trap door at the farther end of the tunnel through which Barabas intends to lead the Turks and with it an "inner-stage" from which Barabas can emerge:

> Fear not, my lord; for here against the sluice,
> The rock is hollow, and of purpose digg'd,
> To make a passage for the running streams
> And common channels of the city.
> Now, whilst you give assault unto the walls,
> I'll lead five hundred soldiers through the vault,
> And rise with them i' the middle of the town,
> Open the gates for you to enter in;
> And by this means the city is your own.
>
> (V.i.86–94)[11]

In each of these instances, the stage—like the play it formerly contained— becomes the protean ground upon which the audience is invited to assemble the speaking picture of Barabas's resourcefulness. Besieging a town and besieging a stage become, as Barabas presents them, equivalent actions. As the stage reveals this enlarged capacity to support a range of theatrical activity that extends outward to embrace the audience itself, the play, so to speak, "snaps," and presents itself as a shared enterprise that actively elicits and relies on the audience's imaginative investment and support. As Simmons observes:

> In the stage action, symbolizing his moral function, Barabas exuberantly leads all the Elizabethan young Turks in undermining the moral pretences of the Establishment and in opening the gates to "unseene hypocrisie." (1971, 104)

Barabas's ultimate defeat at the hands of the politic Ferneze is not necessarily indicative of Marlowe's attempt to slap the hands of an audience that has thoughtlessly allied itself with a rebellious rabble-rouser. Ferneze's

restoration of a more prosaic form of Machiavellism at play's end is insufficient to contain the unruly energies Marlowe has released in the course
of the drama. These energies have not only been directed against Ferneze's
efforts to mystify the nature of his hold on political power, but against the
inhibiting decorum of plays that keep audiences at a safe remove from total
engagement. As Barabas climbs the balcony of the stage in order to super-
vise the construction of his "set" in V.v, revels in his own resourcefulness,
and calls for the applause of his audience—"Now tell me, worldlings, un-
derneath the sun / If greater falsehood ever has bin done?" (V.v.49–50)—
he establishes an irrepressible sense of his own theatrical transcendence.
The fact that he is ultimately made to boil in his own cauldron constitutes
an obvious example of dramatic irony. But, theatrically, it may also constitute a final triumph. Barabas goes out as he came in—spectacularly—first
preening, then pleading, parading, and cursing; not with a whimper, but
with a bang: "Die, life! fly, soul! curse thy fill, and die!" (V.v.89). Like
Dickens's Mr. Krook, Barabas is undone by constant contact with the tools
of his own profession. He dies in character and because of it.

Appropriating Barabas's plot for his own ends, and attributing the destruction of Calymath's soldiers to "A Jew's courtesy" (V.v.108), Ferneze
smoothly reassumes control of Malta at play's end. He sounds the familiar
verities, praising God for his help in putting the devil back into his pot and
the Turk under his foot: "So, march away; and let due praise be given/
Neither to Fate nor Fortune, but to Heaven" (V.v.123–24). But in so doing,
he keeps faith with the spirit of cynical manipulation introduced at the start
by Machiavel and advanced at the level of sensationalism by Barabas. The
imaginative traffic between audience and play established by Machiavel
and stimulated by Barabas is thus not terminated by dramatic closure. The
more reserved Machiavellian, Ferneze, serves as their more prosaic heir-
apparent, hence, as a bridge or intermediary between the play and the
world outside the theater to which the audience is about to return. Machiavellian influence endures as well in the audience's conditioned perception of the deceptiveness and frequently vile underside of civilized surfaces,
and in their experience of the pleasure that release from normative constraints may bring. In this respect, closure simply slows down the momentum of a process that conceivably maintains itself at a lower ebb in the
psyche of the playgoer. Its failure to operate as an effective containing
mechanism confirms Anthony Munday's charge that "The webs [of plays]
are so subtilie spun, that there is no man that is once within them, that can
avoide them without danger" (142).

8. The Unaccommodating Text

Even in a book that claims to depart from conventional comparative procedures, one might expect a comparative appraisal of Shakespeare's *Merchant of Venice* to follow a chapter on Marlowe's *Jew of Malta*. I choose not to satisfy such expectations both because such appraisals have already been made by myself and others (see, e.g., Cartelli 1988, Charney 1979, and Shapiro 1988) and because it is a methodology, not a theory of influence, that I am attempting to delineate and apply here.[1] *Timon of Athens* is my play of choice because its exceptional status in the Shakespeare canon—and its marginal status in the repertory of frequently produced Shakespearean playtexts—makes it unusually suitable for treatment from a perspective that makes exceptional claims of its own. I am especially interested in employing *Timon* as a culminating challenge to the claims I have made regarding the role played by pleasure in theatrical transactions since pleasure is the first word audiences (if not readers and critics) would apply to *The Jew* and the last word anyone would apply to a drama which, for this reason among others, has occupied so anomalous a place in the Shakespearean canon and repertory.

The Trouble with *Timon*

The "corrupt text on the subject of absolute corruption" that is *Timon of Athens* has attracted a disproportionately small number of sympathetic scholars to the task of making dramatic sense of the play's own disproportionate blend of "icy precepts" and "sweet degrees."[2] The text's very corruption, moreover, has encouraged some of the play's strongest supporters to attempt the critical transformation of this obviously unpolished work into an image and likeness that accords with prevailing Shakespearean standards of dramatic integrity and decorum.[3] It has led others, equally sympathetic but more interested in what the play itself has to say, to explore the underpinnings and motivations of Shakespeare's approach to his dramatic art (see, e.g., Handleman 1979 and Fly 1976, 117–42). But probably the most common tendency of recent Shakespeare criticism has been simply to dismiss the play from sustained consideration, not on the basis of its textual corruption, but on account of its apparent single-mindedness, its unaccommodating commitment to its protagonist's stubbornly inflexible point of view. Norman Rabkin formulates his own version of this critical position in the following terms:

> The trouble with *Timon of Athens* is that it is not complementary . . . at no point do we encounter such tensions as Shakespearean tragedy has elsewhere involved us in. . . . Because Shakespeare seems to assume a simple moral position, the play is uniquely unable to call into question the nature of being. It never seems . . . to get down to the unresolvable conflicts with which . . . *King Lear*, *Coriolanus*, *Antony and Cleopatra*, and *Othello* are primarily concerned. (1967, 193)

Rabkin articulates this position with his usual judiciousness and precision; he describes in a very straightforward manner the problem many of us have had in attempting to reconcile *Timon* with plays that hold both the mind and the stage with greater power and authority. But in basing his dismissal of *Timon* on its lack of complementarity (an arguable position in its own right), Rabkin localizes the "trouble" with *Timon* in the context of the play's failure to provide what the critic is looking for and has come to expect, and thus transfers to the play what may well be the trouble with his critical ideology.[4] Since *Timon* does not seem to generate "unresolvable conflicts" of the variety associated with more canonically respectable texts, the conflicts that the play does generate are ignored and the play itself is effectively excluded from critical discourse. In the process, *Timon* is implicitly assigned the status of an unaccommodating text, that is, a text that is inconsistent with the prevailing critical consensus defining what a Shakespearean tragedy is or should be, does or should do. Rabkin's privileging of complementarity thus serves the combined purpose of preserving a canonical distinction and a critical predisposition at the expense of sacrificing a potentially provocative critical encounter with a text that may render suspect the whole process by which such judgments were arrived at in the first place. Given the kind of treatment it has been accorded, *Timon* might just as well have been written by Marlowe.

In taking issue with *Timon*'s critical reputation in this manner, I do not mean to suggest that *Timon* is *not* as single-minded a play or as unaccommodating a text as Rabkin implies; nor do I mean to set into motion a process that will raise *Timon*'s value in the critical marketplace or in the Shakespearean canon. Rather, I mean to clear interpretive ground for readings of *Timon* that are more consistent with the play's peculiar dramatic aims and organization than most past readings have been, and to do so in a manner that is less committed to a critical idiom and ideology that are alien to the peculiar nature of playtexts. It seems to me that what finally distinguishes *Timon* from Shakespeare's other tragedies is not its failure but its refusal to be complementary in the way Rabkin describes. In *Timon* Shakespeare appears deliberately to refuse to accommodate the disruptions of tragic experience to the consolations effected by dramatic strategies that seek to redeem or, at least, moderate the expression of waste or loss. This refusal is combined in the play with an equally bold attempt on Shakespeare's part to have his audience assume an unusually active role in monitoring and evaluating its own responses to the play's protagonist, who similarly refuses to accommodate himself to conventional expectations, but who has no sustained rival in his claim on audience sympathy and attention. The unaccommodating text of the drama becomes in this fashion the occasion for a radical intervention in the prevailing structure of theatrical experience, one that requires the play's audience both to identify, and to engage in a critical dialogue, with a character who is at once its bane and its ideal, its representative and its accuser, the anatomizer and embodiment of its own values and assumptions.⁵ The dialogue between competing points of view that is characteristic of Shakespearean dramaturgy becomes displaced here by a dialogic encounter between a pleasure-denying protagonist and the pleasure-seeking playgoer. This experiment is radical to the extent that it remains faithful to the dramatic logic of its own conclusions, denying Timon as it denies its audience recourse to strategies that might serve to redeem, resolve, or otherwise reduce the prevailing pressure of bitterness and rage which firmly establishes itself at the close of the play's third act and maintains its hold on the drama to the end.

It is, of course, *Timon*'s unswerving devotion to its chosen dramatic idiom that is responsible for its historic failure to command an "understanding auditory" fully sympathetic to what has often been construed as a denial of art itself. As Susan Handelman states in one of the more penetrating appraisals of the play:

> In *Timon of Athens* disillusion is absolute, no substitute is acceptable, there are
> no rituals of atonement, no provisions for mourning. The play is less about the
> experience of loss itself than a demonstration of the rage which refuses to accept

loss. Perhaps this is why it is generally considered to be a bad play—it does not do what we expect of art in general: help us to accept loss. (1979, 47–48)

In making her point, Handelman seems to assign primary responsibility for *Timon*'s failure to find its audience to the play itself, specifically to the play's refusal to accommodate itself to its audience's psychological needs and aesthetic expectations. But her statement also implies that *Timon*'s refusal to "help us to accept loss" is reciprocated by our own refusal to meet the unusual challenges posed by a play that upsets our conventional notions about the uses of art. Although Handelman might well object to the way I am using her argument, she provides a crucial insight into the critical tendency to deny or dismiss works of art that define themselves in terms of refusal or rejection, instead of conforming to an aesthetic of accommodation or compromise upon which Shakespeareans in particular have come too often to rely.[6] In refusing to provide "rituals of atonement" consistent with this aesthetic, *Timon* effectively calls the aesthetic itself into question, attempts to extend the range of tragic expression beyond the pale of dramatic proprieties that serve to defend or protect audiences from unmediated engagement in tragic experience. In so doing, *Timon* may, admittedly, be demanding more than audiences are normally accustomed to give; it may require playgoers to break critical habits of mind that are ineluctably tied to their psychological need for defenses against precisely the kinds of denial with which *Timon* is preoccupied.

It is the possibility that such habits of mind could, indeed, be broken (especially at a time when playwrights like Marlowe and Shakespeare were actively involved in the demystification of cultural assumptions) that I intend to entertain in the following in order to provide *Timon* with the kind of "reading" it deserves: a reading premised on the notion that in *Timon* Shakespeare is consciously engaged in revising his own aesthetic in an effort to bring "unaccommodated man" into the affective orbit of an auditory made susceptible to his aims by its very presence in the theater. Such a notion clearly suggests an insight into Shakespeare's intentions that no one can claim with assurance. I make provisional claim to such insight here in order to give Shakespeare's facility as a playmaker priority in discussing the play's dramatic effects, and also to counter the tendency to see in the playtext's corruption evidence of a compositional breakdown, the formal remains of an unresolved conflict between Shakespeare's actual or original intentions and the intractable matter he had taken for his subject. Of this theory's proponents, Handelman makes the most persuasive case:

All the questions about authorship, which stem from the many confusions and disjunctions in the text, indicate an unfinished play which somewhere broke down, would not allow itself to be composed. But that indeed . . . is itself what the play is about—a breakdown of all those ways in which rage, pain, and loss can somehow be accepted, made sense of, transformed into life-affirming energies. (1979, 48)

Handelman again seems perfectly correct in respect to "what the play is about." But when she connects the play's dramatic breakdowns with a sympathetic breakdown in the compositional process itself, she makes Shakespeare more victim than master of his own intentions and defines the play in the same rhetoric of accommodation that gave us *Timon*'s lack of complementarity.[7] Shakespeare does, of course, go to some trouble in the text of the play as we have it to mediate his audience's generally inescapable engagement with Timon; the Alcibiades subplot, the "normative" incursions of Flavius, as well as the sometimes nagging monomania of Timon himself, all seem to constitute gestures in this direction. But each also seems sufficiently half-hearted and ambiguous to suggest that Shakespeare did not intend his audience to escape so easily from the disturbing implications of Timon's extreme position, which is, in the end, more a culmination of, than a divergence from, Shakespeare's preoccupation (in the compositional period in question) with tragic predicaments and the dramatic forms appropriate to express them. It may, therefore, be more reasonable to assume that compositional strategies which permitted Shakespeare to provide at least the outlines of reconciliation in the "great" tragedies either proved insufficient in relation to *Timon*, or—an alternative I find more convincing—simply inappropriate to the kind of play Shakespeare was writing. The inefficacy of such strategies in *Timon*, rather than serving as evidence of Shakespeare's inability to achieve his intentions, may, in short, help us better to understand just what his intentions were.[8]

Richard Fly approaches the problem of intentionality with a more obvious regard for Shakespeare's control over his own experiment, but, like Handelman, ultimately identifies the process of accommodation as basic to tragedy itself:

In his monomaniac actions and language Timon has been slowly destroying himself as a dramatic entity by attacking the very structure that sustains his being. Shakespeare's apparent willingness to attend the misanthrope on his drift towards non-being suggests his own temporary commitment to a concomitant aesthetic suicide. He appears to have designed a play licensed to pursue its own generic collapse by a perverse rejection of its own medium. (1976, 139)

Especially noteworthy in Fly's formulation is his explicit identification of Timon's rejection of the world's values with Shakespeare's rejection of his own aesthetic standards, his designation as "perverse" Shakespeare's refusal to provide either his play or his audience with what Fly terms "a middle ground of compromise and moderation" (125). The question Fly provokes here is whether "Shakespeare's apparent willingness to attend" Timon so unconditionally really must issue in "a concomitant aesthetic suicide," in "a play licensed to pursue its own generic collapse," as opposed to encouraging the collapse and consequent revision of our own critical categories.

Fly avoids dwelling on the consequences of his own formulation by critically disengaging Shakespeare from Timon in his discussion of the closing movement of the play where he contends that "Timon succumbs to suicidal silence, but Shakespeare goes on to finish the play in a new key" by returning "to the abandoned world of mediation, the carefully excluded 'middle of humanity'" embodied by the now moderate and forgiving Alcibiades (140). But those of us who are less willing than Fly to accept the apparent even-handedness of a character whom Kenneth Burke has aptly termed a "winsome rotter" (1966, 119), and, hence, are less persuaded of the efficacy of what Handelman describes as "an artificial and uncertain resolution" (1979, 67), must continue to dwell on the question Fly has answered to his own satisfaction. We must also begin to examine the ways in which a play that so consistently resists accommodating itself to critical rituals of atonement—framed in the idiom of complementarity, compromise, and mediation—may actually open up areas of theatrical experience left unexplored by more obviously balanced dramatic productions.

The Unaccommodating Text

At the end of *King Lear*, Edgar offers a powerful corrective to Albany's understandably human but dramatically inappropriate attempt to compensate for a tragic loss by formalizing his response to it: "The weight of this sad time we must obey, / Speak what we feel, not what we ought to say" (V.iii.328–29). Although his words are themselves structured in the form of a rhyming couplet, Edgar is ostensibly rejecting here what Nietzsche calls "the mendacious finery" that is the conventional appliance of "the man of culture" in favor of "the unvarnished expression of the truth," which is, in Nietzsche's terms, the true "sphere of poetry" (*Birth of Tragedy*, 61). Edgar's corrective resonates throughout the second half of *Timon of Athens*, but nowhere more crucially than in Timon's interview with the Poet and the Painter in V.i and in his dialogue with Apemantus in IV.iii. In the former scene, Timon responds to the Poet's chronically verbose hypocrisy—"I am rapt, and cannot cover / The monstrous bulk of this ingratitude / With any size of words"—by offering a corrective of his own regarding the frequently duplicitous relationship that obtains between words and feelings: "Let it go naked, men may see't the better" (V.i.63–66). Without overrating the importance of this one statement in relation to the play as a whole, I would submit that its advocacy of "unvarnished expression" occupies a pivotal role in Shakespeare's attempt to give the unaccommodating spirit of Edgar's remark a more sustained hearing than it could receive within the confines of the earlier play.[9]

Letting feelings "go naked" is not, of course, a characteristic procedure of art. Indeed, it can, as Fly suggests, constitute a "rejection" of artistic control that could be construed as "perverse" if in the act of rejection it fails to communicate its purpose to an audience. But there is a second half to Timon's statement that endows his injunction with just such a purpose, and thus makes it appear less a rejection of art than a rejection of the gilded sophistries that pass themselves off as art. The Poet should, according to Timon, let his ingratitude go naked that "men may see't the better," so that it may be made plain and clearly discernible to everyone, hence, impossible to deny. It is here, I believe, that Timon's voice can be confidently identified with that of its author whose evolving aesthetic involves the same uncompromising approach to tragic experience that Timon brings to his succession of dramatic encounters. Shakespeare seems to be engaged here in rewriting the terms of his own relationship to an art that, like the fabrications of ideology, readily subordinates the "real conditions of existence" to an "imaginary distortion" of the same. That such an approach continues to elicit far more negative critical appraisal than the similarly disturbing but comparatively more "complementary" *King Lear* suggests that we are, ourselves, more like the Painter and the Poet than we are like Edgar or Timon. As a consequence of our general uneasiness with feelings that go naked and truth-claims that remain unvarnished, we are likely to be on the lookout, throughout the second half of *Timon*, for other characters with whom we can identify our interests and for dramatic encounters that will serve either to discredit Timon, or to place him at a sufficient remove from us so that he might become the object of our critical scrutiny, instead of our anatomizer and accuser.

Shakespeare seems to supply just such relief when in IV.iii Apemantus delivers what has appeared to many to be the fatal critical blow against Timon's uncompromising indictment of the world's corruption:

> The middle of humanity thou never knewest, but
> the extremity of both ends. When thou wast in thy
> gilt and thy perfume, they mock'd thee for too
> much curiosity; in thy rags thou know'st none, but
> art despis'd for the contrary.
>
> (IV.iii.301–5)

These are strong and working words. They appeal not only to our need to reduce Timon to manageable proportions, but to our prejudice against people who, like Timon, have never had to endure the perhaps pettier but more perdurable round of daily defeats and frustration, who, suffering now from a loss of fortune, never before had a loss to contend with. In short, Apemantus speaks on behalf of our collective desire to undermine the authority of Timon's pronouncements, to invalidate what he says by invalidating who he is. There is, moreover, a certain justice in this, especially given the arrogance and condescension of Timon's immediately prior attempt to discredit Apemantus: "Thou art a slave, whom Fortune's tender arm / With favour never clasp'd, but bred a dog" (IV.iii.252–53).

Justice, however, seems meant to occupy but a secondary role in our response to the extended address of Timon's that these harsh words initiate. For in the verses that follow, Shakespeare endows Timon's speech with a power, grace, and authority that transcend the ongoing battle of mutual abuse and recrimination. In so doing, he cultivates in Timon a sense of self-possession and dignity that overarches the extreme positions Timon has hitherto inhabited and which he will maintain even in the face of Apemantus's potent counterattack:[10]

> Hadst thou like us from our first swath proceeded
> The sweet degrees that this brief world affords
> To such as may the passive drugs of it
> Freely command, thou wouldst have plung'd thyself
> In general riot, melted down thy youth
> In different beds of lust, and never learn'd

The icy precepts of respect, but followed
The sugar'd game before thee. But myself—
Who had the world as my confectionary,
The mouths, the tongues, the eyes and hearts of men
At duty, more than I could frame employment:
That numberless upon me stuck, as leaves
Do on the oak, have with one winter's brush
Fell from their boughs and left me open, bare,
For every storm that blows—I, to bear this,
That never knew but better, is some burthen.
Thy nature did commence in sufferance, time
Hath made thee hard in 't. Why shouldst thou hate men?
They never flatter'd thee.

(IV.iii.254–72)

This speech, providing as it does an influential preface to Apemantus's re-joinder, constitutes a pivotal moment in the play's complex shaping of au-dience response. The excessive animus toward Apemantus which it betrays both at its beginning and end—"Hence, be gone! / If thou hadst not been born the worst of men, / Thou hadst been a knave and flatterer" (IV.iii.276–78) are the bitter words with which it concludes—may, as noted above, serve to alienate further a playgoer who is not sympathetic in the first place to Timon's bias in favor of the prerogatives of privilege. But I believe that this speech is intentionally geared to break down even this playgoer's resistance to Timon—and to do so *before* Apemantus has an op-portunity to respond—by basing its appeal not on a conscious evaluation of what Timon says, but on a more immediate participation in the story he tells.

Shakespeare proceeds here in a manner consistent with his ongoing at-tempt to make his protagonist's approach to the audience both dramati-cally direct and theatrically provocative, but also in a manner uncharacteristic of his writing for Timon in the second half of the play, which is usually phrased in the shrill idiom of invective. Timon seems meant to surprise us as he recalls with a contagious nostalgia—and, in the process, conjures up in remarkably appealing terms—the life of pleasure he lived when all the world was his "confectionary." His speech awakens in us a shared sympathy for that life (based, perhaps, on our own common fan-tasies about our respective "golden ages"), which works to disarm us of the censorious attitude we may have developed in regard to Timon's earlier prodigality. Clearly, Timon is not "going naked" here in the same way he later suggests the Poet should. But he is going naked in a different sense by giving us sustained insight into an interior life (inhabited by his own common fantasies) which most critics of the play refuse to believe exists. When Timon speaks of "The mouths, the tongues, the eyes and hearts of men" that once surrounded him with a suggestively maternal warmth but have now disappeared, he recreates for his audience its own inner narrative of security and separation, compelling it to identify its earliest experience of loss with his present state of abandonment, even though, on a practical level, the men of whom Timon speaks were mere servants and suitors "At duty." Timon thus effectively privileges (as I do here) a psychological reading of his own experience that strategically mystifies the economic basis of his entitlement and, consequently, enables the playgoer to participate in it.

This largely unconscious (though, perhaps, consciously wrought) bonding between actor and audience is, I would submit, precisely the "stuff" theatrical experience is made on, a point easy to lose sight of when speeches like this one are read with a more attentive regard for verbal display than for a play's interactive dynamics. The dynamics of this moment are such that after Timon reaches the peak of his expression of abandonment—in the evocative tree / leaves simile—the point he has been moving toward— "I, to bear this"—is made with far greater impact than it could command were we to encounter it in complete isolation from performative considerations. In short, these too are strong and working words and, as such, they make a case for Timon's "extremity of both ends" that no representative of the "middle of humanity" can wholly discredit, especially when the latter must compete with the audience's desire for engagement, which generally proves a more dominant force than resistance in the economy of theatrical experience.

In its full performative context, Apemantus's critique of Timon thus loses a great deal of the choric authority that is frequently claimed for it. We may, of course, continue to rely on it as a buffer between ourselves and Timon's more icy precepts, as an endorsement of an ethic of accommodation that opposes itself to Timon's rather subversive claim on our sympathies. But to do so would be at odds with Shakespeare's prevailing approach to such situations throughout the second half of the play, which involves turning our search for areas of relief from Timon into a renewed respect for Timon's rejection of the same. In the present instance, we first expect Apemantus to drive Timon out of his misanthropic humor but actually witness a reversal of roles. In an ironic variation on Jonsonian practice, the "fantasist" eventually confutes the "counterfantasist" and disarms him of his presumptive claim to the role of professional demystifier by revealing his own embeddedness in a "middle of humanity" he once professed to disdain.[11]

An even more pronounced reversal characterizes Timon's encounter with Alcibiades in the first half of IV.iii, which, like the ensuing encounter with Apemantus, focuses on a normative character with whom an audience might easily identify its interests, but whose own interests come to seem increasingly mercenary. Critics who like to envision Alcibiades as the restorative embodiment of balance and moderation at play's end tend to pass lightly over the company Alcibiades keeps in this scene, and thus fail to make the connection Timon makes in linking the soldier's pursuits with those of his prostitute companions:

> I know thee too, and more than I know thee
> I not desire to know. Follow thy drum;
> With man's blood paint the ground, gules, gules.
> Religious canons, civil laws are cruel;
> Then what should war be? This fell whore of thine
> Hath in her more destruction than thy sword,
> For all her cherubin look.
>
> (IV.iii.57–64)

Restating here the critical equation of war with lechery that Thersites makes in *Troilus and Cressida*, Timon speaks neither in the idiom of the professional detractor, whose satiric thrusts are indistinguishable from sarcasm, nor in that of the professional moralist, who views the world's "sweep of vanity" from the patronizing perspective of an outsider. Rather, Timon speaks in the more authoritative vein of an exile who has become sufficiently estranged from the world he formerly inhabited—a world he once held to be a "confectionary" of "sweet degrees"—to be able to anatomize its most common values and assumptions. Indeed, Timon "reads" the face of Alcibiades's "fell whore" with the same interpretive facility Macbeth brings to the reports of Duncan's murder and Lady Macbeth's death. And though his insight into the cruelty of religious and civic institutions may be more sudden and unmediated than the jeremiads King Lear delivers in the course of his tragic education, this is largely the result of the dramatic shorthand Shakespeare employs throughout *Timon* to move his former

concern with narrative development into the background, and to fore-
ground what is most unaccommodating in his dramatic text.

Surely, Timon *is* too wholesale in his condemnations, and Alcibiades
does, conceivably, remain a more sympathetic character than Timon portrays. But this does not change the fact that most of what Timon asserts
constitutes a faithful anatomy of the world the play presents and of the
characters who inhabit it, as the following, consciously enigmatic exchange
seems meant to illustrate:

> *Alcib.*   I have heard in some sort of thy miseries.
> *Tim.*   Thou saw'st them when I had prosperity.
> *Alcib.*   I see them now; then was a blessed time.
> *Tim.*   As thine is now, held with a brace of harlots.
>
> (IV.iii.78–81)

Timon's attempt here to turn upside-down Alcibiades's notions about what
constitutes misery and what constitutes prosperity meets with a complete
lack of understanding on the part of a character presumably meant to embody the audience's own normative estimate of the same. This being the
case, what could Shakespeare have expected his audience's response to be?
Clearly, Shakespeare would be asking as much of his audience as Timon is
asking of Alcibiades were he to require it to reverse entirely its most in-
grained notions about what *really* constitutes "a blessed time." The point
is that Shakespeare *is* asking a lot of his audience, perhaps more than Timon (who knows very well that "then" had its share of blessings, as his
later discourse on its "sweet degrees" makes plain) is asking of the irrevers-
ibly limited Alcibiades, who is more interested in Timon's gold than his
"counsel" (IV.iii.131).

Timon's baiting of Alcibiades seems intended to provoke the audience
into making the kind of intellectual leap Alcibiades is plainly incapable of
making. It is specifically designed to draw the audience out of its compla-
cent identification with a set of values Timon is in the process of trans-
valuing and with a way of life Alcibiades is seeking to sustain. Shakespeare
provides Timon with appropriate tools for his seemingly quixotic task by
making the rest of Alcibiades's visit demonstrate that his values are, indeed,
"held with a brace of harlots." As the scene proceeds, and Phrynia and
Timandra respond to Timon's injunction, "Be strong in whore," by saying,
"Believe 't that we'll do anything for gold" (IV.iii.143, 152), the audience's
normative associations with Alcibiades are performatively broken down

and displaced by the performatively more appealing spirit of indignation embodied and advanced by Timon, whose anatomy of the world now commands an enhanced admiration and respect.

The Pleasures of Invective

This dramatic transaction (like others in the play, including Timon's exchange with Apemantus) is complicated by the extreme form Timon's indignation takes and its unpredictable effect on an audience conceivably unaccustomed to identifying its interests with so harsh and unrelenting a dramatic vehicle as invective:

> Consumptions sow
> In hollow bones of man; strike their sharp shins,
> And mar men's spurring. Crack the lawyer's voice,
> That he may never more false title plead,
> Nor sound his quillets shrilly. Hoar the flamen,
> That scolds against the quality of flesh,
> And not believes himself. Down with the nose,
> Down with it flat, take the bridge away
> Of him that, his particular to foresee,
> Smells from the general weal.
>   (IV.iii.153–62)

Probably the most common strategy employed by playwrights who wish to have their audience identify with a character onstage is to make that character the walking embodiment of a fantasy it too desires to see fulfilled. Such a character must be able to awaken and bring to the surface impulses or aspirations that playgoers generally repress in their daily lives, and he must give these feelings at least the illusion of unbridled play before it is time to restrain them at play's end. In this way the playwright provides his audience with an area of licensed relief from the pressures of the quotidian, with a temporary, enabling haven from the limitations of its daily round, and gives it an ephemeral, though sustaining, taste of freedom.

In *Timon of Athens* Shakespeare seems to have set himself the task of experimenting with and, in the process, of complicating his usual procedures. From the start, Timon's position in relation to the audience is rendered ambiguous. On the one hand, he regales both on- and off-stage audiences with visions of apparently unlimited abundance, and should, on that count alone, provide for most playgoers a realization of their dreams of wealth-in-idleness and for some a composite projection of an all-caring, all-providing, rather maternally inclined father.[12] On the other hand, Shakespeare discernibly tries throughout the first act to inhibit our impulse to identify with Timon by warning us that "admiring Timon the prodigal is precisely what we are *not* intended to do" (Lancashire 1970, 42).[13] This warning is, moreover, conveyed as clearly by Timon himself as it is by the sarcastic Apemantus, the concerned steward, Flavius, and the flagrant insincerity of Timon's suitors. What Terry Eagleton terms Timon's "projected egoism" may generate in performance the feeling that Timon's generosity is as remarkably self-satisfied and self-satisfying as it is ingratiating, and that it constitutes a characteristic gesture of self-aggrandizement and exclusivity which seeks to invalidate the possibility of magnanimity in others (1967, 172–76). As Timon says to Ventidius as the latter attempts to repay a loan, "there's none / Can truly say he gives, if he receives" (I.ii. 10–11), a remark Ventidius seems to have expected, indeed, to have banked on, much as Timon seems to expect from it a round of applause (which a performance-oriented reading of the ensuing nine lines suggests he gets, a standing ovation in fact).

The self-aggrandizing pomposity of Timon's liberality thus serves to undermine the very fantasy he embodies, making it an object of the audience's critical scrutiny. When Timon later effects his dramatic transformation into a misanthropist, the audience is consequently prepared to accept this reversal as the logical realization of its own suspicions, as a turn in the performance it has anticipated and, perhaps, even desired. Compelled by the failure of the original fantasy to do more than provoke its ambivalence, the audience plays a cooperative role in the reformulation of that fantasy into more immediately identifiable terms. This reformulated counterfantasy of misanthropy exploits the audience's cultivated distrust in the duplicitous arrangements of society as the first three acts of the play present them, as well as its equally cultivated desire to maintain its imaginative ties with a character who has at least stimulated its capacity for engagement and who now defines himself in direct opposition to duplicity itself. The appeal of this counterfantasy is communicated to the audience through the immediate and unambivalent medium of invective, which supplies the audience the vicarious means to express its own understandable resentment at the dissolution of its original terms of engagement with the play and, perhaps, its dissatisfaction with the inequitable social and economic arrangements that prevail outside the theater.

If we return now to the problem raised by Timon's insistent reversion to invective in the second half of the play, we may better appreciate how a mode of speech that appears in the abstract to constitute an alienating approach to theatrical experience may performatively serve to express the audience's own interests. Clearly, a device such as Marlovian hyperbole would seem to have more to recommend it than does invective in the context of a theatrical environment uniquely disposed to raise an audience's sights above and beyond the struggles and pressures of the quotidian. But, as Kenneth Burke contends in a remarkably probing essay on *Timon*, invective may claim an appeal of its own which is not as immediately obvious as the appeal of hyperbole:

> *Invective*, I submit, is a primary "freedom of speech," rooted extralinguistically in the helpless rage of an infant that states its attitudes by utterances wholly unbridled. In this sense, no mode of expression could be more "radical," unless it be the closely allied motive of sheer *lamentation*, undirected wailing. . . .
>
> Obviously, the Shakespearean theater lends itself perfectly to the effects of invective. Coriolanus is an excellent case in point. Even a reader who might loathe his politics cannot but be engrossed by this man's mouthings. Lear also has a strong measure of such appeal, with his impotent senile maledictions that come quite close to the state of man's equally powerless infantile beginnings. (1966, 120)

Burke concludes his survey of Shakespeare's use of invective by stating that "with *Timon* the function [of invective] becomes almost total," and goes on to claim for Timon himself "a certain categorical or universal appeal," based mainly on his ability to give "full expression" to the impulse described (120–21). Although I am unwilling to accept all of Burke's pronouncements at face value, I believe they strike at the heart of the prevailing critical difficulty with *Timon*, and are particularly useful in addressing the specific problem before us. For if, as Burke contends, invective has its source "in the helpless rage of an infant that states its attitudes by utterances wholly unbridled," in an emotion that refuses to accommodate itself to reason or restraint, how can we possibly expect to position ourselves in sympathetic relation to it? Clearly, we *cannot* sympathize in the theater with an emotion whose surface manifestations we would ordinarily find irritating outside the theater if the source of that irritation is someone or something we are indifferent to or alienated from. But we *can* sympathize with someone or something that elicits or provokes—even against our will—our capacity for engagement, especially when the theatrical apparatus itself has prepared us to make this apparent breach in dramatic decorum the occasion for our own vicarious participation in the freedom from restraint it celebrates. As Burke notes, Timon appeals to us, as Coriolanus and Lear appeal to us despite the "practical discomfitures" engendered by their respective complaints, largely because he indulges a freedom most of us have long suppressed and forsaken in the face of "the fears and proprieties that make up our 'second nature,' " a nature dominated by an ethic of restraint (121).

Viewed in the abstract, Timon's indulgence in this freedom should be expected to garner little conscious support from an audience conditioned by its "second nature" to relegate such childish displays to the province of childish behavior. John Bayley speaks on behalf of such an audience when he states: "What survives . . . in *Timon* is something *hurt*, and that is touching. But how to relate it to the human scene?" (1981, 87).[14] Shakespeare relates it to the human scene by making the expression of the something that is "hurt" in *Timon* strike a responsive chord in the something that is hurt, angry, or simply disappointed in all of us, and by making that chord resonate with the play's concomitant attack on the very same "proprieties" that seek to hold our responsiveness in conscious check. As the most extreme form of unvarnished expression in which the play engages, invective is geared to awaken in the audience that dormant "first nature" which gives us access to feelings as unaccommodating as Timon's, and thus to extend the range of our emotional involvement in Timon's expression of rage and resentment against "the mendacious finery" of the world. Although, like the drama within which it plays so crucial a role, invective may not help either Timon or the audience "to accept loss," it may well provide both with an expressive medium for the cathartic release of feelings that do not necessarily require the "rituals of atonement" theoretically considered mandatory for the achievement of dramatic satisfaction.[15] As Burke suggests in a related essay, "*Coriolanus*—and the Delights of Faction," invective may actually serve a "curative function," consistent with its status as an idiom of denial and refusal, when it is "released under controlled conditions that transform the repressed into the expressed, yet do us no damage" (1966, 94).

In claiming a similarly privileged position for invective in the dramatic economy of *Timon*, and in suggesting that invective may serve a curative function for the audience which is usually associated with more decorous pronouncements on the part of Shakespeare's protagonists, Burke both emphasizes the need to give priority to performance dynamics in the criticism of dramatic texts and confirms the priority of psychological effect, as opposed to "theme" or "meaning," in our experience of plays. Instead of standing back from the insistent presence of Timon in order to legislate a meaning consistent with Shakespeare's status as a humanistic institution—one that would presumably focus on Timon's prodigality, misplaced idealism, or emotional immaturity—Burke grants Timon the dramatic status with which the play of his life endows him, casting him as the prevailing focus of the play's theatrical gravity, as the sustained object of the play's operation on its audience's capacity for engagement. In so doing, he relieves us of our groundedness in a corrupt text which we attempt to piece together with the help of strategies borrowed from our experience of other, more obviously accommodating plays, as well as from the stockpile of traditional literary criticism and received ideas.

In *Timon* invective operates within the "controlled conditions" of a dramatic experiment radical enough to encourage its audience to participate vicariously in the rejection of the audience's own "fears and proprieties," but sufficiently conventional to allow the audience to survive its own act of rejection after the object of its capacity for engagement chooses to repress, once and for all, his capacity for self-expression: "Lips, let sour words go by and language end" (V.i.219).[16] Since Timon's renunciation of language occurs only after he has seemingly exhausted the resources of the medium through which his bond with the audience has been established, the audience should, conceivably, be purged of the impulses that made Timon its spokesman in the first place, and thus should be free to negotiate its way through the closing scenes of the play in a manner more consistent with its previously displaced normative persuasion. In the very scene in which Timon enacts his renunciation, Shakespeare has, however, taken pains to condition the audience to resist the movement toward accommodation which begins with the mercenary visit of the senators to Timon's cave and culminates with Alcibiades's attempt to annex Timon's alienation to his questionable cause: "Those enemies of Timon's and mine own / Whom you yourselves shall set out for reproof / Fall, and no more" (V.iv.56–58). We are treated in V.i to a striking extension of Timon's misanthropic idiom, to a flexibility of manner not generally associated with it, as he parodically plays upon the senators' accommodating rhetoric in his sarcastic response to the same blandishments that will soon win over the "wild" but more politic Alcibiades:

> You witch me in it;
> Surprise me to the brink of tears.
> Lend me a fool's heart and a woman's eyes,
> And I'll beweep these comforts, worthy senators.
>
> (V.i.154–57)

And we are conspicuously reminded by Timon himself that he is as alienated from Alcibiades and his cause as he is from Athens and the senators who represent it: "Go, live still; / Be Alcibiades your plague, you his, / And last so long enough" (V.i.187–89).

Timon's refusal to enact the same compromise Alcibiades enacts in the play's closing scene may, of course, be construed in both psychological and ethical terms as a variety of regressive selfishness, of the kind we are meant to outgrow in the name of maturity. But in performative terms it operates as an influential determinant in shaping an audience's response to Alcibiades's closing appeal to its second nature. Although humanity in the aggregate will do whatever it needs to do to protect itself from incursions against its safety and security, audiences at plays have little really to fear, and may, in fact, draw much pleasure, from theatrical assaults on their characteristic values and assumptions. And this is especially the case when the audience is actually encouraged by both the play in question and the liberty of playgoing to participate vicariously in a licensed release from normative constraints. In short, an audience may, in the closing moments of this play, experience more satisfaction in rejecting Alcibiades's attempt to dissolve the disruptive tensions provoked by Timon than it might experience were it to accept his formula for accommodation at face value. Alcibiades's alternative clearly promises the audience a smoother return to reality than does a continuing imaginative alliance with Timon's misanthropy. But it fails to offer the audience the final (though fleeting) luxury of feeling superior to a gesture playgoers must soon perform in an analogous way of their own, as they re-accommodate themselves to the values and standards of behavior that obtain outside the theater. Once it has sufficiently distanced itself from the affective range of theatrical experience, the audience will, presumably, come to acknowledge its essential resemblance to the normative Alcibiades, and recognize the inescapable otherness of the abnormative Timon. But until the play ends, Alcibiades and the senators who attempt to appease him seem intended to serve as embodiments of what the audience imagines itself to be cured of, not as the welcome agents of a mutually desired reconciliation.

Conclusion: The Imaginary Audience

Having now claimed far more on behalf of *Timon* than it would seem reasonable to claim on behalf of a play that has elicited so many negative estimates in the course of its critical history, it is time to subject my own interpretive strategies to critical scrutiny. Throughout this book I have attempted to offer what I presumptuously term "recoveries" of audience responses which are, strictly speaking, irrecoverable. To compensate for my presumption, I have, whenever possible, attempted to integrate historically oriented speculation with observations that are decidedly more subjective. In my discussion of *Timon* I have, however, failed to offer any specific insight into the play's historical context, apart from occasionally calling its audience "Jacobean," as opposed to "Elizabethan." Yet even this cosmetic distinction is disabled by the strong possibility that no Jacobean audience ever attended a production of *Timon*. As H.J. Oliver notes in his introduction to the play's Arden edition:

> There is no reason to think that the play was ever acted in Shakespeare's lifetime and there is no contemporary mention of it. Nor does it contain a single allusion to any event or person such as generally forms the "external" evidence for dating Elizabethan work. (1959, xl)

The probability that *Timon* was never performed in Shakespeare's lifetime is enforced by Oliver's bibliographical analysis which leads him to conclude "that the copy for *Timon* was not prompt-copy or any kind of manuscript that had been used in a theatre" (xvi–xxii).

Although Oliver's more disputable allegation regarding the absence of allusions to contemporary persons or events provides insufficient grounds to consider *Timon* unresponsive to or unexpressive of topical concerns, as Coppélia Kahn's recent essay on *Timon*'s relation to "the cultural forms that constituted patronage in the Elizabethan and Jacobean periods" demonstrates (1987, 35), the play's apparent failure to find an auditory (understanding or otherwise) at its moment of composition would seem to preclude discussing it as I have addressed so proven a theatrical success as *The Jew of Malta*. Nevertheless, one must assume that however corrupt or unfinished the text of *Timon* may be, and however insufficient it may seem as an authoritative map or supplement to a contemporary Jacobean performance, Shakespeare composed his play for the purposes of production. One may consequently conclude that some obstacle stood in the way of the play's production. Kahn suggests that "perhaps the play was never performed—and as some critics believe, never finished—because it represented powerfully the fears of courtiers caught up in the vortex of patronage and dependent on James" (1987, 55). But such a possibility runs against the grain of the play's effort to elicit and psychologically reward audience identification with Timon, who functions, in Kahn's reading, as a surrogate for the king.

I believe that the playtext's possible failure to receive dramatic realization in its time has more to do with its aggressive refusal to accommodate itself to the "rituals of atonement" which generally characterize Shakespeare's treatment of tragic and comedic disruption and which will again become Shakespeare's stock-in-trade in *Antony and Cleopatra* and the series of romances that follow shortly thereafter. Far from serving either as the moralized embodiment of prodigality, or as a surrogate for the profligate King James, Timon stands most surely as the unforgiving anatomizer and accuser of an entire way of life, which may, if one chooses, be associated with the Jacobean court. But it seems to me that Timon's indictment embraces more broadly the same sense of a world in which trade, love, and friendship are all negotiated out of a supreme self-regard that Marlowe treats to entirely different effect in *The Jew of Malta* and *Edward II*. For Marlowe, the idea that individuals are motivated purely by self-interest, and that any disavowal of the same is sheer hypocrisy, constitutes nothing less than common sense. Absorbed as he was in his own identification with power and the powerful, Marlowe makes such ideas seem positively liberating in dramatic practice. In so doing, he may be said to be perfectly attuned to the actual (if unofficial) operations of his medium which, as the antitheatricalists understood, had little finally to contribute to the moral enrichment of playgoers. Rebel and blasphemer that he was in relation to the official ideologies of his culture, Marlowe appears to have made himself the willing servant of a theatrical enterprise rooted in the entertainment of the kinds of fantasies Shakespeare sets out to explode in *Timon*.

In *Timon* Shakespeare refuses to play the role of "dutiful servant," negatively capable of fading into the woodwork of his culture, subsequently delegated to him both by traditional bardolaters and by more sophisticated critics like Stephen Greenblatt.[1] As is the case throughout the equally un-accommodating *Troilus and Cressida*, and in the resistance to mystification he cultivates in such ostensibly orthodox playtexts as *Henry V* and *The Merchant of Venice*, Shakespeare assumes a position here that runs counter to the prevailing theatrical interests of playgoers at the same time as it attempts to serve their "real" interests. This is not a position that was likely to encourage confidence of a commercial success in Shakespeare's sponsors and colleagues. Indeed, the abrupt shift that Shakespeare requires an audience to make between engagement in a fantasy of effortless abundance and engagement in a counterfantasy of strident rejection may have seemed to Shakespeare himself too ambitious a challenge to mount, too radical an experiment to indulge, in the context of a theatrical apparatus that "saw a daily offring to the God of pleasure, resident at the Globe on the Bankeside" (Vennar 1614, B6).

Given the difficulty of developing a more historically specific insight into the contemporary perception of *Timon of Athens*, I have conducted in the above a reading of *Timon* that is, perhaps, more faithful to my model of theatrical experience than it is to the range of responsiveness that any audience, Jacobean or otherwise, could probably enjoy. All the "audiences" to which I refer in the course of this book are, of course, always largely imaginary, although they are also always constituted in potential in the playtexts I discuss and in the social conditions I describe, and, hence, are always susceptible to acts of reconstitution. As Herbert Blau writes:

> The audience . . . is not so much a mere congregation of people as a body of thought and desire. It does not exist before the play but is *initiated* or *precipitated* by it; it is not an entity to begin with but a consciousness constructed. The audience is what *happens* when, performing the signs and passwords of a play, something postulates itself and unfolds in response. (1990, 25)

To say that the host-audience I have developed to animate and respond to a performance of *Timon* is more imaginary than the other audiences I have entertained would, consequently, be to privilege my earlier efforts in ways they may not deserve, or to conclude that the "consciousness" I have constructed in the name of that audience is unidentifiable with what a contemporary performance of *Timon* may have precipitated or caused to unfold. I find my position in this respect to resemble that of the "Never Writer" who attempts to bring "News" to the "Ever Reader" in the preface to the 1609 quarto edition of *Troilus and Cressida*.

In asserting that "you have here a new play, never stal'd with the stage, never clapper-claw'd with the palms of the vulgar, and yet passing full of the palm comical," the Never Writer claims that the pleasures of the play-text exceed those capable of being generated in a playhouse, especially one dominated by the indiscriminate applause of the vulgar. I claim quite the opposite for *Timon of Athens*, but in so doing assume the same complicity with my imaginary audience that the Never Writer assumes in relation to his Ever Reader. Leslie Fiedler finds it "tempting to believe that [Shakespeare] himself prompted or even ghost-wrote the defensive advertisement of the Quarto" (1985, 51). Although I do not concur, I consider it more than plausible that the willful complexity Shakespeare cultivates in *Troilus* prompted the kind of advertisement the Never Writer wrote. I call the complexity of *Troilus* "willful" because the play's aggressive tone and structure suggest less a confident attempt at artistic risk-taking or experimentation than a studied refusal to write in a vein opposed to the expression of social concerns and personal preoccupations.[2] As in the case of *Timon of Athens*, we find Shakespeare not at all in the mood to accommodate an audience's desire for a good story well told and satisfyingly concluded. But unlike *Timon*, *Troilus* does not even provide an audience (imaginary or otherwise) with an occasion to act out its fantasies or supply a medium through which it may exercise its capacity for engagement. As the Berliner Ensemble has recently demonstrated, *Troilus* makes the case for a theater of alienation as well as any of Brecht's plays.[3]

I am certain that much the same could be said of *Timon* were it to be accorded similar treatment. The "news" I offer here is that *Timon*'s corruption—as well as its potential to alienate—derives as much from our failure to give critical priority to imagining the interplay between performance and response as it does from the unaccommodating status of the playtext itself, and that our responses to other, more accommodating, playtexts may also be considered corrupt—unfinished, partial—to the extent that they remain unanimated by performative considerations. The additional news I offer, through the readings of the playtexts I have considered here, is that in the realm of theatrical experience—where effect generally outpaces intention, subversion often eludes containment, and resistance usually yields to engagement—Shakespeare could be as radical a dramatist as Marlowe.

This is, perhaps, a predictable conclusion for one to reach at the end of a book jointly committed to the interpretive equivalent of fair play on behalf of Marlowe and the Shakespeare-who-isn't-Shakespeare. But it is also a conclusion that has quite literally emerged out of a more active commitment to theatrical justice which, as I read it, often operates at some remove from social justice. What I choose to call Shakespeare's radicalism makes itself felt in a variety of ways. Within the parameters of this book, it is discernible not only in his fabrication of transgressive fantasies that resist erasure but in his resistance to some of the same fantasies Marlowe is devoted to fulfilling: a resistance that has seemed to many to be rooted in moral proprieties but which seems to me to be rooted in a political persuasion often opposed to the theatrical economy enforced by plays and playmaking. This is, finally, matter for a different book and, perhaps, an entirely different approach. For now, it should be sufficient to note that, with only a few exceptions, bardolaters and alleged bardicides alike continue to consign an arguably heterodox Shakespeare to the judgment of imaginary audiences for the understanding auditory he claims.[4] One imagines that the cultural normalization of the Marlowe-who-isn't-Shakespeare —a process in which this book participates—will do much the same for this particular "critical construction," though I prefer to think that nothing I have said here will prevent his plays from constructing audiences of their own that they will continue to shock and unsettle in entirely verifiable ways.

Notes

Introduction: Marlowe and/or Shakespeare

1. Some important recent exceptions are Danson (1982, 1986); Huebert (1984); and Shepherd (1986).

2. In two groundbreaking articles (1961, 1964), Nicholas Brooke makes a strong case for Marlowe's skill as an "experimental" dramatist and as a provocative influence on Shakespeare's early writing for the stage. But in neither instance does his acknowledgment of Marlowe's status as an accomplished playwright in his own right completely displace the traditional estimate of Marlowe's artistic deviance or marginality.

3. See Huebert (1984); Shepherd (1986); Goldberg (1984) Summers (1988); and Porter (1989).

4. Levenson made this observation in a paper she submitted to a seminar on Marlowe and Shakespeare that convened under my direction at the 1985 meeting of the Shakespeare Association of America in Nashville, Tennessee; it has since been published in revised form in Friedenreich, Gill, and Kuriyama (1988, 99–115).

Chapter One: The Terms of Engagement

1. The second article is "Text against Performance: The Gloucester Family Romance" (1985). Also see "Sneak's Noise: Rumor and Detextualization in *2 Henry IV*" (1984).

2. See Jonas Barish's evaluation of Berger's point of view in "Shakespeare in the Study; Shakespeare on the Stage" (1988, 38–39). In his more recent *Imaginary Audition* (1989), Berger offers a series of correctives to his earlier position and presents a more stage-friendly overview of the debate. He writes, e.g., that "The simplistic and tendentious privileging of reading over audition . . . was caused by misplacement of the polarity, and in my second formulation I noted that the conflict is not between reading and audition but between two interpretive emphases within reading, one that promotes the constraints of performance/audition to the status of norms that should govern *literary* response, and one that doesn't" (xiii). Berger now proposes "a tripartite scheme: reading that respects both the [psychological] constraints [that playgoing imposes on interpretation] and the [theatrical] circumstances; reading that respects the circumstances but not the constraints; and reading that ignores both. My focus in the book is on the first two. I shall call the first the *theatrical* model of stage-centered reading and the second the *literary* model of stage-centered reading" (xiii–xiv).

3. Berger comes close to a similar position in the following reformulation of his earlier argument:

"Centered on the practice of imaginary audition, attentive to the structure and conditions of theater, maintaining the fiction of performance as a control on reading yet firmly committed to the practice of decelerated microanalysis, the literary model of stage-centered reading perforce shuttles back and forth between two incompatible modes of interpretation, reading and playgoing. Whether one chooses to privilege the page or the stage, neither can do without the other" (1989, 140). However, in choosing to privilege "the literary model of stage-centered reading"—as opposed to what he elsewhere calls the *theatrical* model of stage-centered reading (see note 2 above)—Berger continues to view performative considerations as constraints on interpretation.

4. Another exception is David Scott Kastan (1986) who observes: "In general, it is the opponents of the theatre, however obsessive their hostility appears, who seem to have the best of the argument. The defenders offer only a narrowly homiletic conception of drama that is belied by virtually every play of the period. The detractors come closer to understanding how the plays actually function; their fears respond to the subversive threat the theatre potentially posed" (464). See, also, Jonathan Crewe (1984) who suggests that "it is . . . possible to see both dramatists and antitheatricalists as participants by 1587 in a cultural dialogue about theatre" (321) and that "drama discovers itself (i.e., at once finds and displays itself) in responding to antitheatricalism" (321, n. 2, and *passim*).

5. This is assuredly not the position of S.P. Zitner who writes that "despite Gosson's undoubted knowledge of the theatre, there is a question whether *The School of Abuse* and *Playes Confuted in Five Actions* give us eyewitness accounts of the Elizabethan audience or only clever enlargements of satiric passages in Ovid's *Art of Love*" (1958, 206), passages that Zitner believes Gosson misread, mistaking as "serious description" what Ovid intends as "sly fun" (207). Zitner also reiterates William Ringler's contention that "There is reason to believe that [*The School of Abuse*] was written at the request of an agent of the City authorities, and that the relatively large run of the first edition is attributable to a subsidy" (207). See Ringler (1942, 26–28) who makes the same claim with respect to Anthony Munday's *A Second and Third Blast of Retrait from Plaies and Theaters*. For an opposing point of view, see Kinney (1974, 17) who also contends that "Gosson's work stands as a monument to contemporary opinion, providing us with the best route to understanding the Elizabethan attack on the stage" (67). Jean Howard offers a brief summary of this debate, as well as an informed commentary on the ideology of antitheatrical literature in "Renaissance Antitheatricality and the Politics of Gender and Rank in *Much Ado About Nothing*" (1987, 184, n. 11; 165–72), though the last word on the subject should belong to Zitner who concludes that "If we believe what Gosson says about audience behavior, we must believe it not because Gosson was an Elizabethan who attended the theatre, but because what he wrote accords with our understanding of human behavior" (208).

6. See Moody Prior (1951, 105ff) for an illuminating review of condescending approaches to the Elizabethan audience which has historically served as the scapegoat for Shakespeare's supposed excesses and inadequacies.

7. See, e.g., Dollimore (1984), Dollimore and Sinfield (1985), and Howard and O'Connor (1987) for representative essays in cultural materialism. See Beier (1985), Manning (1988), Wrightson (1982), and Underdown (1985) for examples of the new social history.

8. In discussing the frequent alignment of *Jack Straw* with Shakespeare's *2 Henry VI*, Annabel Patterson notes that while the former is "generally assumed to have had a law-and-order agenda . . . even [the historian R.B.] Dobson observes that the author 'gives the best lines' to the radical priest John Ball, who thereby recirculates through the London audiences the central ideologemes of 'peasant' ideology" (1989, 46). Michael Bristol makes much the same point regarding "the powerful political and discursive indiscretion" constituted by "the speeches of Jack Cade and his followers" in *2 Henry VI* (1985, 89). Although "Shakespeare's play presents the audience with scenes of official retribution, . . . the expression of popular resentment nevertheless escapes being totally repressed" (90). See also Walter Cohen on "the contradictory significance of the popular dimension in the national history play" (1985, 221).

9. This is not to suggest that a single principle of spectatorship may be held to transcend social or historical considerations—or, for that matter, considerations of gender—regarding the construction of the playgoing subject. Rather, my aim is temporarily to defer such considerations in order first to distinguish the role played by the theatrical apparatus in the construction of audience response.

10. I have effectively appropriated here C.L. Barber's well-known conception of the "saturnalian pattern" which, according to Barber, "can be summarized in the formula, through release to clarification" (1959, 4). Montrose offers a more historically specific and politicized rendering of this formula (1983; rep. 1988).

11. For an interesting discussion of the playgoer's movement between the frameworks of theatrical and ordinary experience, see Goffman (1974, 124–55).

12. In his seminal essay on the Elizabethan audience and Shakespeare, Moody Prior uses the same scene from *King Lear* to critique the "circularity" of arguments that use the "circumstances of life outside the theater" to explain why Shakespeare staged such violent acts (1951, 103). He notes that the attributed taste for violence of the *Lear* audience works against the entire play's attempt to show how "unmistakably appalling" it is that the "pitiable things which happen to Lear and Gloucester are unfelt by Regan, Goneril, and Cornwall" (121). I perfectly agree with Prior regarding the play's overt meaning and intentions, but I do not believe that he accurately appraises the scene's psychological effects.

13. For astute analyses of how distinctions between seemingly "good" and "bad" characters are repeatedly disabled in *Lear* and *Macbeth*, see Berger, "The Early Scenes of *Macbeth*" (1980) and "Text against Performance" (1985).

Chapter Two: The Audience in Theory and Practice

1. Given Andrew Gurr's recent contention that women "were in numbers at the Globe from 1599 to 1614" and that "the assumption that female playgoers were motivated by sex . . . remained a male prejudice throughout the period" (1987, 63), I

would submit that the responses of both sexes to a Jacobean performance of the scene in question may well have resembled those outlined above. A contemporary Jacobean audience might particularly recognize in Leontes's jealous violence an image of the "strained gender relations" which some modern social historians attribute to the period in question. See, e.g, Underdown (1985, 116–36). Since male playgoers in any age will soon discover how terribly destructive and misguided Leontes's fantasies are, and will notice as well that the initially admirable Polixenes is himself not immune from abuses of power, I would also submit that *The Winter's Tale* offers an unusually powerful representation of the dangers of patriarchal dominance in the family and the state.

2. In employing the term "transacted," I am alluding to Norman Holland's psychoanalytically based models of reader response, specifically, to a seminal work in the development of his theoretical preoccupations, "Transactive Criticism: Re-Creation through Identity" (1976). In a later article, "How Can Dr. Johnson's Remarks on Cordelia's Death Add to My Own Response?" (1978), Holland directly addresses the problem of consensual validity in relation to what he terms the "outmoded and confusing" notion of "the 'power' of the text" (40). Although they differ in crucial ways regarding the dynamics of reader response, Stanley Fish shares Holland's conception of the priority of the interpretive process. See, e.g., "Interpreting the *Variorum*" (1976). Wolfgang Iser, on the other hand, claims a more significant role for the text itself in manipulating reader response and thus provides a supportive context for the argument I am advancing on behalf of dramatic texts. See *The Act of Reading* (1978, 152–53).

3. Stephen Orgel (1988) notes that "the acting text of a play always was different from the written text—this means not simply that it was different from the printed text, though it certainly means that, but that it was different from the *script*, what the author wrote" (7). See also Carlson (1985, 5–11).

4. Cf. Fish: "In my model . . . meanings are not extracted but made and made not by encoded forms but by interpretive strategies that call forms into being" (1976, 485).

5. A common objection to reader response criticism can be summarized in Robert Holub's critique of Iser's theory of reading: "Iser's predicament originates in his adoption of an ahistorical, phenomenological starting-point. By conceiving the text-reader relationship in terms of constant or timeless concepts, he forecloses an integration of historical information in anything but a superficial fashion" (1984, 99). Although my own approach is grounded in a psychological model of theatrical experience and, hence, may also be said to proceed from a "phenomenological starting-point," it derives its frameworks and parameters from the material practices it sets out to analyze, practices that are themselves the products of specific social and economic conditions. In this respect, I take very seriously Holub's injunction that "A historical perspective . . . must be integrated into the very conceptual apparatus of the system" (99). However, I depart from other, more deterministic devotees of historical (or materialist) criticism who hold that the ideology of a specific ruling class and the "social mode of reception determined by it" unequivocally shape and control the responses of varied classes of readers and audiences (see Holub, 128). Such a perspective is itself drawn from "constant or timeless concepts." And, as

Holub writes in summarizing a point made by Leo Lowenthal, it specifically fails to acknowledge that "reception entails both a socially conditioned and a psychologically conditioning force; ideology as well as the resistance to ideology; both a gratification of needs and the displacement of gratification" (47). In stressing the central role played by "unconscious stimulants . . . in the psychological triangle of writer, literature, and recipient," Lowenthal contributes an indeterminate variable to the unvarying determinism of materialist analysis (quoted in Holub, 46). What is more, he locates the possibility of resistance to the existing order in the psychological substructures of artworks and their recipients, drawing an implicit connection between psychic economy and the ideological content of aesthetic transactions: "Although . . . in the total social process [art] has the function of reconciliation with the existing order, it also encompasses an element of dissatisfaction that has to be reconciled. In its very fabric is contained in principle the resistance, the contradiction to the existing order" (quoted in Holub, 47). In locating the possibility, indeed the inevitability, of resistance to the existing order in artistic transactions, Lowenthal approves a position that Elizabethan antitheatricalists addressed with disapprobation: namely, that even the most morally or politically didactic texts can be redirected to opposing ends in the act of transmission.

6. See *The Birth of Tragedy* (1968, 67–72), for Nietzsche's discussion of "Greek cheerfulness."

7. As a recent example of ideological assumptions besetting the subject of audience composition, we might notice that in his otherwise telling critique of Ann Jennalie Cook's argument on behalf of privileged playgoers, Michael Bristol opposes what he terms Cook's "elitist description of the sociology of the theater" in favor of a more populist model consistent with his own thesis (1986, 108–10).

8. One of the more curious pieces of evidence Gurr advances to support his view is that "the presence of citizens' wives at plays confirms the inference that citizens themselves were likewise regular playgoers, since no respectable wife could easily attend a play without a male escort" (1987, 63–64).

9. Butler's objections to Cook's thesis, advanced in an appendix of his *Theatre and Crisis 1632–1642* (1984, 293–306), are profoundly convincing. Especially noteworthy is Butler's use of Cook's own citations to support his opposing estimate of audience composition (see 299–300).

10. See, e.g., Fisher (1948), and Beier and Finlay (1986).

11. While Stone's thesis and methodology alike have been disputed by several of his fellow historians, the evidence he has assembled regarding social mobility and social stratification has been repeatedly confirmed and elaborated by Beier (1978), Wrightson (1982), and Hill.

12. Cf. Walter Cohen's treatment of the same issue in the context of the drama's representation of the ruling class: "What place . . . can the concern with individualist aspiration, widespread among English dramatists, occupy in the portrayal of a ruling class? An obvious answer is that an aristocrat may try to become a king" (1985, 237).

13. Alan Macfarlane (1979, 165–75) uses some of the same examples to demonstrate that "almost every aspect of [English] culture was diametrically opposed to that of

the surrounding nations" (165) and, in particular, to emphasize English individualism.

14. Roger Finlay and Beatrice Shearer note that there were five outbreaks of plague between 1563–1665, "four of which claimed at least one-fifth of the total population as victims" (1986, 48). Also see Pelling (1986, 97ff) on outbreaks of syphilis.

15. Christopher Hill writes that "Fear of atheism seems to have been at its height in the early fifteen-nineties, when the government's campaign against the sectaries was under way" (1965; rep. 1982, 170, n. 5).

16. The Lord Mayor's letter is dated 3 November 1594 and reprinted in Chambers (1923, Vol. IV, 316–17). See Ingram (1978, 168–70) on the formulaic pattern of these annual pleas of the City for the suppression of plays and playhouses.

17. David Klein has summarized the topics of these attacks under three general headings in his useful book, *The Elizabethan Dramatists as Critics* (1963). These are: variety of demand; instability of demand; and contempt for the judgment of the masses, with the last topic by far the most frequently addressed (173–84). Nashe's contribution can be found in his prologue to *Summers Last Will and Testament* (ca. 1592).

18. The first phrase, generally taken to be an allusion to the Tamburlaine plays, can be found in the prologue to *Doctor Faustus*; the second, which directly refers to two of Shakespeare's romances, occurs in the Induction to Ben Jonson's *Bartholomew Fair* (lines 131–32).

19. In fact, Crewe supplements his assertion of the probable irreversability of "The conception of the dramatic protagonist . . . as a negative exemplum" with the following note: "The commentaries of Sidney and Puttenham on this subject are too well known to need detailed citation" (1984, 325, n. 11).

20. I prefer the term "receptive auditory" to "understanding auditory" because, like the playwrights themselves, I am not confident that Elizabethan playgoers always understood all that plays attempted to communicate. I make this statement less from condescension to ignorant or inattentive playgoers, than from a healthy respect for the daunting conditions of playgoing. In addition to the obvious discomforts that chronically unpleasant weather probably produced at outdoor playhouses, the playgoers themselves generated a series of distractions. A brief summary of such distractions would include the buying, selling, and consumption of food and drink; the lack of toilets; and the wearing of hats and ruffs that would impede sightlines (see Gurr 1987, 36–44).

Chapter Three: The Tamburlaine Phenomenon

1. Levin also notes that the general allusions to Tamburlaine "all agree in testifying to his mightiness—his power and success," and that this tendency is reinforced by a series of specific allusions "all of [which] single out one of three episodes that vividly enact Tamburlaine's tremendous power and complete success" (1984, 57).

2. According to Levin, these critics "are all agreed not only in condemning Tamburlaine themselves, but also in asserting that he is unequivocally condemned

by Marlowe and hence by the play" (51). Such opinions can be found most conspicuously in Battenhouse (1941; 2nd ed., 1964) and in the chapters on *Tamburlaine* in Cole (1962); Godshalk (1974); Masinton (1972); and Cutts (1973).

3. In his introduction to Pavel (1985), Wlad Godzich asks, "what if Tamburlaine were nothing but the rediscovery of agency as an autonomous force?," and provides the following response: "His lack of a moral dimension would precisely correspond to the amorality of the world flux and be free of any pathos. Marlowe may well have represented at the beginning of our modernity the loosening away of what had until then been an attribute of God" (xxii).

4. Mark Thornton Burnett (1987) uses the same phrases from Part I in identifying Tamburlaine as a masterless man: "Above all, he resembles the vagabond in rejecting 'servitude' and choosing instead 'to live at liberty' " (310). Burnett has done ground-breaking work in relating Marlowe's portrayal of Tamburlaine to contemporary Elizabethan representations of vagabonds or masterless men. While I differ from Burnett in the uses to which I put these resemblances, my subsequent references to masterless men owe much to his work.

5. With respect to generational conflicts, Esler writes that "the apparent hypocrisy and obvious irrelevance of their parents' Christian humanist code" had important effects on the development of the aspiring minds of the Elizabethan younger generation. "How could Anthony and Francis Bacon take seriously their father's motto, *Mediocria firma*, when old Sir Nicholas himself had begun life as a sheep reeve's son and died Sir Nicholas Bacon, K.G., P.C., Lord Keeper of the Great Seal of England?" (69–70).

6. Burnett (1987) observes that "an obvious parallel emerges between Tamburlaine and the contemporary aversion towards masterless men, reviling God and indifferent to the consequences of their irreverance" (314). Burnett also connects Tamburlaine's "band of 'disordered troops' " to bands of disordered soldiers against whom two proclamations were circulated in 1589 (316–17). However, in the present instance, as throughout *1 Tamburlaine*, the play's representatives of secular authority speak of "the band" Tamburlaine assembles in an older idiom reserved for nominating and denigrating "the many-headed monster."

7. I borrow this terminology from Paul Brown (1985) who writes that the discourse of masterlessness "analyses wandering or unfixed and unsupervised elements located in the internal margins of civil society. . . . [It] reveals the mastered (submissive, observed, supervised, deferential) and masterful (powerful, observing, supervising, teleological) nature of civil society" (50).

8. As I note in my first chapter, the authorial intention to discredit the peasant leaders of *Jack Straw* and Jack Cade in *2 Henry VI* cannot be held equivalent to the effect the words and actions of such characters may have on playgoers. See Greenblatt (1983) for a comprehensive discussion of the representation of rebellion, and Hill (1975) on the "many-headed monster."

9. Since in its first version Tamburlaine's question has already been answered by his onstage interlocutors, its rephrasing in the form, "And so would you, my masters, would you not?" appears to be directed over their heads. The aim of this gesture is to generalize the choric expression of desire across the length of the stage by means of a suspensory pause which extends itself into the audience's range and,

conceivably, resonates with its own "suspect" fantasies and aspirations. Marlowe's decision to have Tamburlaine address the audience as his "masters" in preference to the formulation, "What says my other friends, will you be kings?" (II.v.67) employed to address his confederates, exemplifies his effort to bring about a sense of mutual empowerment. To fully bridge the discourse of masterlessness, every participant in this theatrical transaction must feel singled out as more than a submissive onlooker. Playgoers must feel that they too, if only for as long as the performance lasts, are masters of their fates. They must feel that they applaud Tamburlaine's fortunes as *they* please, and not be too conspicuously reminded that the imaginative confederation with Tamburlaine's onstage company of aspiring minds is effected by a playwright eager to exploit such connections. Cf. Pavel (1985): "From his first speeches, Tamburlaine makes it clear that he is addressing everybody else from a privileged vantage point. His poetic discourses hint, from the beginning, that he looks over the heads of his interlocutors" (38).

10. I make this statement in the context of recent materialist re-readings of plays like *King Lear* which channel the frequent filial and fraternal conflicts in Elizabethan plays through the nexus of "power, property and inheritance." See, e.g., Dollimore (1984, 195–202) and McLuskie (1985, 98–106). Cf. Esler (1966).

11. Among the most interesting is its prologue which is presented by "The Ghost of Jack Strawe" and is oddly reminiscent of the prologues to *Doctor Faustus* and *The Jew of Malta*.

12. If one examines the extract "taken from a sequence beginning in 15 June 1594 and ending on 14 March 1595" in Henslowe's diary and reprinted in Rutter (1984, 88), one will notice that the recorded receipts for performances of *2 Tamburlaine* are greater than those for performances of *1 Tamburlaine* in four of the five instances when the plays were performed consecutively.

13. Cf. Greenblatt (1977): "Tamburlaine's violence does not transform space from the abstract to the human, but rather further reduces the world to a map, the very emblem of abstraction" (46).

Chapter Four: Banquo's Ghost

1. See Marvin Rosenberg's comprehensive account of the stage history of the ghost's portrayals (1978, 439–51).

2. In his discussion of this alternative, Rosenberg cites the observations of several of its most influential proponents, among them those of Nevil Coghill, who contends that "What is important is that the audience should see what Macbeth sees, and be identified with him, not his guests" (1978, 443), and Arthur Quiller-Couch: "Who sees [the ghost]? Not the company. Not even Lady Macbeth. Those who see it are Macbeth and you and I. Those into whom it strikes terror. . . . Those whom it accuses are Macbeth and you and I. And what it accuses is what, of Macbeth, you and I are hiding in our own breasts" (444).

3. See Rosenberg's excellent account of this alternative, especially for his description of how the more advanced stage technologies of the nineteenth and twen-

tieth centuries have enabled the play's producers to turn its obvious difficulties to theatrical advantage (1978, 442–43).

4. Bradley concludes his concise review of the hallucination theory with the following summation: "On the whole, and with some doubt, I think that Shakespeare (1) meant the judicious to take the Ghost for an hallucination, but (2) knew that the bulk of the audience would take it for a reality. And I am more sure of (2) than of (1)" ([orig. 1904] 1963, 401–02). Muir's opinion is rendered in the Introduction to his Arden edition of *Macbeth* (1980, lxii–iii, n. 3). Also see Rosenberg (1978, 441–42). Jan Kott anticipates my own position in the following: "Shakespeare's *Macbeth* is not a psychological drama of the second half of the nineteenth century. Macbeth has dreamed of a final murder to end all murders. Now he knows: there is no such murder. . . . The dead do return" (1966, 95).

5. Cf. Willbern (1986): "[The] dagger is the perfect transitional object: both there and not there, real and not real, provided and imagined, his and not his. It appears in authentic answer to his own intent, mirrors his own instrument, and then, as he watches, transforms itself from *present* replica to *future* image: it drips blood" (535). Also see Ide (1975) who writes that "the real dagger will gravitate towards the imaginary dagger his imagination has already bloodied, as if the present moment were dictated by the future vision" (343).

6. Lesser (1976) anticipates both my observation and conclusion in the following: "[Macbeth] is here trying to make himself one with the others lamenting the murder, but . . ., ironically, the occasion provides a welcome opportunity to say something he deeply feels; and his prognosis of his own situation is uncannily accurate" (151–52).

7. I take this phrase from an earlier version of "Phantasmagoric *Macbeth*" (1986) which Willbern contributed to the seminar on the psychology of theatrical experience at the Third International Shakespeare Conference in Stratford-upon-Avon, 1981. The phrase occurs in the following passage: "What ultimately controls this potentially dangerous psychological event is the conventional confine of theatrical space (and genre), as well as the varying scope of our imaginative responses to Shakespeare's questioning vision." Traces of this passage may be detected in the paper's published form where Willbern writes that "In the play of *Macbeth* Shakespeare provides his audience with a framed potential space wherein he presents a character, Macbeth, for whom such space is closed off. This suggests one feature of tragedy as a psychological genre: it can demonstrate the failure of psychic strategies (or defenses) while strengthening its audience's abilities to manage those strategies" (1986, 535). I part ways with Willbern on both accounts. In the first place, I believe that what sets *Macbeth* apart from Shakespeare's other tragedies is its refusal to observe what Keir Elam (1980, 88) terms the "definitional constraint" of the theatrical frame which conventionally serves to hold threatening fantasy material in check. And in the second, I believe Willbern's implicitly therapeutic model of theatrical experience tends to recuperate a moralized reading of *Macbeth* that is at odds with the dynamics of audience engagement.

8. In "The Mated Mind in *Macbeth*," a paper which he contributed to the seminar on the psychology of theatrical experience at the Third International Shakespeare Congress, Kranz proposes that "It might be salutary to calculate what

contextual effects result from Shakespeare's characteristic use of illusion-breakers (plays-within-plays, anachronisms, comments about the Globe theater, etc.) rather than assume that their presence guarantees a static psychic distance from the fictional situation throughout." Although I depart from Kranz's approach to *Macbeth* in a number of crucial ways, I confirm the general usefulness of his proposition in much of what follows.

9. The judgment against Shakespeare's authorship of III.v expressed by Nosworthy (1948, 138–39) remains the prevailing one; see, for instance, Muir's confirmation of it in his Introduction to the Arden *Macbeth* (xxx–xxxiii). But I am of the opinion of Knight—first expressed in "The 'Hecate' Scenes in *Macbeth*" (1932)—and Rosenberg that, given firmer proof to the contrary, there really is no substantive reason "to reject Shakespeare's authorship of the dialogue as part of the original *Macbeth*" (1978, 491).

10. Cf. Ide (1975, 338) where a similar point is made in regard to this "countermovement," the commencement of which is traced to what Ide terms the play's "structural seam," III.vi. I strongly disagree, however, with Ide's rather doctrinaire conclusion that, as a consequence of this shift in emphasis, "those who once looked *with* Macbeth are asked to look *at* him, to judge the murderer from an enormous distance, from God's eye, as it were, who so clearly directs the forces of restoration."

11. I take this suggestive observation from Kranz's ISC paper, "The Mated Mind in *Macbeth*."

12. See Lesser's discussion of what he terms Shakespeare's "double vision of almost every scene of *Macbeth*" (1976, 155–58).

13. Shakespeare "liberates" Richard within the confines of a history play which, because of its fidelity to its sources, must eventually rein him in. The *form* of the play —drawn from its *format* as chronicle—may have served to relieve Shakespeare of the anxiety attendant upon loosing such an appealing villain on the stage in the first place. For an interesting discussion of Shakespeare's approach to history in *Macbeth*, see Kott (1966, 85–87).

14. As Willbern notes, "Imagining Duncan's murder as symbolic patricide is commonplace in psychological (as well as religious and political) readings" (1986, 521). In an intriguing discussion that starts from this commonplace assumption, Willbern makes a persuasive case for an "imagined re-vision of regicide as matricide" (522) and even as "symbolic infanticide" (524).

15. Egan notes that "an undercurrent of uneasiness must mingle with our appreciation of Malcolm's triumph, marked as it is by several echoes of the earliest scenes in the play" (1978, 343). For persuasive reinterpretations of the supposedly sacrosanct moral and political order presided over by Duncan in these early scenes, see Berger (1980) and Hawkins (1982).

16. The question of Macduff's accountability is an old and involved one that deserves (though seldom rewards) more consideration than I have room to give it. It is, however, treated both sensitively and concisely by Bradley ([1904] 1963), whose lead I am pleased to follow: "That his flight was 'noble' is beyond doubt. That it was not wise or judicious in the interest of his family is no less clear. But that does not show that it was wrong; . . ." (312).

Chapter Five: King Edward's Body

1. Like many of his contemporaries, Marlowe was also responsive to ideas that were merely attributed to Machiavelli. See, e.g., Ribner (1954, 349–56). For detailed examinations of popular conceptions and misconceptions of Machiavellism, see Praz (1958) and Raab (1964).

2. In the course of his provocative commentary on the Baines deposition, Jonathan Goldberg observes: "The theater was permitted to rehearse the dark side of Elizabethan culture; it was a recreative spot where sedition could wear the face of play, where authors could make assertions as potent as monarchs'. In the theater, kings were the puppets of writers, greatness was mimed, atheists, rebels, magicians, and sodomites could be publicly displayed. And nowhere, of course, more strikingly than in Marlowe's heroes, . . . Marlowe's identity in his culture comes from his rehearsal of these counterpositions, and the words of Richard Baines, government spy, report how Marlowe, a fellow spy, acquired a counteridentity at once countenanced and denounced by his society" (1984, 376–77).

3. Marlowe's decision to depart from Holinshed's description of Gaveston as "an esquire of Gascoine" (*Chronicles* II, 539), hence, to downgrade his social standing to that of a well-placed commoner or minor gentleman, is itself ambiguous, though it probably has its basis in the repeated placement of his protagonists—e.g., Tamburlaine and Faustus—in the ranks of those who aspire to higher stations than those to which they were born. Cf. Summers (1974, 161–62) and Cohen (1985, 232–37).

4. This kind of "restructuring" may, of course, have been even more difficult for female playgoers to negotiate. Such moments in Marlowe provide perhaps overly suitable examples of Barbara Hodgdon's conclusion regarding female spectatorship, namely, that "there is pleasure, no end of pleasure, only not for a female spectator" (1990, 258).

5. The "elementary" nature of the comparison is, I should add, more obvious to myself than to most other commentators on the play. Cohen (1985), e.g., reproduces a critical commonplace in contending that "greater sympathy" is evoked "for the aristocracy than for the monarchy in the first half of the play." Cohen also asserts that Gaveston and his successors Spencer and Baldock are "treated with far less sympathy" than are characters like Tamburlaine, Barabas, and Faustus who similarly "stand outside the traditional ruling class, with which their aspirations bring them into conflict" (237).

6. It hardly seems coincidental that in order to effect the last stage of Christopher Sly's "transformation" into a lord in *The Taming of the Shrew*, Shakespeare has his "real" lord and that lord's servants liberally borrow from Gaveston's sylvan fantasy:

Second Servant. Dost thou love pictures? We will fetch thee straight
Adonis painted by a running brook,
And Cytherea all in sedges hid,
Which seem to move and wanton with her breath,
Even as the waving sedges play with wind.

Lord.	We'll show thee Io as she was a maid,
	And how she was beguiled and surpris'd,
	As lively painted as the deed was done.

(Ind.ii.49–56)

It is, however, more difficult to determine whether Shakespeare is burlesquing the device he deploys here, criticizing the susceptibility of the low-born and illiterate to such elaborate seductions, or simply confirming the theatrical appeal of such conceits.

7. The most astute discussion of the possible relationship between Marlowe's apparent homosexuality and the social positions maintained in plays like *Edward II* is offered by Huebert (1984) who notes, e.g., that an Elizabethan "homosexual could come to think of himself as an outlaw, living always in defiance of the sacred and secular code, and requiring at all times the support of influential protectors against even the bare possibility of a legal reckoning. Desire, for such a man, would be by its very nature an act of defiance" (212).

8. The negligible attention traditionally accorded the homosexual orientation of *Edward II* is in the process of being redressed by a new generation of Renaissance scholars. Summers (1974) is one of the few, comparatively traditional scholars to acknowledge Marlowe's favorable treatment of homosexuality in *Edward II* (155–86). Kuriyama (1980) breaks some new ground in making Marlowe's sexuality a sustained focus in her psychoanalytically oriented book. More recent and more adventurous appraisals of Marlowe's homosexuality are offered by Huebert (1984), Shepherd (1986), Goldberg (1984), and Porter (1988).

9. While I am indebted to Sanders (1968) for bringing these divergences to light, I find them operating to decidedly different effects from those he describes, which "tempt" him "to mutter piously, 'What a scene Shakespeare would have made of it!' " (130). To support his conclusions, Sanders quotes the following excerpt from Stow, *Annales* (1615, 226): "These champions bring Edward towardes Barkley, being guarded with a rabble of helhoundes, along by the Grange belonging to the Castle of Bristowe, where that wicked man Gorney, making a crowne of hay, put it on his head, and the souldiours that were present, scoffed and mocked him beyond all measure, . . . Moreouer, deuising to disfigure him that hee might not bee knowne, they determined for to shaue as well the haire of his head, as also of his beard: wherefore, as in their iourny, they trauailed by a little water which ran in a ditch, they commaunded him to light from his horse to bee shauen, to whom, being set on a moale hill, a Barbar came vnto him with a basen of colde water taken out of the ditch, to shaue him withall, saying vnto the king, that that water should serue for that time. To whom Edward answered, that would they, noulde they, hee would haue warm water for his beard; and, to the end that he might keepe his promise, hee beganne to weepe, and to shed teares plentifully."

10. Moretti (1981) begins his essay with a discussion of the contention between royalty and aristocracy in *Gorboduc*, the terms of which may easily (and profitably) be transposed to *Edward II*. Moretti argues, e.g., that when "tragedy performs the degradation of the cultural image of the sovereign, it deprives the monarchy of its central bastion, its ultimate weapon" (9) a feat that *Edward II* "performs" repeat-

edly, just as it similarly reduces the prescribed "collaboration between different organs [of the body politic] for the benefit of the whole" to a "contest" of individual wills and self-interest (12).

11. In sexual terms, Edward represents for Lightborn the perfect object of perverse erotic satisfaction, blending the vulnerability of the child with the desperation of a man deprived of all other significant human contact. Toby Robertson (1964), in a discussion of his 1958 Marlowe Society production of the play, calls this episode "almost the last 'love scene' in the play," and describes its enactment in the following manner: "We played this with Edward almost lying in Lightborn's lap and sort of crooning to him. He's very gently stroking him and it became like a child asking for love, wanting love, affection" (179).

12. Cf. Greenblatt (1977, 52) who writes that "in *Edward II*, Marlowe uses the emblematic method of admonitory drama, but uses it to such devastating effect that the audience recoils from it in disgust. Edward's grisly execution is, as orthodox interpreters of the play have correctly insisted, iconographically 'appropriate,' but this very appropriateness can only be established *at the expense of* every complex, sympathetic human feeling evoked by the play. The audience is forced to confront its insistence upon coherence, and the result is a profound questioning of the way audiences constitute meaning in plays and in life." I attempt to provide one kind of answer to this "profound questioning of the way audiences constitute meaning in *plays*." I would add (and hope) that audiences do not "constitute meaning" in the same way in life.

13. Cohen (1985) concludes his discussion of the play by stating that "*Edward II* constitutes a typical act of demystification, powerful in its destructiveness, but incapable of producing a constructive alternative." He adds: "This is to say, however, that Marlowe does what Shakespeare does not and vice versa, . . . (239). It should be clear from each of my discussions of Marlowe that I do not believe Marlowe was at all interested in "producing a constructive alternative." And the following chapter should indicate what it is I think Shakespeare does and does not.

Chapter 6: Radical Shakespeare

1. I have appropriated the term "unitary myth" from Dollimore who disputes the notion that the Tudor myth in particular actually served as a common focus of belief for Shakespeare and his fellow Elizabethans (1984, 89–90). Dollimore contends that not only do "most of Shakespeare's history plays fail to substantiate this (non-existent) unitary myth, but . . . some of them have precisely the opposite effect of revealing how myth is exploited ideologically" (90).

2. According to F.J. Levy (1986), one influential Elizabethan who was capable of a Machiavellian critique of political affairs was Francis Bacon. Taking the 1597 edition of Bacon's *Essayes* as his case in point, Levy observes a shift in Bacon's "emphasis from man's ability to train and control himself to resist the onslaught of fortune to man's ability to control fortune herself, to be the architect of fortune" (113). Levy concludes that "by 1597 [Bacon] had come to adopt Machiavelli's view that it was more important to study what men do rather than what they ought to

do, and to guide one's actions by the conclusions deriving from such a study" (116–17). Greenblatt (1980) analyzes Peter Martyr's account of how the natives of the Lucayan islands were treated by his fellow Spaniards. Greenblatt's emphasis falls on the Spaniards' apparent ability to perceive the status of Lucayan religion as "a manipulable human construct" and their equally apparent inability to come to the same recognition regarding their own religion (226ff). Much the same kind of thought process seems to characterize Shakespeare's Ulysses, as I suggest below.

3. According to Greenblatt (1981)"'subversive' is for us a term used to designate those elements in Renaissance culture that contemporary authorities tried to contain or, when containment seemed impossible, to destroy and that now conform to our sense of truth and reality"(52).

4. Eagleton's summary specifically elaborates on Macherey's contention that "Even though ideology itself always sounds solid, copious, it begins to speak of its *own absences* because of its presence in the novel, its visible and determinate form" (1978, 132).

5. Eagleton admits to having "real difficulties" with the formulation he summarizes. For an earlier, more complete statement of his objections, see Eagleton 1976, 83–85; 89–95. If his remarks about Shakespearean drama continue to represent his thinking, Eagleton would probably resist my application of Macherey's formulation to the Shakespearean set speech: "It is true that Shakespearean drama does not merely 'reproduce' a conflict of historical ideologies; but neither does it press a particular ideology to the point where it betrays its signficant silences" (1976, 96).

6. Rabkin is playing devil's advocate here in describing an "optimistic" approach to the play from which he is, elsewhere in his chapter on *Henry V*, careful to distance himself.

7. Cf. Ornstein (1972) who contends that Henry's "moral awareness is of the mind, not of the heart. He knows intellectually the obligations he does not feel" (189).

8. Henry's observation on the political utility of ceremony closely resembles the observation on the political function of religion attributed to Marlowe in the Baines deposition: "That the first beginning of Religion was only to keep men in awe." Both statements have a common origin in the strong (and generally underestimated) influence of the writings of Machiavelli on contemporary Elizabethan thought. Henry's failure even to acknowledge—and Shakespeare's failure to exploit—the apparent heterodoxy of this position may actually attest to the domestication of Machiavellian habits of mind in Elizabethan intellectual life.

9. This is especially the case with respect to those speeches Shakespeare places in the province of the Chorus who, as Ornstein observes, "is not one to examine unexamined enthusiasms" (1972, 185).

10. This procedure has much in common with the way in which religious and providentialist paradigms continued to operate in the minds of those contemporaries of Shakespeare discussed by Raab (1964, esp. 60–66). See Danson (1983, 40–42) for another account of how Henry's reversion to a religious idiom functions in relation to the speech on ceremony.

11. After calling attention to the similar rhetorical styles of *Henry V* and *Troilus*, Tillyard observes that "in *Henry V* the spirit of criticism plays on the minor char-

acters who are politicians and may even extend to the man of action in general, if only unconsciously. In *Troilus and Cressida* this spirit comes right out into the open and is intensified" (1950, 55–57).

12. Cf. Dollimore (1984): "*Troilus and Cressida* exploits disjunction and 'chaos' to promote critical awareness of both the mystifying language of the absolute and the social reality which it occludes" (44).

13. Eagleton (1980) criticizes Althusser for engaging in "a fairly drastic misreading of Jacques Lacan" in his association of the imaginary with the ideological (150–51). In his more recent *Literary Theory* (1983), Eagleton concedes that Althusser's rethinking "the concept of ideology in terms of Lacan's 'imaginary' " at least constitutes an attempt "to show the relevance of Lacanian theory to issues beyond the consulting room" (172–73).

14. Scholars continue to quarrel about where, when, and if *Troilus* was first performed in London, ca. 1601–10. Indeed, the proposition that *Troilus* can even be considered a *play* composed for performance in its own time is difficult to maintain in the context of the information provided by the "Never Writer" in the 1609 preface and by Kenneth Muir in the Introduction to his "Oxford Shakespeare" edition (1982). For further consideration of this dilemma, see my Conclusion, below.

15. I have borrowed the term "mercifixion" from Harry Berger, Jr., "Marriage and Mercifixion in *The Merchant of Venice*" (1981, 151–62). Berger, however, is so far from villainizing Portia as to suggest that she "is no less an outsider than Shylock, and her 'I stand for sacrifice' is finally not much different from Shylock's 'I stand for judgment' " (161), thus anticipating in some respects my own position.

16. I take up this subject in a recent essay entitled "Shakespeare's *Merchant*, Marlowe's *Jew*: The Problem of Cultural Difference" (1988).

17. Cf. Macherey (1978) who contends that "literature challenges ideology by using it." Macherey continues in a vein that has clear implications for literary studies in general: "If ideology is thought of as a non-systematic ensemble of significations, the work proposes a *reading* of these significations, by combining them as signs. Criticism teaches us to read these signs" (133).

18. I am consciously echoing here Greenblatt's well-known statement that "Shakespeare approaches his culture not, like Marlowe, as rebel and blasphemer, but rather as dutiful servant, content to improvise a part of his own within its orthodoxy" (1980, 253). While Shakespeare may well have been "the servant of the very structures he sets out to subvert," as I suggest (in the long shadow cast by Greenblatt), he was not, I believe, nearly as "dutiful" or "content" with his culture's orthodoxy as Greenblatt contends. It may be more profitable to envision him as the reluctant accomplice—and occasional opponent—of what Greenblatt terms the "normative function" of his own artistic medium, as I suggest in my Conclusion.

Chapter Seven: Machiavel's Ghost

1. Some of the most exciting scholarship in years has been pursued in relation to these issues. See, e.g., Taylor and Warren (1983) on the *Lear* controversy and Warren (1981) on the two versions of *Faustus*.

2. For a summary of textual approaches to the play, see the Bennett edition (1931; rep. 1964, 15–19). The most extreme dismissal of the last three acts, equal to a consignment to oblivion, is offered by Wilson (1953, 65). A more reasonable, though still prejudicial, approach to *The Jew*'s "structural complications" is offered by Sanders (1968, 38–60).

3. See Steane (1964, 166–203); Brooke (1964, 95–96); and Greenblatt (1978, 305).

4. Although it may be argued that what Harry Levin terms the play's "overplot" (presided over by Ferneze) provides just the kind of formal restraint I find lacking, Levin himself contends that, morally speaking, all of the play's interconnected plots "operate on the same level," a fact that, he concludes, "is precisely what Marlowe is pointing out" (1964, 67).

5. Cf. Brooke (1964): "The structure of such a play cannot be considered in simply narrative terms . . . because the rapid changes of theatrical mode which are its chief resource have no narrative significance; still less can it be considered in terms of character, for the actor who takes Barabas's part will have to display a range of theatrical power in which character-definition (though existing) will be quite different things at different times" (95–96). Cf., also, Babb (1957) who contends that the "dramatic standard of reality" in *The Jew* is "completely fluid" (92).

6. I am indebted here to Michael Warren who has allowed me to quote from his unpublished essay on Marlowe's prologues.

7. For complete discussions of Marlowe's knowledge of Machiavelli's writings and use of Machiavelli in *The Jew*, see Ribner (1954); Bawcutt (1970); Babb (1957); Greenblatt (1978, 1980); Hodge (1981); and Minshull (1982). For examinations of popular conceptions and misconceptions of Machiavellism, see Praz (1958) and Raab (1964).

8. Identifying Ferneze as the play's only genuine practitioner of Machiavellian policy has become standard in most recent commentaries on *The Jew*. See, e.g., Hodge (1981, 7) and Minshull (1982, 41ff).

9. Such an action hardly seems to support Greenblatt's rather formulaic observation that "Marlovian rebels and skeptics remain embedded" in "the heart of [a] Renaissance orthodoxy" that is "a vast system of repetitions" insofar as "they simply reverse the paradigms and embrace what the society brands as evil" (1980, 253). In this scene, as in those in which he effects the poisoning of an entire convent and choreographs the demise of the two predatory friars, Barabas operates well outside the pale of such rhetorically constituted moral paradigms. Indeed, the resourcefulness and energy he demonstrates in these scenes appear to derive from Marlowe's efforts to burlesque such high seriousness.

10. It is worth noting on this account that *Tamburlaine* and *The Jew* were particular favorites at the comparatively unprestigious Red Bull playhouse in the 1630s, although *The Jew* was apparently performed with equal frequency for the more privileged playgoers at the Cockpit. See Gurr (1987, 183–85).

11. Simmons substitutes the word "truss" for Tucker-Brooke's generally accepted reading of "sluice" in line 86: "Modern readings should read 'truss,' a deictic word which fuses a part of the actual structure of the playhouse with the imagined wall

surrounding Malta. Barabas points to 'a projection from the face of a wall, often serving to support a cornice, etc.; a kind of large corbel or modillion' (OED, 6b). That image blends with the kind of supporting structure which Burbage, with his knowledge of a joiner, had supplied for the permanent trestles of the Theater (1576)" (1971, 97).

Chapter Eight: The Unaccommodating Text

1. For the application of just such a theory of influence to the plays of Marlowe, Shakespeare, and Jonson, see Shapiro (1991).

2. The quoted phrase is taken from Burke (1966, 115).

3. See, e.g., Knight (1957, 207–39). Knight actually takes his reading of the play beyond the bounds of my formulation by claiming that *Timon* constitutes "the archetype and norm of all tragedy" (220).

4. Rabkin's manner of dismissing *Timon* may serve as a good example of Jameson's assertion that "the working theoretical framework or presuppositions of a given method are in general the ideology which that method seeks to perpetuate." The ideology within which Rabkin works in *Shakespeare and the Common Understanding* (1967) would probably fall under the rubric of what Jameson terms "*ethical* criticism" or, more precisely, "metaphysical thought, which presupposes the possibility of questions about the 'meaning' of life" (1981, 58–60). For his part, Rabkin has revised his critical attitude toward "meaning"; however, he has done so without sacrificing his commitment to humanistic ends which Jameson would consider ideologically exclusive as the following passage from Rabkin (1981) makes clear: "The challenge to criticism . . . is to embark on a self-conscious reconsideration of the phenomena that our technology has enabled us to explore, to consider the play as a dynamic interaction between artist and audience, to learn to talk about the process of our involvement rather than our considered view after the aesthetic event" (27). Given his present emphasis on the process of audience involvement, it is doubtful that Rabkin would now endorse his earlier critical estimate of *Timon*.

5. *Timon*'s status as an experimental drama has already been noted by Ellis-Fermor (1942) and Traversi (1969, 170). According to Ellis-Fermor, Shakespeare was, in *Timon*, "experimenting with structure; again, as in *Troilus and Cressida*, attempting a theme so original that the form it dictated must inevitably be revolutionary" (275).

6. See Jameson's discussion of the similarly accommodating impulses of "ethical" and psychological criticism (1981, 59–60).

7. For Handelman, as for so many psychologically inclined critics, "notions of personal identity, myths of the reunification of the psyche, and the mirage of some Jungian 'self' or 'ego' stand in for the older themes of moral sensibility and ethical awareness" (Jameson 1981, 60).

8. Although I accept here, for the sake of contrast, the conventional critical belief in the efficacy of the great tragedies in transforming the experience of loss

into what Handelman terms "life-affirming energies," I believe that it needs radical revision. The intensification of suffering that attends the closure of *King Lear*, e.g., probably does produce in some readers and most audiences an experience akin to catharsis. But do the closing colloquies of Kent, Albany, and Edgar really accommodate us to an acceptance of loss? Early redactors of Shakespeare did not appear to think so, and their sense of the original play as unrelievedly painful has been echoed in our own time by scholars, directors, and filmmakers alike.

9. Although I agree with Traversi that we should resist the temptation "to think of *Timon of Athens* as a kind of appendix to *King Lear*" and see it, instead, as an attempt on Shakespeare's part at "contriving a new kind of dramatic action" (1969, 170), I believe that the aggressive, comparatively stripped-down dramatic orientation of the later play is a direct consequence of Shakespeare's continuing preoccupation with developing an appropriate language for tragic experience.

10. Traversi begins his own analysis of this scene by stating that "the truth is evenly divided" between Timon and Apemantus, but concludes that "Timon remains distinguished from Apemantus by the ability to turn his life-weariness into distinctive poetry" (1969, 181–84).

11. I have borrowed this terminology from Jackson (1977).

12. Cf. Kahn (1987) who writes that "The play's core fantasy consists of two scenes in the course of which a male self is precipitated out of a profound and empowering oneness with the mother into a treacherous group of men in which he is powerless. It is the mother who betrays him, the whorish mother who singles him out and then spurns him" (35).

13. Although I am in general agreement with what Lancashire has to say about Timon in regard to the first movement of the play (despite her insensitivity to his obvious performance appeal), I disagree altogether with her overall reading of the drama, which derives from an oddly uncritical estimate of its indebtedness to the morality tradition.

14. I find Bayley's chapter on *Timon* (aptly entitled "The Big Idea") consistently illuminating and provocative, and recommend it to anyone interested in a reading of the play opposed to the one advanced here.

15. Cf. Adorno's critique of what Iser terms the "quietistic aspect" of conventional psychological approaches to aesthetic experience: "The conformist acceptance by psychoanalysis of the popular view of art as beneficent to culture corresponds to aesthetic hedonism, which banishes all negativity from art, confining it to the conflicts that give rise to the work and suppressing it from the end-product. If an acquired sublimation and integration are made into the be-all and end-all of the work of art, it loses that power through which it transcends the life which, by its very existence, it has renounced." Quoted in Iser (1978, 47).

16. I have substituted the alternate reading "sour" in place of Oliver's choice of "four." Oliver defends his choice on the grounds that " 'sour' hardly makes sense, since Timon proceeds to further curses" (1959, 132). I would suggest that it makes a great deal more sense than "four" since it announces the imminent, not immediate, termination of speech which will, moreover, be effected in three lines, instead of in the space of four words.

Conclusion

1. My observations here constitute another stage in my running commentary on the remarks Greenblatt makes on Marlowe and Shakespeare towards the end of *Renaissance Self-Fashioning* (1980, 252–54).

2. In her brilliant essay on the play, Elizabeth Freund writes that "*Troilus and Cressida* is probably Shakespeare's most daring experiment in defensive self-presentation, . . . It may yet come to be read as the period's most paradigmatic text" (1985, 35).

3. I refer here to a production of *Troilus* that some participants in the Fourth International Shakespeare Congress had the opportunity to see in April, 1986.

4. In his most recent exercise in reactive debunking, Richard Levin claims that "the death of the author" proclaimed by politically oriented critics of Shakespeare has created "a hermeneutic vacuum" which these critics seek to fill with "a universal law . . . that dictates what one must look for, and must find, in every play" (1990, 502). What one looks for, and finds, according to Levin, is "Concealed-but-Revealed Ideological Contradiction" (502). Levin concludes that "The Death of the Author enables these critics to wage—and to win—a kind of class war against the forces of evil, embodied in the text's hegemonic ideology, and therefore to achieve in this displaced and 'imaginary' arena their avowed political goals" (502). While Levin's prose drips with the sarcasm of the self-constituted authority, impelled to defend his prerogatives against the many-headed (but univocal) monster, he accurately gauges the effort of contemporary critics to circumvent the problem of authorial intention. While I freely identify my critical interests with those of many of the estimable scholars Levin chastises and derides, I differ from most of them insofar as I do choose to speak of Shakespeare's intentions and do consider Shakespeare capable of harboring oppositional positions of his own.

Works Cited

Adams, Robert P. "Opposed Tudor Myths of Power: Machiavellian Tyrants and Christian Kings." In Dale B.J. Randall and George Walton Williams, eds. *Studies in the Continental Background of Renaissance English Literature: Essays Presented to John L. Lievsay*. Durham, NC: Duke University Press, 1977, 67–90.

Adelman, Janet. " 'Born of Woman': Fantasies of Maternal Power in *Macbeth*." In Marjorie Garber, ed. *Cannibals, Witches, and Divorce: Estranging the Renaissance*. Selected Papers from the English Institute. Baltimore: Johns Hopkins University Press, 1985, 90–121.

Althusser, Louis. "Ideology and Ideological State Apparatuses." In *Lenin and Philosophy*. Ben Brewster, trans. New York and London: Monthly Review Press, 1971.

Babb, Howard. "Policy in Marlowe's *The Jew of Malta*." *ELH* 24 (1957): 85–94.

Barber, C.L. *Shakespeare's Festive Comedy*. Princeton, NJ: Princeton University Press, 1959.

———. *Creating Elizabethan Tragedy*. Richard P. Wheeler, ed. Chicago: University of Chicago Press, 1988.

Barber, C.L. and Richard P. Wheeler. *The Whole Journey: Shakespeare's Power of Development*. Berkeley: University of California Press, 1986.

Barish, Jonas. "Shakespeare in the Study; Shakespeare on the Stage." *Theatre Journal* 40:1 (1988): 33–47.

Battenhouse, Roy W. *Marlowe's "Tamburlaine": A Study of Renaissance Moral Philosophy*. Nashville: University of Tennessee Press, 1941.

Bayley, John. *Shakespeare and Tragedy*. London: Routledge & Kegan Paul, 1981.

Bawcutt, N.W. "Machiavelli and Marlowe's *The Jew of Malta*." *Renaissance Drama*, N.S. III (1970): 3–49.

Beier, A.L. "Vagrants and the Social Order in Elizabethan England." *Past and Present* 64 (1974): 3–29.

———. "Social Problems in Elizabethan London." *Journal of Interdisciplinary History* 9 (1978): 203–21.

———. *Masterless Men: The Vagrancy Problem in England 1560–1640*. London: Methuen, 1985.

Beier, A.L. and Roger Finlay, eds. *London 1500–1700: The Making of the Metropolis*. London: Longman, 1986.

Belsey, Catherine. *The Subject of Tragedy: Identity and Difference in Renaissance Drama*. London: Methuen, 1985.

Berger, Harry, Jr. "Theatre, Drama, and the Second World: A Prologue to Shake-speare." *Comparative Drama* II:1 (1968): 3–20.

———. "The Early Scenes of *Macbeth*: Preface to a New Interpretation." *ELH* 47 (1980): 1–30.

———. "Marriage and Mercifixion in *The Merchant of Venice*." *Shakespeare Quarterly* 32 (1981): 155–62.

———. "Text Against Performance in Shakespeare: The Example of *Macbeth*." *Genre* 15:1 and 2 (1982): 49–79.

———. "Sneak's Noise: Rumor and Detextualization in *2 Henry IV*." *Kenyon Review*, N.S. 6 (1984): 58–78.

———. "Text Against Performance: The Gloucester Family Romance." In Peter Erickson and Coppélia Kahn, eds. *Shakespeare's "Rough Magic": Renaissance Essays in Honor of C.L. Barber*. Newark: University of Delaware Press, 1985, 210–29.

———. *Imaginary Audition: Shakespeare on Stage and Page*. Berkeley: University of California Press, 1989.

Bevington, David M. *Tudor Drama and Politics: A Critical Approach to Topical Meaning*. Cambridge, MA.: Harvard University Press, 1968.

Blau, Herbert. *The Audience*. Baltimore: The Johns Hopkins University Press, 1990.

Bradley, A.C. *Shakespearean Tragedy*. Cleveland: World Publishing, 1963.

Bristol, Michael D. *Carnival and Theater: Plebeian Culture and the Structure of Authority in Renaissance England*. London: Methuen, 1985.

Brooke, Nicholas. "Marlowe as Provocative Agent in Shakespeare's Early Plays." *Shakespeare Survey* 14 (1961): 34–44.

———. "Marlowe the Dramatist." *Elizabethan Theatre*. Stratford-upon-Avon Studies 9 (1964): 87–106.

Brown, Paul. " 'This thing of darkness I acknowledge mine': *The Tempest* and the discourse of colonialism." In Jonathan Dollimore & Alan Sinfield, eds. *Political Shakespeare: New Essays in Cultural Materialism*. Ithaca, NY: Cornell University Press, 1985.

Burke, Kenneth. "*Coriolanus*—and the Delights of Faction." In *Language as Symbolic Action*. Berkeley: University of California Press, 1966.

———. "*Timon of Athens* and Misanthropic Gold." In *Language as Symbolic Action*. Berkeley: University of California Press, 1966.

Burnett, Mark Thornton. "Tamburlaine: An Elizabethan Vagabond." *Studies in Philology* LXXXIV:3 (1987): 308–23.

Butler, Martin. *Theatre and Crisis: 1632–1642*. Cambridge: Cambridge University Press, 1984.

Carlson, Marvin. "Theatrical Performance: Illustration, Translation, Fulfillment, or Supplement?" *Theatre Journal* 37:1 (1985): 5–11.

Cartelli, Thomas. "Shakespeare's *Merchant*, Marlowe's *Jew*: The Problem of Cultural Difference." *Shakespeare Studies* XX (1988): 255–60.

Chambers, E.K. *The Elizabethan Stage*, vol. IV. Oxford: Clarendon Press, 1923.

Champion, Larry S. *Perspective in Shakespeare's Histories*. Athens: University of Georgia Press, 1980.

Charney, Maurice. "Jessica's Turquoise Ring and Abigail's Poisoned Porridge: Shakespeare and Marlowe as Rivals and Imitators." *Renaissance Drama*, N.S. X (1979): 33–44.

Clemen, Wolfgang. *English Tragedy Before Shakespeare*. New York: Barnes & Noble, 1961.

Cohen, Walter. "*The Merchant of Venice* and the Possibilities of Historical Criticism." *ELH* 49 (1982): 765–89.

———. *Drama of a Nation: Public Theater in Renaissance England and Spain*. Ithaca, NY: Cornell University Press, 1985.

Cole, Douglas. *Suffering and Evil in the Plays of Christopher Marlowe*. Princeton, NJ: Princeton University Press, 1962.

Cook, Ann Jennalie. *The Privileged Playgoers of Shakespeare's London, 1576–1642*. Princeton, NJ: Princeton University Press, 1981.

Cox, John D. *Shakespeare and the Dramaturgy of Power*. Princeton, NJ: Princeton University Press, 1989.

Crewe, Jonathan V. "The Theatre of the Idols: Marlowe, Rankins, and Theatrical Images." *Theatre Journal* 36:3 (1984): 321–33.

Cutts, John. *The Left Hand of God: A Critical Interpretation of the Plays of Christopher Marlowe*. Haddonfield, NJ: Haddonfield House, 1973.

Danson, Lawrence. "Christopher Marlowe: The Questioner." *English Literary Renaissance* 12:1 (1982): 3–29.

———. "*Henry V*: King, Chorus, and Critics." *Shakespeare Quarterly* 34 (1983): 27–43.

———. "Continuity and Character in Shakespeare and Marlowe." *Studies in English Literature* 26:2 (1986): 217–34.

Davenport, Arnold, ed. *The Poems of Joseph Hall*. Liverpool: Liverpool University Press, 1969.

Dekker, Thomas. *The Shoemaker's Holiday*. R.L. Smallwood and Stanley Wells, eds. Manchester: Manchester University Press, 1979.

Dollimore, Jonathan. *Radical Tragedy: Religion, Ideology and Power in the Drama of Shakespeare and His Contemporaries*. Chicago: University of Chicago Press, 1984.

Dollimore, Jonathan and Alan Sinfield, eds. *Political Shakespeare: New Essays in Cultural Materialism*. Ithaca, NY: Cornell University Press, 1985.

Eagleton, Terry. *Shakespeare and Society*. New York: Schocken Books, 1967.

———. *Criticism and Ideology: A Study in Marxist Literary Theory*. London: New Left Books, 1976.

———. "Text, Ideology, Realism." In Edward Said, ed. *Literature and Society*. Selected Papers from the English Institute, 1978. Baltimore: Johns Hopkins University Press, 1980, 149–73.

———. *Literary Theory: An Introduction*. Minneapolis: University of Minnesota Press, 1983.

Egan, Robert. "His Hour upon the Stage: Role-Playing in *Macbeth*." *Centennial Review* 22 (1978): 327–45.

Elam, Keir. *The Semiotics of Theatre and Drama*. London: Methuen, 1980.

Ellis, John. *Visible Fictions*. London: Routledge & Kegan Paul, 1982.

Ellis-Fermor, Una. "*Timon of Athens*: An Unfinished Play." *Review of English Studies* 18 (1942): 270–83.

———. *Christopher Marlowe*. Hamden, CT: Archon Books, 1967.

Esler, Anthony. *The Aspiring Mind of the Elizabethan Younger Generation*. Durham, NC: Duke University Press, 1966.

Finlay, Roger and Beatrice Shearer, "Population Growth and Suburban Expansion." In A.L.Beier and Roger Finlay, eds. *London 1500–1700: The Making of the Metropolis*. London: Longman, 1986, 37–57.

Fish, Stanley. "Interpreting the *Variorum*." *Critical Inquiry* 2:3 (1976): 465–85.

Fisher, F.J. "London as a Centre of Conspicuous Consumption in the 16th and 17th Centuries." *Transactions of the Royal Historical Society* 4th series, xxx (1948).

Fly, Richard. *Shakespeare's Mediated World*. Amherst: University of Massachusetts Press, 1976.

Freud, Sigmund. "Psychopathic Characters on the Stage." *Standard Edition*, vol. VII. James Strachey, trans. London: Hogarth Press, 1953.

Freund, Elizabeth. " 'Arachne's broken woof': the rhetoric of citation in *Troilus and Cressida*." In Patricia Parker and Geoffrey Hartman, eds. *Shakespeare and the Question of Theory*. New York & London: Methuen, 1985, 19–36.

Friedenreich, Kenneth, Roma Gill and Constance Kuriyama, eds. *"A Poet and a filthy Playmaker": New Essays on Christopher Marlowe*. New York: AMS Press, 1988.

Girard, Rene. " 'To Entrap the Wisest': A Reading of *The Merchant of Venice*." In Edward Said, ed. *Literature and Society*. Selected Papers from the English Institute, 1978. Baltimore: Johns Hopkins University Press, 1980, 100–19.

Godshalk, W.L. *The Marlovian World Picture*. The Hague: Mouton, 1974.

Goffmann, Erving. *Frame Analysis: An Essay on the Organization of Experience*. New York: Harper & Row, 1974.

Goldberg, Jonathan. "Sodomy and Society: The Case of Christopher Marlowe." *Southwest Review* 69 (1984): 371–78.

———. "Speculations: *Macbeth* and Source." In Jean Howard and Marion O' Connor, eds. *Shakespeare Reproduced: The Text in History and Ideology*. London: Methuen, 1987, 242–64.

Goldman, Michael. "Marlowe and the Histrionics of Ravishment." In Alvin Kernan, ed. *Two Renaissance Mythmakers: Christopher Marlowe and Ben Jonson*. Baltimore: Johns Hopkins University Press, 1977, 22–40.

Gosson, Stephen. *Plays Confuted in Five Actions*. In William Hazlitt, ed. *The English Drama and Stage*, London, 1869.

———. *The Schoole of Abuse* (1579). In Edward Arber, ed. English Reprints, no. 3. London: A. Murray & Son, 1869.

Greenblatt, Stephen J. "Marlowe and Renaissance Self- Fashioning." In Alvin Kernan, ed. *Two Renaissance Mythmakers: Christopher Marlowe and Ben Jonson*. Baltimore: Johns Hopkins University Press, 1977, 41–69.

———. "Marlowe, Marx, and Anti-Semitism." *Critical Inquiry*, 5:2 (1978): 291–307.

———. *Renaissance Self-Fashioning: From More to Shakespeare*. Chicago: University of Chicago Press, 1980.

———. "Invisible Bullets: Renaissance Authority and Its Subversion." *Glyph* 8

(1981): 40–61. Rep. in Jonathan Dollimore and Alan Sinfield, eds. *Political Shakespeare: New Essays in Cultural Materialism*. Ithaca, NY: Cornell University Press, 1985.

———. "Murdering Peasants: Status, Genre, and the Representation of Rebellion." *Representations* 1 (1983): 1–29.

———. "Psychoanalysis and Renaissance Culture." In Patricia Parker and David Quint, eds. *Literary Theory / Renaissance Texts*. Baltimore: Johns Hopkins University Press, 1986.

Guⁿr, Andrew. *The Shakespearean Stage: 1574–1642*. Cambridge: Cambridge University Press, 1970.

———. *Playgoing in Shakespeare's London*. Cambridge: Cambridge University Press, 1987.

Handleman, Susan. "*Timon of Athens*: The Rage of Disillusion." *American Imago* 36 (1979): 45–68.

Harbage, Alfred. *Shakespeare's Audience*. New York: Columbia University Press, 1941.

———. "Innocent Barabas." *TDR*, 8:4 (1964): 47–58.

Hattaway, Michael. *Elizabethan Popular Theatre: Plays in Performance*. London: Routledge & Kegan Paul, 1982.

Hawkins, Michael. "History, Politics and *Macbeth*." In John Russell Brown, ed. *Focus on Macbeth*. London: Routledge & Kegan Paul, 1982, 155–88.

Heywood, Thomas. *An Apology for Actors* (1612). Richard H. Perkinson, ed. New York: Scholars' Facsimiles and Reprints, 1941.

Hill, Christopher. *Puritanism and Revolution*. London: Secker & Warburg, 1958.

———. *Intellectual Origins of the English Revolution*. Oxford: Oxford University Press, 1965.

———. "The Many-Headed Monster," in *Change and Continuity in Seventeenth-Century England*. Cambridge, MA: Harvard University Press, 1975, 181–204.

Hodgdon, Barbara. "He Do Cressida in Different Voices." *English Literary Renaissance* 20:2 (1990): 254–86.

Hodge, Bob. "Marlowe, Marx and Machiavelli: Reading into the Past." In David Aers et al., eds. *Literature, Language and Society in England 1580–1680*. Dublin: Gill & Macmillan, 1981, 1–22.

Holland, Norman N. *The Dynamics of Literary Response*. New York: Norton, 1975.

———. "Transactive Criticism: Re-Creation through Identity." *Criticism* 18 (1976): 334–52.

———. "How Can Dr. Johnson's Remarks on Cordelia's Death Add to My Own Response?" In Geoffrey H. Hartman, ed. *Psychoanalysis and the Question of the Text*. Baltimore: Johns Hopkins University Press, 1978, 18–44.

Holub, Robert. *Reception Theory: A Critical Introduction*. London: Methuen, 1984.

Howard, Jean E. *Shakespeare's Art of Orchestration: Stage Technique and Audience Response*. Urbana and Chicago: University of Illinois Press, 1984.

———. "Renaissance Antitheatricality and the Politics of Gender and Rank in *Much Ado About Nothing*." In Howard and Marion O' Connor, eds. *Shakespeare Reproduced: The Text in History and Ideology*. London: Methuen, 1987, 163–87.

Huebert, Ronald. "Tobacco and Boys and Marlowe." *Sewanee Review* XCII:2 (1984): 206–24.

Hurstfield, Joel. "The paradox of liberty in Shakespeare's England," in *Freedom, Corruption and Government in Elizabethan England*. London: Jonathan Cape, 1973.

Hurstfield, Joel and Alan G.R. Smith. *Elizabethan People*. London: Edward Arnold, 1972.

Ide, Richard. "The Theatre of the Mind: An Essay on *Macbeth*." *ELH* 42 (1975): 338–61.

Ingram, William. *A London Life in the Brazen Age: Francis Langley, 1548–1602*. Cambridge, MA: Harvard University Press, 1978.

Iser, Wolfgang. *The Act of Reading: A Theory of Aesthetic Response*. Baltimore: Johns Hopkins University Press, 1978.

Jackson, Gabriele Bernhard. "Structural Interplay in Ben Jonson's Drama." In Alvin Kernan, ed. *Two Renaissance Mythmakers: Christopher Marlowe and Ben Jonson*. Selected Papers from the English Institute, 1975–76. Baltimore: Johns Hopkins University Press, 1977, 113–45.

Jameson, Fredric. *The Political Unconscious: Narrative as a Socially Symbolic Act*. Ithaca, NY: Cornell University Press, 1981.

Jauss, Hans Robert. *Aesthetic Experience and Literary Hermeneutics*. Trans. Michael Shaw. Minneapolis: University of Minnesota Press, 1982.

Jonson, Ben. *Bartholomew Fair*. E.A. Horsman, ed. London: Methuen, 1967.

Kahn, Coppélia. " 'Magic of bounty': *Timon of Athens*, Jacobean Patronage, and Maternal Power." *Shakespeare Quarterly* 38:1 (1987): 34–57.

Kastan, David Scott. "Proud Majesty Made a Subject: Shakespeare and the Spectacle of Rule." *Shakespeare Quarterly* 37:4 (1986): 459–75.

Kinney, Arthur. *Markets of Bawdrie: The Dramatic Criticism of Stephen Gosson*. Salzburg Studies in English Literature, 4. Salzburg: Salzburg University, 1974.

Klein, David. *The Elizabethan Dramatists as Critics*. New York: Philosophical Library, 1963.

Knight, G. Wilson. *The Shakespearian Tempest*. Oxford: Oxford University Press, 1932.

———. *The Imperial Theme*. 3rd ed. London: Methuen, 1953.

———. *The Wheel of Fire*. 5th ed. New York: Meridian Books, 1957.

Kott, Jan. *Shakespeare Our Contemporary*. Garden City, NY: Doubleday, 1966.

Kranz, David. "The Mated Mind in *Macbeth*." Unpublished paper.

Kuriyama, Constance Brown. *Hammer or Anvil: Psychological Patterns in Christopher Marlowe's Plays*. New Brunswick, NJ: Rutgers University Press, 1980.

Lancashire, Anne. "*Timon of Athens*: Shakespeare's *Doctor Faustus*." *Shakespeare Quarterly* 21 (1970): 35–44.

Lesser, Simon O. "*Macbeth*: Drama and Dream." In Joseph P. Strelka, ed. *Literary Criticism and Psychology*. University Park: Pennyslvania State University Press, 1976.

Levenson, Jill. " 'Working Words': The Verbal Dynamic of *Tamburlaine*." In Kenneth Friedenreich, Roma Gill, and Constance Kuriyama, eds. *"A Poet and a filthy Playmaker": New Essays on Christopher Marlowe*. New York:AMS Press, 1988, 99–115.

Levin, Harry. *The Overreacher*. Boston: Beacon Press, 1964.

———. "Marlowe Today." *TDR* 8:4 (1964): 22–31. Rep. as "Reconsidering Marlowe," in *Shakespeare and the Revolution of the Times*. New York: Oxford University Press, 1976, 61–73.

Levin, Richard. "The Contemporary Perception of Marlowe's Tamburlaine." *Medieval & Renaissance Drama in England* I (1984): 51–70.

———. "The Poetics and Politics of Bardicide." *PMLA* 105:3 (1990): 491–504.

Levy, F.J. "Francis Bacon and the Style of Politics." *English Literary Renaissance* 16:1 (1986): 101–22.

Macfarlane, Alan. *The Origins of English Individualism*. Oxford: Blackwell, 1979.

Macherey, Pierre. *A Theory of Literary Production*. Geoffrey Wall, trans. London: Routledge & Kegan Paul, 1978.

Mack, Maynard. "Engagement and Detachment in Shakespeare's Plays." In Richard Hosley, ed. *Essays on Shakespeare and Elizabethan Drama: In Honor of Hardin Craig*. Columbia: University of Missouri Press, 1962, 275–96.

Manning, Roger. *Village Revolts: Social Protests and Popular Disturbances in England, 1509–1640*. Oxford: Clarendon Press, 1988.

Marlowe, Christopher. *The Complete Plays of Christopher Marlowe*. Irving Ribner, ed. New York: Odyssey Press, 1963.

———. *The Jew of Malta* and *The Massacre at Paris*. H.S. Bennett, ed. New York: Gordian Press, 1966.

———. *Tamburlaine the Great*. J.W. Harper, ed. New York: Hill & Wang, 1973.

Masinton, Charles. *Christopher Marlowe's Tragic Vision: A Study in Damnation*. Athens: Ohio State University Press, 1972.

McCann, Franklin T. *English Discovery of America to 1585*. New York: Columbia University Press, 1952.

McLuskie, Kathleen. "The Patriarchal Bard: Feminist Criticism and Shakespeare: *King Lear* and *Measure for Measure*." In Jonathan Dollimore and Alan Sinfield, eds. *Political Shakespeare: New Essays in Cultural Materialism*. Ithaca, NY: Cornell University Press, 1985, 88–108.

Minshull, Catherine. "Marlowe's 'Sound Machevill'." *Renaissance Drama*, N.S. XIII (1982): 35–53.

Montrose, Louis Adrian. " 'Shaping Fantasies': Figurations of Gender and Power in Elizabethan Culture." *Representations* 2 (1983): 61–94. Rep. in Stephen Greenblatt, ed. *Representing the English Renaissance*. Berkeley: University of California Press, 1988, 31–64.

Moretti, Franco. " 'A Huge Eclipse': Tragic Form and the Deconsecration of Sovereignty." *Genre* 15 (1981): 7–40.

Muir, Kenneth and F.P. Wilson, eds. *The Life and Death of Jack Straw* (1594). Oxford: Oxford University Press, 1957.

Mullaney, Steven. *The Place of the Stage: License, Play, and Power in Renaissance England*. Chicago: University of Chicago Press, 1988.

Mulvey, Laura. "Visual Pleasure and Narrative Cinema." *Screen* 16:3 (1975): 6–18.

Mulvey, Laura. "Afterthoughts on 'Visual Pleasure and Narrative Cinema' Inspired by *Duel in the Sun*." *Framework* 15–16 (1981): 12–15.

[Munday, Anthony]. *A Second and Third Blast of Retrait from Plaies and Theaters*. In William Hazlitt, ed. *The English Drama and Stage*. London, 1869.

Nashe, Thomas. *Pierce Penniless His Supplication to the Divell*. In R.B. McKerrow, ed. *The Works of Thomas Nashe*, vol. I. London: A.H. Bullen, 1904.

———. *The Unfortunate Traveller*. In McKerrow, vol. II.

Nietzsche, Friedrich. *The Birth of Tragedy*. In Walter Kaufmann, trans. and ed. *Basic Writings of Nietzsche*. New York: Random House, 1968.

Norbrook, David. "*Macbeth* and the Politics of Historiography." In Kevin Sharpe and Steven N. Zwicker, eds. *Politics of Discourse: The Literature and History of Seventeenth Century England*. Berkeley: University of California Press, 1987.

Nosworthy, J.M. "The Hecate Scenes in *Macbeth*." *Review of English Studies* XXIV (1948): 138–39.

Orgel, Stephen. "The Authentic Shakespeare." *Representations* 21 (1988): 1–25.

Ornstein, Robert. *A Kingdom for a Stage: The Achievement of Shakespeare's History Plays*. Cambridge, MA: Harvard University Press, 1972.

Patterson, Annabel. *Shakespeare and the Popular Voice*. Oxford: Blackwell, 1989.

Paul, Henry N. *The Royal Play of Macbeth*. New York: Octagon Books, 1978.

Pavel, Thomas G. *The Poetics of Plot: The Case of English Renaissance Drama*. Minneapolis: University of Minnesota Press, 1985.

Pelling, Margaret. "Appearance and Reality: Barber-Surgeons, the Body and Disease." In A.L. Beier and Roger Finlay, eds. *London 1500–1700: The Making of the Metropolis*. London: Longman 1986, 82–112.

Porter, Joseph. "Marlowe, Shakespeare, and the Canonization of Heterosexuality." *South Atlantic Quarterly* 88:1 (1989): 127–47.

Praz, Mario. " 'The Politic Brain': Machiavelli and the Elizabethans." In *The Flaming Heart*. New York: W.W. Norton, 1958, 90–145.

Prior, Moody. "The Elizabethan Audience and Shakespeare." *Modern Philology* 49 (1951): 101–23.

Raab, Felix. *The English Face of Machiavelli*. London: Routledge & Kegan Paul, 1964.

Rabkin, Norman. *Shakespeare and the Common Understanding*. New York: The Free Press, 1967.

———. *Shakespeare and the Problem of Meaning*. Chicago: University of Chicago Press, 1981.

Rainolds, John. *The Overthrow of Stage Playes*. London, 1600.

Ribner, Irving. "Marlowe and Machiavelli." *Comparative Literature* 6 (1954): 349–56.

Riggs, David. *Shakespeare's Heroical Histories: "Henry VI" and Its Literary Tradition*. Cambridge, MA: Harvard University Press, 1971.

Ringler, William. *Stephen Gosson: A Biographical and Critical Study*. Princeton, NJ: Princeton University Press, 1942.

R.M. *Micrologia*. London, 1629.

Robertson, Toby. "Directing *Edward II*." TDR 8:4 (1964): 174–83.

Rosenberg, Marvin. *The Masks of Macbeth*. Berkeley: University of California Press, 1978.

Rowlands, Samuel. *Hell's Broke Loose* (1605). In *The Complete Works of Samuel Rowlands* (1880). New York: Johnson Reprint Corp., 1966.

Rutter, Carol C. *Documents of the Rose Playhouse*. Manchester: Manchester University Press, 1984.

Rye, William B. *England as seen by foreigners in the days of Elizabeth and James the First*. London: J.R. Smith, 1865.

Salgado, Gamini. *Eyewitnesses of Shakespeare: First Hand Accounts of Performances 1590–1890*. New York: Barnes & Noble, 1975.

Sanders, Wilbur. *The Dramatist and the Received Idea*. Cambridge: Cambridge University Press, 1968.

Schilders, Richard. "The Printer to the Reader." In John Rainolds, *The Overthrow of Stage Playes*. London, 1600.

Shakespeare, William. *Timon of Athens*. H.J. Oliver, ed. London: Methuen, 1959.

———. *The Second Part of King Henry VI*. Andrew S. Cairncross, ed. London: Methuen, 1965.

———. *The Complete Works of Shakespeare*. David Bevington, ed. Glenview, IL.: Scott, Foresman & Co., 1980.

———. *Macbeth*. Kenneth Muir, ed. London: Methuen, 1980.

———. *Troilus and Cressida*. Kenneth Muir, ed. Oxford: Oxford University Press, 1982.

Shapiro, James. " 'Which is *The Merchant* here, and which *The Jew*?': Shakespeare and the Economics of Influence." *Shakespeare Studies* XX (1988): 269–79.

———. *Rival Playwrights: Marlowe, Jonson, and Shakespeare*. New York: Columbia University Press, 1991.

Sharp, Buchanan. *In Contempt of All Authority: Rural Artisans and Riot in the West of England, 1586–1660*. Berkeley: University of California Press, 1980.

Shepherd, Simon. *Marlowe and the Politics of Elizabethan Theatre*. New York: St. Martin's Press, 1986.

Simmons, J.L. "Elizabethan Stage-Practice and Marlowe's *The Jew of Malta*." *Renaissance Drama*, N.S. IV (1971): 93–104.

Sinfield, Alan. "Against Appropriation." *Essays in Criticism* XXXI:3 (1981): 181–95.

Snow, Edward A. "Marlowe's *Doctor Faustus* and the Ends of Desire." In Alvin Kernan, ed. *Two Renaissance Mythmakers: Christopher Marlowe and Ben Jonson*. Baltimore: Johns Hopkins University Press, 1977, 70–110.

Stallybrass, Peter. "*Macbeth* and Witchcraft." In John Russell Brown, ed. *Focus on Macbeth*. London: Routledge & Kegan Paul, 1982, 189–209.

Steane, J.B. *Marlowe: A Critical Study*. Cambridge: Cambridge University Press, 1964.

Stone, Lawrence. *The Causes of the English Revolution: 1529–1642*. New York: Harper & Row, 1972.

Styan, J.L. *Drama, Stage, and Audience*. Cambridge: Cambridge University Press, 1975.

Summers, Claude J. *Christopher Marlowe and the Politics of Power*. Salzburg: Salzburg Studies in English Literature, 22, 1974.

Summers, Claude J. "Sex, Politics, and Self-Realization in *Edward II*." In Kenneth Friedenreich, Roma Gill, and Constance Brown Kuriyama, eds. *"A Poet and a filthy Playmaker": New Essays on Christopher Marlowe*. New York: AMS Press, 1988, 221–40.

Taylor, Gary and Michael Warren. *The Division of the Kingdoms: Shakespeare's Two Versions of "King Lear"*. Oxford: Oxford University Press, 1984.

Thomas, Keith. *Religion and the Decline of Magic*. London: Weidenfield & Nicholson, 1971.

Thomson, Peter. *Shakespeare's Theatre*. London: Routledge & Kegan Paul, 1983.

Tillyard, E.M.W. *Shakespeare's Problem Plays*. Toronto: University of Toronto Press, 1950.

Traversi, Derek A. *An Approach to Shakespeare*. Vol. 2, 3rd ed. Garden City, NY: Doubleday, 1969.

Turner, Victor. "Variations on a Theme of Liminality." In Sally F. Moore and Barbara G. Myerhoff, eds. *Secular Ritual*. Amsterdam: Van Gorcum, 1977, 36–52.

Underdown, David E. *Revel, Riot and Rebellion: Popular Politics and Culture in England 1603–1660*. Oxford: Oxford University Press, 1985.

———. "The Taming of the Scold: the Enforcement of Patriarchal Authority in Early Modern England." In Anthony Fletcher and John Stevenson, eds. *Order and Disorder in Early Modern England*. Cambridge: Cambridge University Press, 1985, 116–36.

Vennar, Richard. *An Apology*. London, 1614.

Warren, Michael. "*Doctor Faustus*: The Old Man and the Text." *English Literary Renaissance* 11:2 (1981): 111–47.

———. "Marlowe's Prologues." Unpublished paper.

Whigham, Frank. "Ideology and Class Conduct in *The Merchant of Venice*." *Renaissance Drama*, N.S. X (1979): 93–115.

Willbern, David. "Phantasmagoric *Macbeth*." *English Literary Renaissance* 16:3 (1986): 520–49.

Willett, John, ed. *Brecht on Theatre*. New York: Hill & Wang, 1964.

Williams, Clare, ed. *Thomas Platter's Travels in England, 1599*. London: Jonathan Cape, 1937.

Wilson, F.P. *Marlowe and the Early Shakespeare*. Oxford: Clarendon Press, 1953.

Wilson, Thomas. "The State of England (1600)." F.J. Fisher, ed. In *Camden Miscellany*, 3rd ser. 52 (1936): i–vii, 1–47.

Wrightson, Keith. *English Society: 1580–1680*. New Brunswick, NJ: Rutgers University Press, 1982.

Zitner, S.P. "Gosson, Ovid, and the Elizabethan Audience." *Shakespeare Quarterly* 9 (1958): 206–8.

Index

This book has been set in Linotron Galliard. Galliard was designed for Mergenthaler in 1978 by Matthew Carter. Galliard retains many of the features of a sixteenth century typeface cut by Robert Granjon but has some modifications which gives it a more contemporary look.

Printed on acid-free paper.